John Richard Digby Beste

Nowadays

Courts, Courtiers, Churchmen, Garibaldians, Lawyers and Brigands at Home and Abroad -

Vol. I

John Richard Digby Beste

Nowadays

Courts, Courtiers, Churchmen, Garibaldians, Lawyers and Brigands at Home and Abroad - Vol. I

ISBN/EAN: 9783743410800

Manufactured in Europe, USA, Canada, Australia, Japa

Cover: Foto ©Andreas Hilbeck / pixelio.de

Manufactured and distributed by brebook publishing software (www.brebook.com)

John Richard Digby Beste

Nowadays

NOWADAYS:

OR, COURTS, COURTIERS, CHURCHMEN, GARIBALDIANS, LAWYERS AND BRIGANDS,

AT HOME AND ABROAD.

By J. RICHARD DIGBY BESTE, ESQ.

AUTHOR OF "THE WABASH," "MODERN SOCIETY IN ROME,"
ETC., ETC.

IN TWO VOLUMES.

VOL. I.

LONDON:
CHAPMAN & HALL, 193, PICCADILLY.
1870.

PREFACE.

"The Wabash," which was published in 1855, told the adventures of a family, consisting of a father and mother and twelve children, in the interior of America. But 1855 is so long ago that I cannot hope to be still remembered; and I am tempted to reprint, even in this place, some of the opinions of the press which greeted that work and the other book* mentioned on my title-page. They may serve as letters of introduction to remind the reader that we were already on friendly terms when I began chatting with him again in the opening pages of these volumes. Thus, then, were those books spoken of by, perhaps, too-friendly critics:

"Encouraged by the brilliant success of *The Wabash*, Mr. Beste has followed up that very charming record of travels and adventures in America, by a book yet more remarkable."—*Sun*.

"This work cannot fail to do good service to the reputation of its author, in whom we recognise the writer

---

* "The Siege of Rome" was the title I originally gave to this historical novel and, indeed, is the printed heading to every page. The publishers thought to make it more attractive by calling it "Modern Society in Rome"—a change which annihilated all my historical pretensions, and led people to believe that it was a mere personal satire.

of the delightful books of travel published under the name of *The Wabash*."—*Morning Post*.

"All the talent which Mr. Beste evinced in his instructive volumes published under the singular title of *The Wabash*, is evinced in these volumes."—*Bell's Weekly Messenger*.

"Mr. Beste's book is interesting. In literary merit, it is above the majority of books of travel."—*Athenæum*.

"The work is singularly interesting."—*Literary Gazette*.

"Mr. Beste has awakened interest in all the persons of his narrative. The journals of the children, by the effect which a perfectly natural tone produces, may put to shame many a laboured composition. Nobody will read the book without being the wiser for it."—*Examiner*.

"We have been tempted to multiply our extracts from these amusing volumes."—*John Bull*.

"The constant presence of the family feelings and interests imparts a species of dramatic character to this agreeable book of travels."—*Spectator*.

"We recommend this book to the public."—*Standard*.

"There is a sort of 'unbookish' novelty in *The Wabash*."—*Globe*.

"Full of lively sketches which give it an air of family history, which has a charm of its own, making it a very amusing production."—*Guardian*.

"The novelty of the design of *The Wabash* has given it a personal interest, and we would especially recommend it should be placed in the hands of young persons."—*Critic*.

"The journals kept by the young ladies are marked by that feminine observation of trifles which makes ladies' letters so much more amusing than those of the sterner sex. Good stories are plentifully scattered over these pages."—*Times.*

"Carefully written, and has many interesting sketches of life in the Prairie."—*Daily News.*

"As good a sketch of the people, their manners and their country—fresh, racy, and natural—as could be desired."—*Press.*

"There is a wholesome and enthusiastic spirit running through *The Wabash* which renders it extremely delightful as well as instructive."—*Sunday Times.*

"These entertaining volumes are valuable in a practical point of view."—*Weekly Dispatch.*

"*The Wabash* is as charming a book of travel and adventure as it has been our good fortune to light upon. Mr. Beste's information, not merely upon the present state of the American wilds and backwoods, but on its facilities for colonisation, are invaluable."—*Messenger.*

Thanking all these kind reviewers, I would only add that the volumes now published may be properly considered as a continuation of *The Wabash.* The same individuals are actors in the scene; only, instead of being cast among the pioneers of the backwoods, their experiences lie amongst the cities, the courts, the society, the revolutions of the Old World. The reader is called upon for a deeper degree of sympathy as he traces the sad destinies of the now grown-up children; and is shewn the fearful consequences of travel in those climates to which thousands of our countrymen betake themselves yearly in search of health.

Those who seek for amusement only, and those who care for historic information, may equally rely upon the authority of these pages; for light, anecdotical, superficial, as they may seem, they record nothing unadvisedly or maliciously. The public acts of public men, whether English or foreigners, are public property, and are freely spoken of; the privacy of individuals is ever respected.

I regret not to be able to describe the present state of Italy as rapturously as English friends of that country would wish me to do. It were ever impertinent in a foreigner to declare himself a political partisan in any country in which he may temporarily reside, as I have resided in Italy; but I must record those of its malpractices from which I have suffered. I must record the unmethodical laziness of its administrative departments; the inefficiency of its soldier-police; the treacherous secrecy of its tribunals; the inadequacy of its punishments; the sloth and indifference of all to everything;—a sloth which keeps two-thirds of the electors from every polling booth in the kingdom; an indifference which almost amounts to connivance in every crime, since none care to express pity for the victim, or to bid the journals record the trial or punishment of the criminal; an indifference or connivance which, when the head of the police was stabbed to death last year at midday in Ravenna, caused every door and window to be instantly shut against his cry for help, and permitted the corporation of the city to present, to the central authority, an apologetic address which said not one word in execration of the crime!

CONTENTS OF VOLUME THE FIRST.

CHAPTER I.
EN ROUTE FOR EVERYWHERE.

The Wabash.—A medical consultation.—A roving commission.—An election at Southampton. - - 1

CHAPTER II.
THE MAIL PACKET.

The P. and O. Company and my horses.—The muster-roll.—Pleasant anchorage.—Diversions in a storm.—The Admiralty agent. - - - - 10

CHAPTER III.
THE BAY OF BISCAY.

Royal presents.—The storm.—The "novena."—Saved. 18

CHAPTER IV.
NEW SHORES.

Lost ships.—Vigo.—The brutal first-mate.—The ill-used horse.—Money versus letters.—Our log.—Coasting.—The other Tagus.—The custom house.—Night walk in Lisbon. - - - - 25

CHAPTER V.
A NEW LOCATION.

Lisbon by daylight.—Hissing in Portugal and Australia.—No lodgings.—A retrospective quotation.—Christmas Eve.—A terrific hotel bill.   -   -   36

CHAPTER VI.
SOCIETY AT LISBON.

A celebrated traveller.—The royal family.—Presentation at court.—The king, Don Pedro.—Court receptions.—Toilettes.—The Duke of Terceira.—The Saxe Coburgs.—The English legation.—The papal nuncio.—A bull-fight.—The ships at anchor.—Mourning ceremonial.   -   -   -   -   -   49

CHAPTER VII.
THE KING OF PORTUGAL.

The House of Peers.—The cholera.—Seclusion of Lisbon.   -   -   -   -   -   -   74

CHAPTER VIII.
ECCLESIASTICAL.

The clergy of Lisbon.—St. Vincent and the ravens.—Scandals.—Religious observances.—Procession of the Passion.—Churches.—St. Roque.—English nuns and Sion House.—The Estella.—Penha de França.—Theology below stairs.—Mr. Murray and the wondrous lizard.—Belem.—My butler, Stevens.—The rector of West End.   -   -   -   79

CHAPTER IX.
THE GREAT EARTHQUAKE.

Prognostics.—Present dread.—The minister, De Pombal.—Attack on the king.—Funny conspiracy.—Uncertainties.   -   -   -   -   -   101

CHAPTER X.
THE NEIGHBOURHOOD.

Climate.—Flowers.—H.R.H. the Infanta Isabel.—Quinta of Lumiar.—Of Oeiras.—The grape disease.—Oranges.—Horse races.—Mafra.—Another horse.—Cintra.—The Royal Palace.—Dom Sebastian.—The Duke of Wellington and the ring.—The Pena.—D. John de Castro.—Mr. Beckford.—The cork convent.—The pinch of snuff and Prince Torlonia - 109

CHAPTER XI.
INTERIOR OF PORTUGAL.

A Portuguese railroad.—Caldas.—An inn-keeper's bill.—Battle of Aljubarota.—Batalha.—Monastery of Alcobaca.—Don Pedro and Ines de Castro.—Portuguese inns. - - - - - 129

CHAPTER XII.
A LOCATION IN LISBON.

The Minister of Finances.—House hunting.—The tobacco contractor.—Lady O'Shaunessy.—A Brazilian speculator "stumped."—Another Minister of Finances.—The House of Peers and the author.—The English minister afraid. - - - - 138

CHAPTER XIII.
SPAIN.

Difficulty of going to Spain.—L'Helvétic.—The medical lecturer.—Cadiz.—A Spanish family.—Gibraltar.—Malaga.—A "bull-fight." - - - 151

CHAPTER XIV.
THE CALCUTTA.

The coast of Africa.—A dream.—Second sight.—Shipwreck. - - - - - - 169

CHAPTER XV.
AFRICA.

Oran.—Variety of costumes.—Mount Atlas.—"Isidora."
Walter Scott.—Future fame.—Old Vidal.—Lord
Exmouth's bombardment.—The French consul and
the dey.—Algiers.—The Arab quarter.—An Arab
mansion.—The Kasbah.—Amount of booty. - 173

CHAPTER XVI.
THE SOUTH OF FRANCE.

The great mosque.—Shopping.—Climate of Algiers.—
The Balearic Islands.—Marseilles and old acquaintance.—Prosperity of France.—Aix.—Eating and
washing.—La Crau.—The new archbishop.—Arles.
—The giant bones.—The man market.—Nîmes.—
The wisdom of doctors.—Montpellier.—The pig
market.—Silly bees of Narbonne.—Cheap Tea.—
Street processions.—Cafés et billards.—Battle of
Muret.—Approach to the Pyrenees.   -   - 192

CHAPTER XVII.
CAUTERETS.

Drinking and bathing.—Le Raillère.—Modern French
and the Queen of Navarre.—The Bad-hole.—The
doctors and the sore throat.—The doctor and the
lungs.—Progress of medicine.—Lac de Gaube.—
Pleasant walks.—The Pic du Midi.—The Cagots.—
The Republic of Luz and its finances.—Barèges.—
Madame de Maintenon.   -   -   -   - 208

CHAPTER XVIII.
THE PYRENEES.

Carriage and horses seized for debt.—Lourdes and the
Ages of Faith.—Legend of the Chateau de Benac.—

Bagnères de Bigorre.—Bagnères de Luchon.—The old guide.—Bear-hunting.—A funny story.—Isard hunting.—A sad story. - - - - 227

CHAPTER XIX.
THE LAWSUIT.

Character of the Bearnais.—Begging.—The coat button.—The picture.—The asylum.—Henry IV.—Bernadotte.—Arrested.—The President of Tribunals.—Denaturalised.—The trial.—Judgment - - 253

CHAPTER XX.
PAU.

Betheram.—A legend.—Birthplace of Henry IV.—Abd-el-Kader.—Dearness of Pau.—Unhealthiness of Pau.—Eaux Bonnes.—Pass of Hourat.—Little statue of the B. V. M.—Talking rocks.—Eaux Chaudes.—Climate. - - - - 265

CHAPTER XXI.
FORBIDDEN BOOKS IN ROME.

From Pau to Rome.—Roman turncoats.—The Temporal Power. - - - - - - 279

CHAPTER XXII.
ANTE-RAILROAD TRAVELLING.

Tailors at court.—A J.P. in the olden time.—F.M. the Duke of Wellington.—Taking the oath.—Schaffhausen and Niagara.—St. Gothard.—An American traveller.—Lugano.—Blockade of the Ticino.—An Austrian corps de garde.—San Salvadore.—Frontier of Lombardy.—General Singer.—Again at Lugano.—Again the frontier.—The cow and the sword.—Away! away! - - - - - 296

CHAPTER XXIII.

A MURDER.

An Italian inn.—The waggoner.—A mysterious youth.—The pretore.—The gensdarmes.—Catholic deputy-lieutenants.—How Austria lost Italy.—Mahomet and the Arab. - - - - - 327

CHAPTER XXIV.

SHADOWS OF COMING EVENTS.

Papal Ceremonial.—The Santo Bambino —New Cardinals.—Pasquinades.—Death of a Roman Prince.—Confirmation.—Head of St. Laurence.—French army of occupation, and the Romans. - - 337

CHAPTER XXV.

COUNTS, QUEENS, PRINCES, AND CARDINALS.

Inventory of my furniture.—English toadyism.—The lady and the guardia nobile.—The same and the French prelate.—A letter and the censorship.—The English language.—Judgment by a Roman tribunal.—Queen Cristina of Spain.—My passport withheld.—Festas and Sundays - - - - - 349

CHAPTER XXVI.

CONVENTS AND KIDNAPPERS.

Tableaux Vivants.—Florence Nightingale and the Nuns.—Catherine of the Wabash.—Rev. Mother at Sentari.—Pious lies.—Cardinal Wiseman and his attornies.—Ecclesiastical property.—Pio Nono and the Monks.—A suggestion. Division of property. 363

NOWADAYS.

CHAPTER I.

EN ROUTE FOR EVERYWHERE.

The Wabash.—The medical consultation.—A roving commission.—An election at Southampton.

"And now forgive me that I ask one question," said good old Dr. Latham, after pummelling and tapping and stethoscoping her collar-bones and her shoulder-blades to his heart's content; "forgive me," he repeated, as he looked at the visiting card I had sent in, "if I ask whether I have the pleasure of seeing one of the young ladies of THE WABASH—of that book of travels in the interior of the United States, which I have read with so much enjoyment?"

Our conscious smiles shewed that he had rightly judged of the country visitors who had come up to town to consult him.

"Curious coincidence!" exclaimed the kind-hearted old doctor, again feeling his little patient's pulse with still greater interest than before.

I myself did not see anything "curious" in the "coincidence"; but I thought that the expression might be a catch-word with the lively physician, as it had been with my neighbour, the solemn Colonel Shedden, who, when the late Duchess of St. Alban's took a ring from her finger and explained to him that Charles the Second had given it to Nell Gwyn and that the Duke of St. Alban's had given it to her, thoughtlessly exclaimed, as he did on every imaginable and unimaginable occasion, "Curious coincidence! A very curious coincidence!"

"Well, then," resumed Dr. Latham, "I am happy to be able to declare that there is nothing whatever the matter with the lungs :—only a bronchial affection which must be taken care of this winter. Your daughter had better remain in-doors whenever the wind is in the north or the east, or when the air is damp and the sun does not shine.". . . .

"But the sun never does shine in the winter, except when the wind is in the north or the east," I interposed.

"True. I own that is pretty much the case during our English winters," replied the doctor. "Of course, it would be safer if you could go abroad."

"If such is your opinion, abroad we must go!" I answered with a heartfelt sigh: for it is not pleasant to break up one's establishment, to forego one's pursuits and interests,—in a word, to leave one's home at the beginning of winter, or, I am Englishman enough to think, at any time.

"Whither are we to go?" I asked.

"I don't much care," replied Dr. Latham: "the case is not so serious but that I would prefer giving you a roving commission to go wherever you like. You probably know the different climates of the Continent better than I do. But you may safely stay in England until Christmas. Our cold weather does not set in till Christmas."

This consultation had taken place on the 4th of November, 1856. We returned on the same day by railway to Botleigh Grange.

A large family cannot be unhoused and transported abroad without many preparations. The doctor had given us till Christmas; but we knew the dangers of travelling through France by land at that late season of the year, and of lodging an invalid for several nights in unfrequented French hotels. The weather was open and mild; and our packing went on slowly. On the 28th of November, an unaccustomed fall of snow surprised our

South of Hampshire climate; and a hard frost set in which lasted for a week. Then came warm cloudy weather, with blasts from the south-west, and frequent showers. Such was the morning of the 8th of December when, having sent all the rest of my family into Southampton before us, I drove in, with my wife, in the pony-carriage, drawn by the two little Black-forest ponies, now twenty-six years old, but which did the six miles in the accustomed forty minutes.

The town of Southampton was then in a state of unusual excitement. An election of a member of Parliament was impending, to replace Sir A. Cockburn, who had taken office. Two candidates from a distance were canvassing the borough on liberal principles; and were opposed by Mr. Richard Andrews, the liberal coach-builder and mayor of the town, though discountenanced by Lord Palmerston and the great ironmonger, who had endeavoured to put a spoke in his wheel. Encouraged by these divisions in the liberal ranks, my friend and neighbour, the Hon. Sir Edward Butler, was putting forth seductive addresses, and hoping to slip into the vacant seat on conservative principles.

I pulled up my ponies at the door of my printer's shop—

"Have at you all, Mr. Marshall!" I exclaimed: "Get this thing printed as soon as possible, and posted about the town."

In the course of the afternoon, the following address was read by many an elector—with what sentiments I cared not. I copy it here in order that those who will have to accompany me through many revolutionary scenes may know, at starting, what were my political principles :—

"TO THE LIBERAL ELECTORS OF SOUTHAMPTON.

"GENTLEMEN,—The constituency of Southampton is so immensely increased within the last ten years, that many of you may not be aware of its previous electoral history. At about that period, it was deemed advisable to secure a LIBERAL CANDIDATE connected by property with the neighbourhood, and whose position would entitle him to the honour of representing the borough in Parliament. In conformity with that opinion, Mr. Richard Andrews headed a deputation to my house, and presented a requisition, at the head of which stood his own name, inviting me to offer myself at the next ensuing election. I assented to the honour proposed to me; and, after I had explained my political principles at a large meeting of the then important Reform Association, Mr. Andrews proposed the following result :—*Resolved.*—'That a requisition, inviting J. R. Beste, Esq., to become a candidate for the representation of this borough upon liberal principles, having been accepted by that gentleman, and this meeting, having heard Mr. Beste's eloquent address and declaration of his opinions, do hereby pledge themselves to give him their unflinching support, and use their utmost strenuous exertions to secure his election at the next vacancy.' 'The resolution' (I quote from the *Hampshire Independent* of January 3rd, 1846) 'was agreed to unanimously.'

"The election came on in the following year, and I was at my post, prepared to fight your battle against two CONSERVATIVE candidates; but, in the meantime, some of the 'Liberals' of Southampton, who had been used to cheer at every meeting the sentiment of Civil and Religious LIBERTY, had the impertinence and inconsistency to question the private religious opinions in which I was born, and object that my religion, as an English Catholic, disqualified me for a seat in Parliament. Mr. Andrews and the Whig Government took up the recreant bigot cry : Sir A. Cockburn was sent down to oppose me, and I was obliged to withdraw from the contest.

" But, in my parting address, I took leave of you only for a time. I repeated to you what my principles were, and had ever been—a Free Trader before Free Trade was thought of—opposed to all State endowments and legal exactions whatsoever, in support of whatsoever religion, in whatsoever part of the world, before the excellent society for the liberation of religion had a being—an advocate for the extension of the suffrage and vote by ballot from my youth upwards. I referred you to my printed and published opinions which I have put forth for the last thirty years—for I began life early—and I told you that, if ever you should think the principles you PROFESS worth contending for, I would be ready to advocate them with you and for us all.

" Such was the state of the borough ten years ago. An election is again impending, and Mr. Andrews (your present mayor, and a most skilful coachmaker) is now, with two other liberal candidates from a distance, dividing the liberal constituency of the borough. It is not my purpose to divide it still more. The conservatives have found the advantage of securing for their candidate a gentleman of position and property in the neighbourhood. I merely put forth this address to inform the new blood amongst you that, should you ever think it wise to recur to the same plan, you will find me, as I have ever been, prepared to advocate what I believe to be the interests of the people and the rights of man. One of the oldest magistrates in this division, a deputy-lieutenant for the county, connected with your town by extensive landed property and many ties, I will be with you should you ever wish to go to the poll for the sake of PRINCIPLE. The liberation of all religions from state control is the only principle I now think worth contending for. I care not to stand on any other.

"I should not have addressed you now but for the disunion brought into the liberal ranks by Mr. Andrews. What will be the upshot, it rests with you to say. The health of one of my family compels me to go to Lisbon during the severity of the winter season. But the election will not be yet ; and, if you care for principle rather than for expediency, if you will not be dictated to by half a score of bigots who call themselves liberals, I shall be within hail, and always

"Your faithful neighbour and servant,

J. RICHARD DIGBY BESTE."

"*Botleigh Grange, 8th December,* 1856."

I left Mr. Marshall perusing the above address; and our ponies rattled down to the Docks.

CHAPTER II.

THE MAIL PACKET.

The P. and O. Company and my horses.—The muster-roll.—
Pleasant anchorage.—Diversions in a storm.—The
Admiralty agent.

THE old *Tagus* of the Peninsular and Oriental Company, lay in the same place where I had before seen it, along side the quay. My family and carriage were on board. One of my horses—the iron-grey one which, confidingly and intelligently, always, in any difficulty, first followed me or the coachman, that he might encourage the other—was swinging in mid air above the ship's side; trembling, but yet neighing to the other that stood under an open shed awaiting its turn. My coachman came and complained to me that the Company had provided two boxes of unequal size; and that one of them was too small for horses nearly seventeen hands high ; and that the agents had refused to change it, alleging that they had no other. Let this be borne in mind. Let it be borne in mind also that our places had been taken a fortnight before, and that the Company had charged one hundred pounds for our passage. Our party consisted of my wife and me, our three daughters, and two little boys; two maids, our butler, coachman, carriage and these two horses.

The sky was overcast. Broken clouds hung low. The air was warm; gusts of wind rushed over us; and rain came down in frequent showers.

"What do you think of the weather?" we asked, with nervous anxiety, of the officer on deck; who, with blue cap strapped under his chin and his hands in his breeches pockets, was dividing his attention between the lowering sky and our horses swinging in air. The little man grinned with apparent delight, and showed his white teeth from ear to ear.

"If ever you had a rough passage by sea in your life," he said, "prepare for one now. You had better go and insure those horses."

This was not encouraging. But we were regularly booked for Lisbon, and there was no escape. I went on shore to the Company's office and proposed to insure my horses. The Company could only insure against loss by shipwreck, but not against any other accident. Of shipwreck, I had no fear.

"You need have no fear of anything, sir," exclaimed the agent, Captain Engledew: "The weather looks ugly in port; but the wind is going down and it will be all right before you get outside the Isle of Wight."

I returned on deck, and told my grinning friend what I had heard. He grinned more than ever: pulled the collar of his rough great coat around his ears, and thrust his hands deeper into his breeches pockets. At half-past three, Captain Christian, our skipper, came on board. We shook hands with our domestic chaplain, who returned on shore, promising that he would offer up many a prayer for us. The chimney hissed. The paddles plashed. The *Tagus* moved its unwieldy bulk; and we went below deck to arrange our cabins. There the ladies occupied themselves while the vessel was in the calm of the Southampton water. I myself returned on deck, where my coachman and the ship's carpenter were arranging a sort of pent-house over the heads of the horses, to protect them against the rain and wind. Curlews circled overhead and amid the ruins of Netley Abbey on the left bank. Returning fishing boats danced, like walnut shells, on the tiny waves. The clouds scudded past, and dashed single rain-drops in our faces.

The muster-roll to dinner was well attended; for we had not yet rounded Calshot Castle; and all our fellow-passengers showed themselves to the right and left of the captain. Leaving a vacant place for the Admiralty agent who kept his cabin, there sat a gouty colonel who was going out to Gibraltar to escape an English winter: there sat an English cavalry officer with his young wife: there sat two or three other English officers without wives: and there sat one who had overstaid his leave, and who expected to be put under arrest so soon as he should land at Gibraltar. There sat a lady and gentleman with their old father going to Malaga, by medical advice, in the hope that the climate might prolong the old man's life: and there sat an elderly man—a great wine merchant of Cadiz—hastening to rejoin his wife, and with solemn mockery pooh-poohing the grave looks which the weather called up in us all and even in the ship's officers. He and one or two others were seasoned sailors and defied the briny influences: the rest of us round the dinner table were as jolly as fresh-caught fish gasping in a wicker-basket. The motion of the steamer increased; and most of the company rushed on deck with the pretence of wishing to see her round Calshot Castle.

Calshot Castle, indeed, was there; and there was *The* Island, as we Hampshire men call it, rising on our left hand—its bleak downs blending with the darkening skies and the lowering clouds. Nearer to us, these were streaming in the likeness of horse-tails swept by the rushing blast. The tops of the short waves were lashed into foam around us; and sea-gulls careered and circled wildly overhead. My friend, the second mate, who had foretold us a rough passage, was keeping the quarter deck, and touched his cap with a triumphant grin, as I passed by him. The Admiralty agent came up and paced the deck with the captain, often pausing to look anxiously at the threatening sky. We watched him as one on whom our fate depended. "Would he were fatter!" I exclaimed as we noted his tall spare form and the quiet glance with which he eyed the horizon.

"He is a hard, stern man!" whispered my wife, "and there is no hope that he will order the captain to put back. It is evident that he will carry on his mail bags to the bottom of the sea."

Disconsolately we plodded our anxious way

between the island and the low lands of the New Forest; and noted the falling back of the coast on either hand and the opening of the waters in front. We came upon several tall vessels and steamers, and were rejoiced to see the crew of our own vessel casting anchor amongst them. We felt like doomed prisoners suddenly reprieved; and the night wore quietly away as we lay thus in Yarmouth Roads.

TUESDAY MORNING.—The wind was evidently higher than it had been yesterday. But the thin admiralty agent and Captain Christian, who looked as impassive as he, consulted together; the anchor was heaved on board, and at half after nine we pushed out into the open channel. Suffice it to say that the following hours were disgusting— whether we passed them reclining in our cabin or in the saloon, or on the wet and storm-swept deck, I knew not, and scarce heeded which way we were going; and it was with a grunt of dubious satisfaction that, at half-past four in the afternoon, I found that we were again anchored in our old moorings of Yarmouth Roads. Again the criminals were unexpectedly reprieved. We dined and spent a pleasant evening. The admiralty agent, Lieutenant Loyd, unthawed, and proved that he was not so stern a man. Captain Christian, too, shewed that he had human sympathies, as we all laughed at the impatience of the old Cadiz wine merchant who surlily insisted that we ought to have pushed on through the gale in order the sooner to bear him to the arms of his venerable wife.

WEDNESDAY.—No abatement of the gale. Hard as ever, it blew from the south-west directly in the teeth of our course. Up with the anchor; and again we struggle out into the storm, while stern determination again comes over Mr. Loyd and the captain of the *Tagus*. We left the great steamer, *The Avon*, quietly anchored in the Roads; and through the rising waves we splashed and cut our way. My coachman staggered to me on the quarter-deck, and requested me to have the horses seen to, for that he was going to lie up for the rest of the voyage. I examined the state of the poor animals. The one in the larger box seemed to be doing well; the chest of the poor grey was swollen, owing to his constantly striking it against the top rail of the box, which ought to have risen to his throat. He neighed as I felt his ears and had a sack, filled with hay and chaff, placed, as a cushion, between his chest and the rail. I then lay myself disconsolate on the deck until my old friend, the second mate, took pity on my state; and, without any show of triumph that his prophecy was fulfilled, led me to his own cabin on the deck, where I remained for hours apart from the noisome noises that disturbed the main saloon. The sea broke over the cabin and splashed on the deck outside; but I pulled to the door and tried to interest myself in reading Cooper's novel, "The Pilot." Breakfast, luncheon, dinner, tea, and supper held, however, their accustomed hours with such of us as felt no ill effects from the sea, or valiantly battled against them; and our daughters learned to like "crab," made for them with Cheshire cheese and mustard by the old gouty Colonel, or bravely paced the deck with the admiralty agent, Lieutenant Lloyd, who interested them in the fate of his own children, or in the sympathy he evinced for themselves. We no longer looked at the kind sailor's intelligent grey head and light blue eye with wishes "that he were fatter."

CHAPTER III.

THE BAY OF BISCAY

Royal Presents.—The Storm.—The Novena—Saved.

WE had left Southampton dock on Monday, and now, on Thursday, we ought to have been entering the Tagus; but here we were, still tossing about in the old tub of that name, and able only to congratulate ourselves that if she was the slowest, she was the safest sea boat belonging to the Peninsular and Oriental Company : that our captain and stewards were most attentive ; and that in the opinion of all the children and ladies on board, the stewardess, Mrs. Paul, was worth her weight in gold—though so vast a nugget was never dug out of Australian or Californian mine. One or two of the cavalry officers came to me with evil prognostications about my poor grey horse. His ears were cold, and blood was running from his nose and mouth. The people of the ship said that it came from his head: but we observed that it gushed out more copiously whenever the motion of the vessel threw him against that top rail of his low horse-box. My feelings towards the Company which had sent a valuable horse to sea in a box unsuited to it became very savage. The second mate, Mr. Shrubsole, and the sailors, did all they could: the first mate, a man named Johnson, whose nature did not seem to be freighted with an over-cargo of sympathy or politeness, contented himself with saying that, " of course, all horses fared ill on board the Peninsular steamers: that they had taken on board three presented by the Queen of England to the King of Portugal, and that two of them had died on the passage, and the other as soon as it was landed."

My friend of the cavalry replied that he himself had brought home scores of horses from the Crimea without the slightest difficulty or accident.

Captain Christian was anxious and wholly engaged in the management of his vessel. We were entering the Bay of Biscay, and the gale blew harder than ever.

FRIDAY.—Still the storm seemed to increase, and our discomforts certainly did so. My wife and I had a four-berth cabin to ourselves. She had occupied the berth nearest the side of the ship, that she might have air from the port-holes. These, however, had necessarily been shut down at starting; though it had been early discovered, with the rising of the waves, that they could not be effectually closed. Again and again the ship's carpenter had been sent for; but he could not prevent the water from oozing through: so that now the mattrass on which she lay was thoroughly saturated; and the clothes in her carpet bag and on the lower berth, which we used as a table, were all wet through with the brine. Such was the accommodation on board the *Tagus*, for which the P. and O. Company charged ten pounds per head!

As we lay in our berths, it was evident to us, from the motion of the vessel, that the gale and the waves had increased during the night. The tossing of the ship had upon me the same effect that the rocking of a cradle has upon a sleeping child. It made me drowsy beyond measure; and I felt that I could have slept away successive days. My poor wife crawled across the cabin and, kneeling beside my berth and clutching to it to steady herself, tried to convince me that we were all in great danger.

"From what?" I drowsily asked. "There are no rocks near, and how can the broad old tub sink unless she has a hole in her bottom to let in the water?"

Through all my impassiveness, however, the thought was ever present to my mind that we might, perchance, go to the bottom; and then I looked on the bronze crucifix hanging in front of me, and which was already turned quite green, with the washing of the brine through the porthole. I said prayers and commended ourselves to the Almighty; and then I consoled myself with the thought that, if we did go to the bottom, we should all go down together—that no daughters or young children were on land to suffer the want of guardianship; and then I thought, with Cæsar, that there could be nothing to fear, because that I —great I—was on board: and anon it occurred to me that the world had gone on without Cæsar, and that it might go on as well even without me or mine, and that the utmost result of our loss to the public would be a paragraph in the papers saying how sadly a whole family had sunk together—while those who read the paragraph would rather that we had gone down than that they should have missed the reading of the account: and so I again prayed and dozed, and dozed and prayed; and at length I roused myself, dressed, and went upon deck.

Truly enough the wind had increased and the waves were running what is called "mountains high." Lieutenant Lloyd told me that the captain was fearful that his stock of coal would not last out across the Bay, and had been doubting whether he should not try to work in towards Bordeaux: he would not have hesitated to do so had he known the coast, although there would have been danger in attempting to alter the course of the vessel. While we were conversing, the captain came up, and said to Mr. Lloyd, "Let us hoist the trysail and make a run for our lives." It was done, and away we staggered for a few hours in a direct line across the Bay.

In the evening, while we were down in the saloon, this sail was blown out of its bolts with a tremendous clash; and while it flapped and bellied out on every side, we heard a scrambling on the deck as if the whole crew were being washed overboard. Tears began to stream down the cheeks of the surly Cadiz wine-merchant, who bemoaned his folly in having come by sea rather than face a nine days' journey by land—although he still maintained that all our danger was owing to our having lain so long in Yarmouth Roads rather than rush at once into the storm. The gouty colonel and the captain of cavalry looked grave, like sensible men; the young gentleman who expected to be put under arrest on his arrival at Gibraltar, with one or two other of his brother officers, played at chuck-farthing against the wine-glasses on the table, and laughed and talked uproariously and nervously-loud to conceal their fears. Suddenly the ship staggered under a dull blow, as from a mountain of mud cast against its side: a part of the paddle-box was washed away; and another huge wave, emulating its predecessor, leaped upon the top of the skylight of our saloon; stove it in; and brought it, with all its glass and framework, upon the dining-table before us. Lieutenant Lloyd hastened on deck. Captain Christian was there—self-collected and giving all the needful orders with the coolness of an experienced sailor. He knows not that he was heard to whisper to himself, "Oh God, what will become of my poor wife and children!"

The invalid passengers who were going to Malaga

were, like ourselves, Catholics. That lady, also, had her husband and child on board. That evening she went quietly round to all the cabins occupied by my family, and by such other of our co-religionists as were on board, and urged that all should immediately begin a "novena"—certain and the same prayers to be said by all at the same time and with the same common intent; but she proposed that, instead of being said every day, they should be said whenever the bell struck—for, amid all our danger, the ship-discipline was maintained. The suggestion was joyfully adopted by all. I know not why it was not mentioned to me—I believe I was not in my cabin at the time. I only know that, after the second striking of the bell and the second repetition of the prayers, one of the noisy Gibraltar officers was heard on the companion ladder exclaiming,—

"Hallo! The wind has veered to the northwards!"

"Aye: quite unexpectedly," replied another. "There must be some good soul on board that has been praying for us."

CHAPTER IV.

NEW SHORES.

Lost ships.—Vigo.—The brutal first-mate.—The murdered horse.—Money *versus* Letters.—Our log.—Coasting.—The other Tagus—The Custom House.—Night-walk in Lisbon.

SATURDAY.—Although it had slightly moderated, a stiff gale was still blowing, but rather from the north. My poor grey horse was now evidently in much suffering. The blows of the upper rail of his box, against which he had been thrown so long, had brought on inflammation of the chest, which he now relieved by a constant swinging motion—throwing himself back and then against it ; while every fresh pressure caused more blood to issue from his mouth. The quarter-master, who had taken my coachman's place about him, kept it washed out and supplied him with the water he incessantly craved by unmistakeable signs : while the foolish people around insisted that he must be doing well because he eat the hay that was placed before him.

They knew not that a horse will die with food in its mouth.

Sunday.—The gale had sensibly decreased; and although, to passengers who had not been exposed to such a storm, the sea would have still appeared to run "mountains high," we felt it to be comparatively still water; and our daughters delighted to walk the quarter-deck by the help of good Lieutenant Lloyd's arm; and heeded not that it inclined on one side at an angle of forty-five degrees, and that, every now and then, the rising and sinking of the prow and stern gave them a steep hill to breast, or made them run down to the further end. Thus were we advancing with renewed hope and spirits, when a large steamer met us from the south-west and hailed us. Both tried to lie to; but were carried beyond the range of the speaking trumpet. Again both wore round; and then, borne along the blast and over the foam-curled waves, came the rough inquiry,—

"What has become of the *Ripon* steamer? Long due at Vigo."

"Left Southampton four days before us. Not seen her. Had enough to do to look after ourselves."

Again we rolled forward through the sea: but

at a slower rate: for, as our captain had foreseen would happen, his coal had fallen short, and we were now burning the refuse, of which, fortunately, a large quantity seemed to have accumulated in the lower regions.

MONDAY.—We had passed Corunna: had rounded Cape Finisterre. Land was in sight on our left hand. The sun shone bright. The sea was comparatively smooth. The air was warm. Our invalid daughter, for whom we had undertaken this voyage, came on deck. All looked bright and fair. We passed inside some picturesque rocky islands on the right; steamed up a quiet bay; and cast anchor before a picturesque town surmounted by an old castle, by wooded hills, and by a massive church. We were in Vigo harbour: one of the safest and best and largest harbours in the world; but the shipping of which was now represented by our own battered steamer, and by one or two Spanish coasting luggers.

My first care was to land my poor murdered horse—destroyed by the negligence of the P. and O. Company. I thought he might possibly recover after a few days' rest on shore, and could rejoin us by land, or by another steamer. My coachman had reappeared as soon as we were under the shelter of the Spanish coast, and now anxiously busied himself about him. The poor beast seemed scarcely able to stand; but was lowered, in his ill-fated box, into the barge that came alongside and was to convey him to shore.

"I say," cried the first mate, Mr. Johnson, of whose unprepossessing ways I have already written; "I say," he cried to a sailor, "unloose those slings from under the horse and throw them up here."

I expostulated that the horse was too weak and battered to support himself on his legs without slings until he reached the shore.

"We have nothing to do with him when he is once off the ship's side," replied Mr. Johnson.

A murmur of disgust arose from the English officers around, who had taken an interest in the sufferings of the noble horse; and when I took out my tablets and showed the mate that I had written down his very words, and should report what care he took of the property entrusted to the P. and O. Company, he muttered something about being personally responsible for the slings, and ordered the sailors to bring them back so soon as the horse should be landed.

We watched the poor beast rolling from side to

side with the motion of the barge; and heard his frequent neigh to his companion remaining on deck. He was alongside the quay and, staggering, stood upon dry land again, and was led out of sight. Let me finish the history of the poor murdered grey, and let me be excused for saying so much about him, for that we had done much together. I had first seen him a three year old, five years before, in the stable of a dealer in Oxford Street, the property of a Norfolk landowner who had bred him, and who valued him at £170. He had served me well in Hampshire; and I had driven him myself through France and Switzerland, and over the St. Gothard to Rome. We understood one another. My coachman, who landed at Vigo with him, rejoined me a few days after: but without the grey. He told me that his sufferings throughout the night had been most apparent; that his shrieks—those strange wild shrieks that horses so seldom emit even in their agony—had disturbed all the hotel; on the following morning he had looked the coachman steadily in the face and died.

At Vigo, we learned that the *Ripon* steamer, respecting which so much anxiety had been expressed, and which had left Southampton four days before us, was lying safely in the harbour of Corunna. She had on board no mails, but a very large amount of specie; and, to secure its safety, she had run from the storm into port. Our *Tagus* carried the mails and passengers; but these latter, being less valuable than specie, had been endangered by keeping the sea.

Mem: Never to go to sea again in a mail packet; but always to prefer one carrying specie.

The *Alhambra*, respecting which our captain was anxious, and which we ought to have met long ago, had put back to Lisbon. The powerful Brazilian steamer, the *Avon*, which we had left anchored in Yarmouth Roads, was only now passing southwards. I record these details to prove that we had been out in no common gale. We were delighted afterwards to see that the English journals of that day did justice to the severity of the weather. Indeed when, on my arrival, I claimed of the Peninsular and Oriental Company compensation for my horse, destroyed by being placed in too small a horse-box, I received, in answer, Captain Christian's report, which stated—
"The weather was such that I myself am perfectly surprised that either of them lived, or, in fact, that carriage, horses, and everything on deck was

not washed overboard. The gales and sea from the 10th to the 13th in the Bay and Channel being of such a furious character that I do not remember to have encountered anything like it for many years; in proof of which I beg to refer you to the remarks in the log."

No compensation was given. We had to console ourselves with the thought that matters might have been worse. I would not, however, leave Captain Christian and his second mate, Mr. Shrubsole, without bearing testimony to their very great civility, kindness, and attention to the comfort and security of all on board.

And now all was calm and sunshine as we steamed out of Vigo bay, and took our course along the rock-bound coast of Spain. Gradually it became less and less precipitous, and towns and villages showed themselves in the light of the setting sun. We held our steady way; nor felt a regret that our steamer did not approach and lie off Oporto. To land once and for all, was our only anxiety.

Tuesday morning arose bright and warm and balmy in the gentle breezes from the spreading western sea. The Berlingas rocks stood up, bold and fantastic, from the water, and, after passing before them, the coast again rose in boldness. The towers of Mafra loomed gloomily on the mainland; and pinnacles that we were told arose in Cintra, engaged every eager eye. We rounded the promontory and the low sandbanks, and steamed quietly up the yellow Tagus.

And yellow, indeed, were its tiny waves and the rocks and villages on its shores in the glow of the December sun. It was the 16th of December; and it looked and felt like a beautiful summer's day. The windows in the picturesque old castle of Belem were spangled with yellow and ruddy glint as they stood out in the river course; and pile above pile of the town of Lisbon crept up the steep hill-side and overlooked the glassy stream. A few English vessels of war were there quietly anchored; and a boat pulled off from one of them for despatches. We gave them and proceeded on our course; and, at four o'clock in the afternoon, anchored on the outside of a mass of shipping which lay between us and a handsome building which they told us was the custom-house. The shores of the upper river about the city looked flat and uninteresting: and altogether the shores of the Tagus lacked the massive woodland, or the clumps and single trees and the bold cliffs and pinnacles of rock that are needed to the composition of a picturesque landscape. An expanse of water was, indeed, there. The town rose on steep acclivities on our left; the high shores on the opposite side were brown with the bare rock and earth, or verdant with partial vegetation: but this was all—all, save the glorious sun that was now sinking in splendour behind them. I left all the passengers at dinner in the saloon; and, with the help of Mr. Vanzaller, the Company's agent, who came on board and showed much zeal, activity, and good humour, I overlooked the landing of my carriage and of the remaining one of my horses. The carriage was detained in the customhouse, as being something almost worse than contraband goods. They pitied the state of the horse, and permitted it to be led at once to a stable in the town.

I returned on board to fetch my family; and after the usual amount of wrangling amongst boatmen and porters, we all landed at the customhouse steps at seven o'clock. The people had left work for the night,—all but one, who civilly told us to bring forward our "bag-nights," as he ingeniously called our carpet-bags; and, having satisfied himself by a glance that their contents were really of the kind which he wished to denote by that expressive word, he politely wished us good night, and sent us forth with a retinue of porters.

It was now quite dark, and we groped our way under the tropical evergreen trees beside the custom-house; and, remembering the descriptions in *Childe Harold* and other writers, dreaded to think of the walk that lay before us through the streets of Lisbon. The porter opened the wide gates of the yard; and, going forth, we found ourselves in a vast space, the sides of which were too distant for us to perceive the architecture of the buildings around, although the size and outline of the square were plainly marked by the lines of brilliant gas lamps that circled it. We crossed the space diagonally, and came upon a cluster of gas lamps in the centre, surrounding a large pile surmounted by an equestrian statue. This, then, was what the English call "Black Horse Square." We threaded our way along a handsome street, still well lighted with gas, and paved on either side; and we sought lodgings at different hotels. All were too full to accommodate us; but the mistress of the Bragança good-naturedly offered to lodge us for the night in her own private house.

After a hearty supper, we sank into beds that appeared—oh! so luxurious, after the wet holes in which we had been "cabined, cribbed, confined," for nine days in the wretched *Tagus!* Soon, however, how mine began to rock and spin beneath me! All night, I seemed to be climbing waves and sinking into their hollows; and for two days afterwards, everything swam around me, and I staggered on level ground, as that vessel herself had laboured and rolled across the Bay of Biscay.

CHAPTER V.

A NEW LOCATION.

Lisbon by daylight.—Hissing in Portugal and Australia —
No lodgings.—A retrospective quotation.—Christmas
Eve.—A terrific hotel bill.

WHEN we awoke next morning, we found that we had slept with a large window of our bedroom open to the north. It mattered not. It was the 17th of December; but, in that beautiful climate, what mattered it whether a window were open or shut at night?

Again I returned to the custom-house, and claimed my luggage, which had been landed and left there. It was but slightly examined, if at all, and passed without difficulty. England is the only country in the world in which custom-house officers are really troublesome. To get my carriage was, however, a more difficult matter. The importation of carriages seems to be strictly forbidden; and it was only by the favour of the

Portuguese Minister of Finance, whom I waited upon in person, that I was permitted to have it, after paying down to the treasury £90 as a deposit, to be returned whenever I should take it out of Portugal.

But how magnificent were the public buildings that I had to visit in order to accomplish this arrangement! Seen by night, as we had walked to our hotel, the streets and squares through which we passed, brilliantly as they were lighted by gas, had most unexpectedly impressed me; but when I got acquainted with them now by daylight, I could but marvel at a vastness of design, and a grandeur of architecture, that I had nowhere seen expended on such establishments. All this part of Lisbon, having in fact been destroyed by the great earthquake, arose again, like London after its fire, on one uniform plan of rectilinear grandeur; and it would be difficult to find handsomer districts, in any city, than " Black Horse Square" (as the English call the Praça do Commercio) than the Rocio, and the streets about them. Other parts of the city justify still all that *Childe Harold* says against it. No sewers there exist, and the street is the common receptacle of everything that is thrown out of the window, and that does not alight upon the person of the passer by.

But the population of the streets, the strange dress and habits of those who throng them, offer an endless fund of amusement, until the freshness of comparison is worn off. The great cloaks that hang loosely over the shoulders of the men; the white kerchiefs pinned over the heads and under the chins of the women; the tall sugar-loaf broad-brimmed hats of the peasants: their gaudy dress; their trowsers tied up with a long red sash; their jackets, with dangling silver buttons, thrown over their left shoulders like Figaro in the play; their shirt fronts fastened by large gilt clasps; their long brass-bound cudgels, which they often manage to bring with them into the city, instead of leaving them, according to police regulation, at the gate, as if they were going into a museum and the citizens' heads were objects of art that might be cracked or broken; the blue coats and trowsers and straight black Hessian boots of the priests, whose sacerdotal dress is certainly that of a church militant; the heavy-loaded carts and waggons drawn by magnificent oxen, and creaking along the streets as the lumbering axle turns with the lumbering wheels which are fastened to it;—the greatest thoroughfare in the town is called the "Rua do Sciados—creaking street," from the number of these vehicles that pass along it; the little loose-swinging tumbril carriages jerking and jolting hither and thither, and drawn by a pair of little mules—carriages in which the very first of the gentry, and my valued friend, Marshal Duke of Terceira among the rest, delight—his beautiful Duchess had a more modern equipage; the long livery coats of the coachmen and servants, which come down to their heels, and so render other livery unnecessary because unseen; all these, and a thousand more strange objects, delighted me during my first walk, and until the novelty of all I saw wore gradually away.

I remembered me of the prints in a little edition I had left at home of *Gil Blas*. There were many carriages, mules, men-servants, and personages who must, methought, have been drawn from the life I now saw around me. And yet those purported to represent Spaniards.

The manners of the people were not less curious. I had been talking to one, and, having parted from him, had gone half down the street, when I heard a succession of violent sounds of "hish! hish!" behind me. I turned round to see what poor devil could be incurring such a hissing from the mob, when I perceived my Portuguese acquaintance signing to me that he wished to say something more. I paused, and he came up panting; but no one of the crowd paid the least attention to the call, except one or two horses that I noticed to stand still, till their drivers gave them to understand, that it was not addressed to themselves. I should now stop in any street in Europe at the sound of this well-learned "hish"! which is as peculiar as the "coe" of the Australians; one of whom, we are told, looking out of a second-floor window in the Strand, saw a settler, whom he had not known to be in England, pass on with the crowd on the opposite side of the street. "Coe!" cried the Australian from the window; the other in the street instantly paused and gazed around and above, till he discovered who it was that called him by the only sound he could have distinguished in the hubbub.

My *hisser* was just taking leave of me when up rushed a friend of his, who seemed as surprised at the meeting as the two Australians in London had been; and, catching my Portuguese round the waist, lifted him three times fairly off his legs, in the heartiness of his delighted and friendly hug.

I went on my way—passing many a labouring man, or Gallician water-carrier, who, meeting a friend of the same class, would greet him with a low bow, and pray that God would give him good days, and then politely inquire into the health of every member of his family.

All this was very well and very amusing; but I could not find nor hear of any house or apartment to be let—no, not even unfurnished, if I could have hired furniture to put into it. I was told that, as soon as Brazilians had made their fortune, they returned to settle in the mother-country and bought up every house before it was built, or in the market; and, as no travelling English or other strangers ever came to Lisbon, apartments to let were not provided. Formerly, when the rest of the Continent was shut against us by the wars or policy of the first Napoleon, our country people, as we all know, ventured to Lisbon to enjoy a mild winter climate; but since the South of France, Italy, and Egypt have been open to them, none would brave a voyage across the Bay of Biscay when they could secure what they believed to be an equally good climate without risking a lengthened sea-route. I was in despair, and would have put up with almost any lodging rather than remain in an hotel,—for, though we had moved into good rooms in the Bragança on the day after our arrival, and were well satisfied with that hotel, still an hotel could not be a comfortable home for a family of young girls and children.

At length our minister, the Hon. Mr. Howard, and Mr. Smith our consul, both of whom kindly interested themselves for us, brought me word that a Mrs. Jones, who kept a respectable boarding-house in a good quarter of the town, offered to give it up to us. I went to see it; found much that I did not like, and would have turned away from, but that our friends assured me that I must either take that or stay in the hotel. It was Hobson's choice. I bargained, however, with Mrs. Jones that she and all her own family and servants should leave the premises and give up the whole to us; and for £100 she agreed to these terms, and surrendered it to us for four months from Christmas Day.

And here let me return once more upon the past to quote two or three pages which, in looking over memoranda of our journeys, I have just found in the handwriting of one whom, those who have read the "Wabash" will, I am sure, be glad to meet with again. I can form no better wish for them and for myself, than that we may all meet again my dear, my beautiful daughter Lucy. Thus, then, runs her little manuscript:—

"Everything was now prepared for our departure from Botleigh Grange, and I believe every one was sorry to go. Papa and mamma disliked the crossing of the sea. For some days, the weather had changed. Instead of the bright frost and snow, we had nasty, warm, close weather, and very high winds, almost hurricanes; but we were to start on the 8th of December, and I felt that, whatever the weather, we should be safe. Dr. MacAuliff, our chaplain, gave us all medals that had been blessed with prayers for the wearers of them; and, on the morning of the 8th, papa, mamma, and I received Holy Communion. We had all done the same on the 6th. At half-past two the boat started. Every one expected bad weather, and at night, we anchored off Yarmouth because the weather was too rough for us to go on. I was in high spirits and felt sure that we should come to no harm. Next morning, we started again; the sea was very high, and we were tossed about terribly, and every plank creaked. I was very bad. At midday, I heard that we had turned back, and at four, we were in still water again,

Next morning we tried it again, and this time we went on; but I was obliged to go down to the cabin with the captain's help, and was very sad. It was very awful to feel the rolling and tossing; to hear all the planks creaking and moaning; and, every now and then a smash of glasses. The storm continued all night; and next day, Thursday, it was as bad. Every sailor was sick: nobody had seen such weather for years: still I felt, 'We are quite safe—no harm will come to us.' On Friday, it was worse than ever; but though I was so sure that we were quite safe, I was praying all the time. I was quite ready to die, and knew that we were in great danger, but still I felt that we should be saved. Friday night, a great sea came into the saloon: for a moment I thought we had sprung a leak, and that all was over; but when I heard the water coming from above, I knew it was all right. I heard them put up a sail to steady us, and then that it was blown away like a ribbon. Still we prayed, and I never lost my faith. I could not think that God would disregard the mass that was daily offered for us by Dr. Mac Auliff, at home; I could not doubt that the Blessed Virgin would pray for us, and so I was not afraid, for my Jesus was with me. I had been very sick and had not got up since Wednesday, but had eaten hardly anything; on this Friday, I was better. I heard that every one on board was in bad spirits, except some one who had tried to jest with the captain, who had told him that it was no jesting matter. Mamma had been very sick, and was in low spirits.

"At nine o'clock, Mrs. Roupe came and proposed that we should all say a novena. We said the prayers directly. After we had said them the second time, I heard some one coming down stairs, saying the glass was rising, etc. I went to mamma and found her crying and very ill. I tried to comfort her, and went upstairs. Mr. Loyd helped me, and stayed with me some time. The captain took me to his cabin, and shewed me on the chart where we were—about one-third across the Bay of Biscay; and I realised our position. The sea was running mountains high; but they said it had gone down in a most surprising manner. Mrs. Roupe and I were the only ladies up. Saturday; still improving. The wind was favourable; and, on Sunday, we went on beautifully to Vigo. And now gratitude instead of prayer took possession of me. While we were stopping at Vigo, I said the Te Deum and Gloria in Excelsis and the Litany of Glory. But I was often obliged to stop; and God understood my silence; for it spoke better than words. And now I was all gratitude; and my gratitude was so great that it made me miserable; and I was obliged to hide the tears that *would* come, and keep them in till night. But then, when I was in bed, and I thought of the dangers we had gone through, I let my tears flow freely; for I knew not how to thank God, but I thought that these tears were the best prayers of praise that I could offer to Him. And for three days, I had to go and hide them and to keep them back; but at night they came again for two hours, till at last I fell asleep. I had such a delightful feeling as I drank in the beautiful scenery and felt the sun so warm; I could not work or read or do anything but look and look and drink it all in.

"And then came Christmas Day. I woke up and heard the bells. Oh, how beautiful they were! Not solemn, but so full of joy! It was daybreak; and all was quiet and harmonious like those bells. But I could not enjoy them properly, nor Christmas Day, nor *the* Hymn, for I had been angry the day before, and all my nice feeling was gone, and I have not been right since; for I have not been to Confession, and I have been very bad. But last night I prepared myself, and it is again a beautiful day, and I have been reading; and I feel rather better. I want to feel nice again, but I can't quite yet. The hills in front are all covered with a blue haze, and it is lovely."

That is all, reader. Was it not worth copying out? It has done us both good.

Yes; those Lisbon bells were very sweet. We had been delighted first to hear them on the night before, on Christmas-eve. The thermometer stood at 64 as we went out to go to midnight mass. It was a bright starlight night. Suddenly, a slight cloud suffused the sky, and a little shower of rain fell while the stars shone on, visible through the transparent veil. Who could not but remember the words of the Psalmist:—
"Rorate cœli desuper et nubes pluant justum, Drop dew, ye heavens, from above, and let the clouds rain down the just one"? We went into the church. A partition divided the great door and was carried down the nave. It parted the women on one side from the men on the other side of the church. All was a blaze of light. The music was soft and harmonious as the bells. There was no braying serpent from French cathe-

drals: there were no noisy fiddles and violoncellos from Italian sacred choirs. The music was sweet and devotional.

Two days afterwards, we moved into our new house, No. 44, Rua da Sacramento da Lapa, Buenos Ayres; having paid our bill at the Hotel of Bragança—one hundred and eighty-two thousand nine hundred and thirty reis;—so they please to keep their accounts in Portugal, in a nominal coin which does not exist, and of which about 4500 go to the pound sterling; so that the apparently awful amount of my bill reduced itself to little more than forty pounds,—not an exorbitant charge for carriage-hire, board, lodging, service, and horse-keep during ten days for ourselves and five children, four servants and one horse—the survivor of the P. and O. Company's neglect.

CHAPTER VI.

SOCIETY AT LISBON.

A celebrated traveller.—The Royal Family.—Presentation at Court.—The King, Don Pedro.—Court Receptions.—Toilettes.—The Duke of Terceira.—The Saxe Coburgs.—The English Legation.—The Papal Nunzio.—A bull-fight.—The ships at anchor.—Mourning ceremonial.

THE *Jornal do Commercio*—which was then the leading journal of Lisbon—published the following paragraph in its number of 27 December, 1856:—

" Viajante celebre.—Chegou a Lisboa, e acha-se hospedado no hotel de Bragança o celebre viajante inglez Mr. Beste, o qual com a sua familia tem percorrido a major parte da Europa e da America.

"Mr. Beste é author de algumas obras religiosas; e são tambem suas as *Recollections of Rome, Wabash ou aventuras de um inglez e sua familia no interior da America,* obras muito apreciadas na Gran Bretanha.

"Mr. Beste tenciona na proxima primavera fazer uma digressão pelo faiz. Parece que viajara na sua propria carroagem como sempre costuma."—

"Celebrated traveller. There has arrived at Lisbon and lodged himself at the Hotel Bragança the celebrated English traveller Mr. Beste, who, with his family, has visited the greater part of Europe and America. Mr. Beste is the author of some religious works, and also of the *Recollections of Rome, Wabash, or Adventures of an English Family in the Interior of America;* works that are much appreciated in Great Britain. Mr. Beste intends next spring to make a digression through the country. It appears that he will travel in his own carriage, as he is always in the habit of doing."

Now all this was very flattering, notwithstanding its absurdity. Notwithstanding the absurdity of supposing that I should have carried my family to Portugal for the purpose of visiting the country, and that I intended to travel in my own carriage through provinces in which there are no roads, it was very flattering. Whence the learned editor could have had his information about me, I could not guess. English families, as I have said, seldom land at Lisbon; a stray arrival, therefore, created the more sensation. I found everybody very civil. While waiting in the anteroom of the Minister of Finance to get permission to land my carriage, I had made acquaintance with the Conde de Sobral, Civil Governor of Lisbon, with all the members of whose family we had afterwards the pleasure of being intimate; the Prime Minister, Marquis Loulé (who had married the aunt of the king) was prompted, by the Portuguese innate spirit of politeness, to call upon me two or three days after my arrival; and, as I have before-mentioned, I experienced from our English minister and consul all those attentions which all diplomatists, when they are not ashamed of their country, pay to the countrymen whom they represent. In a very short time, we were acquainted with most of the society of Lisbon; and we as soon learned to consider it one of the pleasantest with which we had ever mingled. Let me here give a general idea of this society,—respecting the privacy of individuals, as in duty bound.

The present King of Portugal, Don Pedro V, was born in 1837. His mother, D. Maria da Gloria, had died in 1853, leaving her second husband, Don Ferdinando (of Saxe-Gotha), regent of the kingdom during Don Pedro's minority. This had ended in September 1855 : so that His Majesty was now but little more than nineteen years of age, and had been king only fifteen months. His father, Re Fernando, as he was always called, was but forty years of age; and was generally reported to be as fond of pleasure as his son was of study; and to be in the habit of calling that son Padre Pedro. He seemed, however, to be well-liked in popular estimation, and, as regent, had given much satisfaction. There were other younger brothers and sisters of the king.

On the morning of the 4th of the new year 1857, we received a note from Mrs. Howard, who told us that the Legation had just been informed that the first royal reception was to take place that evening; and that, in order to be able to attend it, we must be presented that very morning: the world had not then imagined the royal court balls of Florence, to which thousands were to be invited who had never been presented to the sovereign. My wife put on her best morning dress and bonnet; and I donned my English deputy-lieutenant's uniform; and we drove at about midday to the Palace das Necessidades.

The situation of this palace, on the heights of Buenos Ayres, is very beautiful. Its windows, like those of our own house, overlooked the spreading Tagus, (usually, and even now, charged with seven or eight English ships of war) and the vine-covered hills beyond. This royal residence, this "palace of want", received its curious name from a small chapel built and dedicated in former ages by some pious people who had escaped a dreadful pestilence, to the Blessed Virgin, who had prayed for them in their necessities—in their wants. One of the kings, the magnificent Don John V, believed himself to have been delivered from a dangerous illness by her prayers, which had been invoked for him in this chapel; and, in return, purchased all the land about the little sanctuary, enlarged it, and enclosed it within the palace which he built on the spot; and which, from its vicinity to Lisbon, is the most convenient and usual residence of the royal family.

On our road, we called for Mr. and Mrs. Howard, whose residence was between our own and the palace; and proceeded thither together. We went up a very handsome staircase, and were shown into a drawing-room hung with satin damask, and where gilt chairs, covered to match, were placed formally against the walls. Here we chatted together for some time; and, at last, began to be rather tired of standing, and impatient for the arrival of the sovereign. A door opened, and King Fernando, his father, tripped lightly into the room ; a slim, tall, graceful man, with a handsome face and very black, long, pointed beard. We were presented to him ; and he began talking pleasantly with the two ladies, when his son, Don Pedro, came in from another door. He advanced more staidly towards us, and we were presented with somewhat more formality. The king was a good-looking, tall young man, dressed in a military uniform, but evidently very shy. As he conversed, he leaned upon his sword heavily, and spoke very slowly and without animation or change of features ; the usual expression of which seemed to be a sadness strange in one so young. He addressed us in English ; and I afterwards found that he insisted upon speaking their own native language to each one whom he addressed. He said to us one or two of the stereotyped phrases usual to sovereigns, asking how we liked Lisbon ; and when I launched out, rather more than courtly etiquette justified, in its praises, and remarked on the number of new buildings in course of erection in every street, and on the many improvements that were being made in the town, he answered, with an arch smile, "It is time!" He then asked me if I had seen the Bay of Naples, and whether I noted the resemblance which others told him existed between it and the Tagus at Lisbon. Not all my wish to please and compliment the young sovereign could lead me to flatter so far his beautiful capital;—beautiful, but still not to be compared to that "bit of heaven dropped down upon the earth."

The conversation was continued somewhile longer; and we were then graciously dismissed with an intimation that we should attend the first reception which took place that evening.

At half after eight o'clock—such are the early hours for social gatherings in that pleasant capital—we again found ourselves at the Palace das Necessitades. Our two eldest daughters, Lucy and Louie of the *Wabash*, the latter of whom Dr. Latham had sent to Lisbon for the mildness of its climate, accompanied us. Now a low dress, suited to a court reception, was not compatible with a dread of pulmonary complaint such as had induced a voyage to Lisbon. At the same time, I was unwilling to ask for a dispensation which might be refused, and so deprive our child of a pleasure which might never offer itself to her again. We, therefore, dressed her in a white satin dress that fitted tightly to her slim figure and well-formed bust, and was completely closed up to her throat.

Lucy and my wife wore the usual proper evening dress. I knew that we were the only English family who had been, for many years, presented at the court of Lisbon—where those in commerce are not received;—and I trusted that two pretty, elegant, English girls would be greeted with pleasure, even although one of them shewed by her dress that we had paid Lisbon the compliment of seeking it for the sake of its climate.

Five or six handsome drawing-rooms were opened, in one of which the ladies seated themselves in a semicircle, with their backs to the wall. There might be about five-and-twenty present; and four times as many men stood about or conversed in that and the other rooms. The king came in and began addressing the ladies in the circle, each of whom, of course, stood up as he approached her; he said a few words to each:—pausing long, as is the usage of royal personages, between each phrase, and racking his brain for something to say; which he did not always find. King Ferdinand followed him; and when Don Pedro hesitated for too long a time, or some more attractive lady was ahead, the father skipped past his son, with a disregard of all courtly etiquette, and went on to the other ladies until his Majesty overtook him, when, of course, papa fell back.

Don Luiz, Duke of Oporto, younger brother of the king, and destined ere long to succeed him, was also there and made his round—but more irregularly and without formality—sitting down and chatting with those ladies with whom he was most acquainted. He was a lively lad of eighteen; dressed in a naval uniform, he had much the look and bearing of a merry English midshipman.

When these royal personages had paid their compliments to the ladies, they addressed themselves to such of the gentlemen present as they pleased to select for that honour, and stood about singly or in knots conversing during the rest of the evening. Ices and lemonades were carried round by servants in livery; and so the evening passed in quiet and subdued conversation. Before retiring, the king went and kissed the hand of his father, Re Fernando, wishing him good night. We left with the others, and were home at half after eleven o'clock.

Having now got what I wanted, having presented our invalid daughter, my wife wrote to our friend, the Duqueza de Ficalho, the Camareira

Mör, and asked whether she might be permitted to bring her again in the same toilette, as she still feared to let her put on a low dress. The Duchess answered in French—the language of Portuguese society—that *franchement* the custom of the Court was that ladies should be décolletées and wear short sleeves : but, she added, "you need have no uneasiness. His Majesty is very amiable, and has not said a single word." We, therefore, continued to take both our daughters whenever we attended these pleasant fortnightly receptions, which became more pleasant as we were better acquainted with the people ; and which could not but be interesting, as showing an entirely new society, with new subjects of thought and of conversation.

The society of the Palace was, however, restricted by political considerations. The greater part of the noblesse of Lisbon were Miguellites : —adherents to Don Miguel, uncle of the present king, who, while regent for his niece, had abolished the constitution, declared himself king, and had maintained himself in civil war until he was finally driven out of the country, and the authority of Queen Donna Maria was restored by the Duke of Terceira and Sir Charles Napier in

1834. This personage, however, was still living; and the greater number of the gentry refused to recognise the reigning sovereign, and secluded themselves from Court and from all society, excepting small and comparatively-private reunions amongst themselves.

A few evenings after our first reception at the palace, we were at a small party at the brave Marshall Duke of Terceira's, who, by leading a couple of thousand men by forced marches on Lisbon, had obtained possession of the capital and put an end to the civil war. Pleasant, kind old man! After a long experience of many lands, memory knows not where to find one on intercourse with whom it lingers more agreeably than on this gentlemanly soldier and on his beautiful and elegant Duchess. The only sad thing at this first party at their house was to see what I often observed afterwards in other societies:— to see Marquis Loulé, president of the Council, on one side of the room, and his wife, the Infanta Donna Anna, on the opposite side; while their daughter passed from one to the other, kissing each parent and affectionate with both, who had no other intercourse than through her. At this party, the Duke of Oporto and King

Don Fernando were also present; and the latter sang to the accompaniment of the piano. He sang well and artistically; and I afterwards found that he was a first-rate musician, and a draughtsman of no small ability. Curious that these Saxe-Coburgs should be so frequently accomplished and sensible men—so far beyond the average of princes! Common sense, moderation, and accomplishments would seem to be what the French call their *spécialité ;* and how convenient, too, that there should be a Catholic and a Protestant branch of the same house, so that they can supply husbands to either Catholic or Protestant queens in search of such!

We also met the same royal father and son at a grand ball given by Marquez de Fronteira at their Quinta (or villa) at Bemfica, about four miles from Lisbon. A very interesting old house was this residence in which they most delighted. One or two of the rooms were lined, to the height of about five feet from the floor, with blue porcelain tiles, on which were represented, in bas-relief, the warlike feats of the Conde della Torre, one of the ancestors of this old family, who was a distinguished leader in the wars both against the Spaniards and the Moors.

Most of these right noble families of Portugal can show more to be proud of in the deeds of their ancestors than illustrates the descent of all the other grandees of Europe put together: as Portugal so long owed its independent existence to the heroic deeds of its small but chivalrous population.

But the grandest fête of the winter, from the sumptuousness of its preparations and the number of its guests, was a ball given by the Marquez de Vianna in his splendid mansion. It seemed a curious contrast that, at this ball, our host and hostess asked us to be present at a private celebration in their beautiful chapel, in thanksgiving that they and all their family had escaped the cholera which had scourged the city not long before.

Then there was the Corps Diplomatique at Lisbon, which contributed its share to the amusement of society. Mrs. O'Sullivan, wife of the American minister, gave some dances and a grand fancy ball. Mrs. Howard gave several pleasant parties and dances; and insisted, contrary to the advice of Portuguese friends, on giving a ball at mid-lent; which ball the said Portuguese ladies refused to attend, as being offensive to their religious habits; and Mrs. Howard was, consequently, much annoyed. But our minister, Mr. Howard, an English Catholic, had married a German Protestant, and this lady's piety and the habits of the country to which her husband was accredited, were often in opposition. Thus I remember meeting her Catholic husband one day at the American minister's, when he said to the latter—

"Why have you put out your flag? Is to-day anything particular?"

(Nota bene.—At Lisbon it is customary for all public buildings, Government offices, and foreign legations to be *imbandierate*, or decked with flags, on the days of the principal saints and festivals of the Church.)

"Do not you know," answered Mr. O'Sullivan, "that it is one of your Church festivals? I always pay the country the compliment of hanging out the stars and stripes when they put out their flags. To fail in such an act of courtesy, displeases them."

"Ah, yes; but I leave those matters to Mrs. Howard," answered our English minister.

The system by which England appoints its representatives is different from that which obtains in other countries; and I do not think the result is very satisfactory: it is still less so when, as often happens, the round man is put into the square hole.

Next door to our house at Buenos Ayres, was the residence of the Papal Nuncio, Di Pietra, who was made a cardinal for his services in this mission. It was a great pleasure to become acquainted with this most able statesman of the Sacred College, and we were able to attend the offices of the Church more conveniently in his private chapel than in the rather ill-served parish churches of the town. On taking leave of him after a dinner party, I was surprised to hear from his Eminence that his carriage was waiting to carry him four miles into the country. He only came into Lisbon for business and the duties of his station.

There was also a Club Lisbonense and an Assemblea Portugueza, which gave periodical dances during the winter. These were not only frequented by the nobles of the court, but it was a pleasure to meet there the principal merchants of Portugal with their families, and such a large sprinkling of English Naval officers that the chatter of the middies with their dancing partners, the pretty daughters of the English resident merchants, seemed to make ours the predominant language in the crowd.

In short, there is more society in Lisbon than in any town I am acquainted with out of England; and, unlike the Romans, whom I was accused of treating ungratefully (because, in the historical parts of my "*Modern Society in Rome*," I was obliged to mention the conduct of many during the Revolution which they would now wish to have forgotten)—unlike the Romans whom I am accused of "treating so ungratefully after all their hospitality to me"—they dined and danced at my house—the Portuguese not only made a return of civilities, but gave parties to those from whom they could not expect to receive any equivalent. All knew that our house was ill-adapted to receptions; but our English feelings urged us to do our best to show our sense of all the kindness we were receiving; and we got the promise of the Terceiras, the Saldanhas, the Fronteiras, Sobrals, Ficalhos, De Majors, Mrs. Howard, and other friends, that they would kindly excuse our want of means, and grace our small reception rooms. Then appeared what I have noticed in every part of the Continent where society has been disruptured by political feuds: then appeared the wish of all parties to forget differences, to amalgamate and to meet on neutral ground. The house of an English traveller was necessarily such; and the Lancastres and the Abrantes,* and several whom I had never met in general society and was not even acquainted with, did us the honour of desiring to be introduced to us, that they might come to our little dance. Our girls were delighted. They were all three happy and pretty, and our little party went off to their hearts' content.

The three were walking on the next afternoon, with their two little brothers and the nursemaid, in the garden of the Estrella, which lay at no great distance from our Rua da Lapa, and which will be a delightful pleasure ground when the shrubs are grown into trees. Here they were joined by King Fernando, who seemed to be listlessly sauntering about.

"So you had a dance at your house last night," said his Majesty. "Why was not I invited?" he asked good-naturedly.

"Papa and mama could not take such a liberty."

---

* Not Napoleon's hero—General Junot—but the ancient noble family of Portugal, whose title it was very silly and very bad taste to assume.

"Not at all. I do not see why I am to be excluded from a pleasant party. Tell them that if they give another, I shall come. But why, young ladies, are you not at the bull-fight that is being held at the Praça dos Tauros ?"

"We had no wish to see such cruel sports," answered Lucy.

"Quite right," said the King. "No one with a good heart can enjoy such sights. My little girls are gone. I wish people would not take them there. We have no such amusements in Germany."

"This country must be very different," said one of my daughters. "Does not your Majesty ever wish to see your own ?"

"Not in the least," replied Re Fernando, laughing. "I am very well satisfied to be here. When I remember the frost and the snow of North Germany, I am very well satisfied to be where I am."

I had gone to see this bull-fight, the first of the season, as being a national amusement which so celebrated a traveller and descriptive writer as the *Jornal do Commercio* had proclaimed me to be, was bound to make himself acquainted with. A very large wooden circus, containing several tiers of seats, was crowded with an eager population of sight-seers. The more humanised character of the Portuguese had caused them to abolish, nearly a century ago, the style of bull-fight still practised in Spain, and occasionally in France to gratify the gentle propensities of the Empress Eugenie. On this occasion, therefore, no bulls were slain, no horses were disembowelled. A modified cruelty only was perpetrated for the delight of the Portuguese. Fifteen bulls, of no unusual size, were driven in succession into the circus. A number of performers, dressed in old Spanish attire, were there to receive them. And when the brute, dazzled on leaving a dark stable, by the sudden glare and the shouts of the spectators, stared wildly around him, these gentlefolks danced about and waved small red flags in their hands, till the bull, irritated, made a rush at some one of them. The performer awaited until the horns were lowered to gore, then threw the red flag over them and the eyes of the animal, and with one hand, or, if he were clever, with both hands, threw or stuck one or two little javelins, bearing a tiny flag, into the skin behind the bull's ears. The latter of course threw up its head on feeling the puncture, and the *campino* skipped lightly aside. Another and another succeeded him, till the poor bullock bore a dozen or twenty of these little javelins about its neck, which, only piercing the skin, hung there by their barbed point, but inflicted no great wound. At length, the bull generally found out that every rush he made at his adversaries only drew upon himself another dart and refused to attack any more. A number of cows with bells were then driven into the arena, with which the tired bull trotted quietly off. The darts were then drawn out and the wounds healed.

By way of variety, and to arouse a tame or cowardly bull, one or two negroes occasionally entered the arena with feathers about their heads, like African chieftains, and seated themselves upon a chair, or got behind pasteboard horses, and cajoled the bull till he made a rush to toss them, but entangled his horns on the rungs of the chair, so that all were tumbled over together. This seemed to be considered great sport, perhaps because there was no small danger of injury to the poor blacks!

Such are the spring and summer amusements of the people at Lisbon. I did not go twice to the circus; but enjoyed better the society of our kind friends without the intervention of bulls or blacks. In truth, we were very much pleased with the Portuguese of all classes; with the frank kindness with which we were welcomed by the society of the city; with the civil and civilised bearing of the people. I never heard an oath from a Portuguese during the five months we lived in Portugal. I once saw a prisoner escorted by the police, pause, with their permission, at a tobacconist's; he there bought himself a supply of snuff, which he politely handed round to his escort. There were also English and foreign men of war always in the Tagus; and the morning was occasionally pleasantly passed on board one or other of these. I remember that the religious feelings which Christmas eve had aroused within us, as I have stated, were, however, rudely shocked by the first visit I paid on board the *Cæsar*, two days afterwards. The funeral of a marine was being performed in the fleet—of a marine who had died of overdrink, taken in on Christmas eve.

I remarked a curious escort which always attended these English ships—flights of sea-gulls skimmed the Tagus all around them. The birds were picking up the stray victual thrown over by the crew. Our people were very proud of these flights of birds, and bade me remark that none were seen around a more parsimonious frigate bearing the flag of France. As one who had to pay towards the support of our sailors, I could not join in the admiration of waste which delighted those who lived upon the taxes.

The Portuguese in their habits and manners are more English than the people of any other country on the continent. They drink more tea. Morning and evening, the tea-things are brought in, and few Portuguese ladies do not like a cup of tea also about four o'clock.

I regret, however, to have to state that the manner in which the last days of carnival were kept, was, and is, if there has been no change, a disgrace to a civilised town; though I vainly endeavoured to persuade my good friend the Conde de Sobrel, governor of the city, to think of the practice as I did. Rotten eggs, lime, every filth was thrown from the windows on whoever or whatever passed through the streets below. Here was no fun, no frolic; a few wretched masks alone ventured out: all decently dressed people were afraid of showing themselves; and, contrary to the rules of their own police, which the governor would not enforce, the whole town was given up to license and filth.

Turn we to a sadder scene. A member of one of the first families of Lisbon had died, and had been carried to that most beautiful cemetery, the ground of which was formerly known by the appropriate name of the Alto dos Prazeres—the heights of pleasure. The relatives had not accompanied the departed one; they remain at home to receive the condolence of friends. For eight days, they sit in a room so dark that persons can scarcely be recognised therein. One of them acts as chief mourner, and to him all visitors bend their sympathising steps; to him they bow; then seat themselves in the lugubrious circle in solemn silence for a few minutes. Not one word is spoken. The room, in the instance to which I refer, is perhaps unusually darkened; certain it is that the sky is very bright. And our English minister may well be unable to distinguish anything as he steps hesitatingly into the mournful atmosphere. He cannot distinguish any one around the circle of mourning relatives; but a large china vase, standing in one corner of the drawing-room, is dimly perceptible through the gloom—that must be the chief mourner. He walks up to it. With all the gravity of a diplomatist, he makes it a low bow, and then gropes his way, without speaking, to a chair. No one speaks. Our minister knows the usages of society. He also sits in silence for as long a time as etiquette requires. He then rises, turns once more to the china vase, makes it another bow more expressive of sympathising grief than even the first had been, and then gently and slowly retires. The circle of mourners could not quite preserve their gravity.

"How could you ask me to come and dine in your house to-day?" said the lively Condessa de A— to us, after a friendly dinner. "You should know it was as bad as telling the English admiral, as I heard you do this morning, that the house belonged to Mr. Jones."

"But so it does. What should I have said?" I asked.

"You should have told him the house was his own."

"His own? But it belongs to the other people, and I rent it."

"That makes no difference," she said. "In Portugal, you must always make a present of your house to the person you are speaking to at the time. If we were not in the habit of speaking

French to you, into which we cannot naturally turn our Portuguese politeness, you would have noticed that we always give you our house. Please to walk in—a casa è sua—the house is yours."

"Just as we, in England, beg friends to make themselves at home!" I exclaimed.

"I suppose so!" said the Condessa. "But we go further. In writing a letter we date it—Desta sua casa—from this your house!"

"Said I not rightly that you are the pleasantest and the most polite people in the world?"

CHAPTER VII.

THE KING OF PORTUGAL.

The House of Peers.—The Cholera.—Seclusion of Lisbon.

On the 2nd of January, with tickets to reserved places, with which we were favoured, we witnessed the opening of his Parliament by Don Pedro, the King. We were placed in a comfortable gallery overlooking a handsome but rather small hall in the suppressed convent of St. Bento. A satirical Portuguese writer will not take upon himself to decide whether the useless monks have more useful successors in the Cortes or not. Gradually the hall filled itself with the " Dignos Pares do Reino e Senores Deputados da Nação Portugueza." The worthy peers of the kingdom, as they are called, are in number one hundred and nineteen, including the Cardinal Archbishop of Lisbon, and the Cardinal Patriarch, who is hereditary President of the

House. These Peers are appointed by the Sovereign and their rank is hereditary, as in England. Not, however, as in England, have all of them titles. A title is not necessary to a seat in the House of Peers; and many Portuguese have titles who are not peers. Thus, although there are scarcely one hundred titles in this House of Lords, there are, in all Portugal, seven Dukes, twenty-one Marquesses, seventy-eight Counts, twenty-three Viscounts, and fourteen Barons (*com grandeza* or grandees), and upwards of one hundred and fifty Viscounts and Barons without *grandeza*. Among these latter are Sir Isaac Goldsmid of London and Dr. Kessler, M.D. to King Fernando; so that, I presume, they correspond with the honoured class of civil knighthood in England. The oldest creation of the former class dates from the fifteenth century; of the latter class, all but two are of the nineteenth.

The young King entered, supported by general officers and other Peers of the kingdom. There was the elegant figure of old Marshal Duke of Terceira; the portly and frank bearing of Marshal Duke Saldanha. There were our friends, Marquis Fronteira and Loulé and Ficalho—all men above the middle height, all of fine and noble carriage;

indeed, the personal appearance of the gentlemen now assembling beneath our gallery, struck us as being unusually distinguished. Most of them were of middle age or beyond; scarcely a young man was amongst them except the King himself, whom they appeared to surround with a fatherly courtesy. He ascended his modest throne and, in a sensible and well-toned voice, read rather a long speech.

But his Majesty had much to say. His country had been afflicted since the last session by a fearful visitation of cholera. He did not allude to the noble manner in which he himself had more than performed his duty:—a lad of nineteen, he had not fled to the cool retreats of Cintra or Mafra when his capital was desolated by the pestilence. He had stayed at Lisbon to encourage his people; he had almost lived in the hospitals; he had supported in his own arms more than one poor wretch dying there of what was generally believed to be a contagious malady; he had awakened afresh the dying memory of a soldier of his own regiment whom he found in one of the wards; he had made the poor fellow recollect him, and by speaking words of comfort and promising to the sick man, and that he would again soon be mounting guard under the palace windows, he had so cheered him up that the invalid had battled successfully with the fell disease, and had, indeed, again stood sentry, within a short time, upon the beautiful esplanade. All honour to Don Pedro the Fifth! His father called him Padre Pedro, and he was used to write political disquisitions and to submit them to the opinion of our own Prince Consort; it is also true that, when he had visited London, and been obliged, in the fraternity of sovereigns, to kiss his sister Victoria, he had blushed so deeply that our Queen, turning aside, had laughed at his modesty, for that he was not used to kiss women. All this may be—nay, is true: but he was a brave, a good young man, and won the love of his people, and honoured the crown he wore.

In his speech at the opening of his parliament, he deplored, therefore, the sufferings which the cholera had inflicted upon the kingdom, and bore grateful testimony to the sympathy and assistance which had been afforded by other countries, and particularly by England. He called upon the legislature to promote the cause of public instruction; to extend railroads, and to make highways through the land. Hitherto the Portuguese had always objected to this, because they would facilitate the incursions of their mortal and hated foes, the Spaniards; but now the King even asked for a railroad to unite Lisbon with the frontiers of Spain; and, at Mr. Howard's dinner table, I had met Sir Morton Peto, who had come over to promote such objects.

I could never understand the complaints against the seclusion of Lisbon, which I constantly heard from the members of the diplomatic corps. They complained that they were quite segregated from Europe; and our own minister even declared that Rio Janeiro, from whence he had come, was more in the world. It is true that the land post through Spain did little for us; and that all our foreign intelligence was to be waited for till the packets arrived from Southampton; but I know not how or why, I was satisfied. Perhaps it was something in the Lisbon air that calmed me to content.

CHAPTER VIII.

ECCLESIASTICAL.

The Clergy of Lisbon.—St. Vincent and the Ravens.—Scandals.—Religious Observances.—Procession of the Passion.—Churches.—St. Roque.—English Nuns and Sion House.—The Estella.—Penha de França.—Theology below stairs.—Mr. Murray and the Wondrous Lizard.—Belem.—My Butler, Stevens.—The Rector of West End.

MURRAY's Handbook tells the new-comer to Lisbon that he will be struck by the great number of soldiers and the total absence of clergy, until he finds out that the gentlemen dressed in blue frock coats, tight pantaloons, and Hessian boots, are priests, and that such is the ecclesiastical dress of Portugal. Be it so. *L'habit ne fait pas le moine*, and one dress is as good as another when people are used to it.

Monks, however, in the dresses of their different orders are no longer to be seen. Monasteries have been suppressed; church property has been seized; tythes have been abolished, and a small stipend has been granted by the state for the support of its clergy. When states learn that they have nothing to do with either appointing or supporting clergy, the latter will be selected for their spiritual worth, and will be more decorously maintained by those who wish for their services. I know not what good service the rector of our parish had done to the state for which he had been rewarded with that benefice; but during the time of the cholera, he was said to have fled to the country, and none had cared for his parishioners except a poor Capuchin monk of a suppressed convent, who had dedicated himself to them, and who, this year also, in Hessian boots, fulfilled all those duties which should have been performed by the rector.

I was taken to visit the Cardinal Patriarch of Lisbon, President, by office, of the House of Peers— a weak old man, without energy or courage to stand up for what he believed to be right. The cathedral itself is a heavy gloomy building with no architectural beauty, or historical interest. In the chapel of St. Vincent are the relics of that saint, and in the cloisters two ravens are always kept. They reminded me of the owls in the old tower of Arundel Castle. It is, however, requisite that I explain the connexion between the ravens and the body of the saint.

In the fourth century, Vincent, a Catholic Christian, was put to death, after cruel torments, by the Roman governor of Dacia because he refused to disown the Christ and to sacrifice to the pagan gods; and his lifeless body was ordered to be exposed to the beasts and birds of the woods, but was protected from them by two ravens. So says the legend; and those who believe that a raven regularly carried food to a prophet under the imperfect Dispensation, can have no difficulty in believing that ravens cared for the body of a witness to the more Perfect Law. His body was, however, revered for eight hundred years by the Christians of Algarve, and gave its name to a Cape which Englishmen of our day delight to honour. When the heroic Affonso Henriquez had gained his great battle of Ourique in that neighbourhood, and, with the death of 200,000 Moors, had conquered Lisbon and driven the valiant infidels out of the kingdom, he brought the body of S. Vincent to his capital, and built this cathedral over its tomb:—by the bye, an Englishman named Gilbert was named first bishop to the see—one that had accompanied a body of Crusaders, whose fleet had entered the Tagus during the siege of Lisbon, and who had gallantly aided the brave Affonso.

Two ravens are said to have accompanied the vessel that bore S. Vincent's body; and in commemoration of the event, a ship and two ravens were adopted as the arms of the city; and ravens have been always kept in a courtyard of the cathedral.

All these are pleasing, praiseworthy, or, at least, innocent memorials of the past. Not so, to my mind, were some of the adjuncts of the cathedral. Not so, for example, was the convent of S. Vincent, founded exclusively for monks of noble families, who were forbidden to demean themselves by going out on foot; their profession of humility requiring to be exemplified by carriage equipages. Not so, either, was a chapel in the cathedral set apart as the burial-place of the bastards of successive sovereigns :—too royal to be buried with other men, and not royal enough to sleep with their fathers!

No wonder an avenging Providence should punish such a system by revolutions in church and state! What an intolerable place of oppression and infamy this world would be if it were not for occasional revolutions!

In the refectory of this suppressed convent, are the tombs, or sarcophagi, of the royal family. Methought a curious place of entombment! The coffin of the late queen was of enormous proportions. Here, too, was the coffin of a princess more recently deceased, and which was covered with flowers and garlands. *Ci-gît, hic jacet:* this the inscriptions on all proclaimed: no recognition of any religious opinion!

And yet the churches in Lisbon are well frequented, particularly that of the English college, where, in conformity with the English bump of veneration possessed by no foreigners, the services are decorously performed. Here are seats or benches as in England. In all the other churches, the women kneel on the mat-covered floor, or rather kneel on it and sit upon their own heels; while the men stand on the opposite side of the nave. Before Holy week, also, a couple of old confessionals are brought into every church from some lumber-room; are dusted and cleaned of cobwebs, and placed on each side of the altar rails. Around these, the penitents congregate, and proclaim their sins to the priest, who sits thus *coram populo.* I have described the Lisbonites as an innocent-minded people; and this habit of bringing out their confessionals only once a year should prove them to be so.

This for the lower orders; we presume that the

gentry confess more privately. For these, we had
had the Procession of the Passion, in which a
figure, quite as large as life, was carried through
the streets by the noblest in the land. It was the
privilege of the Duchess Terceira and another great
lady to provide the robe and to clothe this bleeding representation of the Christ as taken from the
Cross. The highest grandees, dressed in full uniform, and preceded by bands of music, carried it
on their shoulders; the most courtly ladies in
mourning and in long black veils followed behind;
and some more devout, amongst whom I knew
two of the noblest and most pious in the land,
concealed their humility and their penance and
their bare feet, bleeding with the gravel of the
streets, by walking even under the stage on which
the figure reclined.

On Maundy Thursday, when the consecrated
Host is placed on an illuminated altar in each
church to await the service of Good Friday, the
whole population of Lisbon seems to turn out into
the streets, and to visit, in a devotional spirit, the
different churches. No carriage of any description
is allowed to circulate; and, indeed, so thick is
the crowd that it could not do so without danger
to thousands.

On Holy Saturday we were taken by friends to a private gallery in the handsome church of S. Nicholas. This we found in almost total darkness. The church was quite full, and Mass was being celebrated. Suddenly, when the priest sang the words of the Credo, "He rose again from the dead," the curtains were all drawn up, and brilliant leaves and flowers were showered from the ceiling on the congregation below; little birds were thrown out of their cages and flew about; and a burst of music, together with a flood of light, represented the joy of mankind for the resurrection of the Saviour. All this was very pretty and innocent, if it helped the devotion of those who witnessed it.

The devotion of all was, however, always unmistakably shown whenever and wherever the Blessed Sacrament was carried through the streets to communicate some dying Christian. So soon as the tinkling of the small bell, carried before the priest, announced the approach of the humble procession, lights appeared at every window, while the inmates knelt beside them. Not long ago, the audience at the great theatre S. Carlos caught a sound of the little passing bell, and calling to the actors to hush the performance, all rose and turned towards the door as the Viaticum passed by.

As this chapter treats of religion and churches, visit we three or four of the more remarkable of the latter. Here are none of architectural magnificence; but several have something remarkable about them. The church of St. Roque, for example, plain in every other respect, contains within it the richest chapel in the whole world. King John V, called the Magnanimous, and who seems to have had more wealth than wit, visited this church early in the last century, and, observing that all the chapels in the church were handsomely adorned by the confraternities to which they belonged, while that dedicated to St. John Baptist was in its original simplicity, as belonging to no particular society, declared that St. John the Baptist was his own patron, and that he himself would embellish this chapel. The dimensions of the chapel were sent to Rome with orders to case and adorn the enclosed space with all that splendour, art, and wealth could combine. This was done, and the little shrine was put up in St. Peter's, where Pope Benedict the XIV consecrated and said Mass in it.

The priest is allowed to live by the altar; and

the Pope did not scruple to accept a million of crowns which the sovereign sent him in payment for the Mass he had said.

The chapel was taken to pieces, brought to Lisbon, and put together again in this place. Who shall describe its gorgeousness? The outer facing of the principal arch is of coral. The arch itself is of alabaster. The pavement is mosaic and porphyry. The walls are of marble panels around mosaic pictures, so beautiful that it is difficult to believe they are not paintings. The doorposts and cornices are of wood and gialloantico and jasper. The roof is supported by eight columns of lapis-lazzuli, with bases of alabaster and amethysts, and capitals of bronze. The rails in front of the altar are of verde antique; the altar itself is of jasper with a frontal of lapis-lazzuli bordered with amethysts. Here are three beautifully wrought lamps of solid silver, and two massive candlesticks, ten feet high, each of which cost 75,000 crowns. In fact, our friend Vasconcellos, who is the honorary keeper of the keys of this chapel, and, indeed, all Portuguese, in the present comparative poverty of their country, seem proud to tell what wealth they formerly had to squander away, and that this chapel cost 14,000,000 crusados, or about one million and a half sterling.

When the French held Lisbon, they had planned to remove this chapel and its contents to Paris; but their own removal from Portugal prevented the completion of the project.

In the church near this chapel, is the tomb of Sir Francis Trajean, an Englishman, with whom Queen Elizabeth is said to have fallen desperately in love. As he resisted her advances, she confiscated his property and imprisoned him for being a catholic. After twenty-eight years, he escaped, and fled to Lisbon, where, the inscription tells us, he died in the odour of sanctity, and that his body, found incorrupt after many years, was removed to this spot by his countrymen. The incorrupt state of a body is certainly no proof of sanctity; but, if it were not unusual, it would not have been remarked upon by those who moved it. An Irish traveller translated the beginning of this epitaph :—" Aqui está em pé—Here lies standing up."

Other curious English reminiscences are aroused by a Brigittine convent of English nuns, near Sao Bento. These ladies are the successors of those who formerly possessed Sion House, which, since the dissolution of our monasteries, passed into the hands of the Duke of Northumberland. The sisterhood wandered from country to country, till, more than two centuries ago, they settled at Lisbon. They were visited here by a late Duke of Northumberland, and showed his grace the original keys of Sion House, which they had carried away with them in token of their continued claim to the property.

What a history they tell of the avenging fate that overtook the first possessors of the property of these poor nuns! Henry VIII kept it for himself, and Catherine Howard was confined here for three months before she went to the scaffold. Henry's body lay in state here; and here the dogs licked his blood. Edward VI gave the place to the Duke of Somerset, who died on the scaffold, and it reverted to the crown. John Dudley, Earl of Northumberland, next held it; and here Lady Jane Grey was persuaded to accept her luckless crown. Then, for a short while, the nuns were reinstated; and then James I again granted it to Henry Percy, Earl of Northumberland. He was suspected of being implicated in the gunpowder plot, and adjudged to be imprisoned for life, and to pay a fine of £30,000. He offered Sion House in lieu of the fine, but it was refused; though, after fifteen years imprisonment, £11,000 was accepted, and he was set at liberty. In the time of his son, it was used as a prison for the children of King Charles; and his grandson, having died without male issue, his daughter, Lady Elizabeth Percy, inherited Sion House, and was left a widow by the Earl of Ogle before she was fourteen. Her second husband was assassinated by a rival on the very day of their marriage; and her third husband, the amiable Duke of Somerset, who left one of his daughters £20,000 less than he gave to the others, because she had sat down one afternoon in the hall, in which he had gone to sleep—her third husband left only one son, in whom his line became extinct. This abbreviation from Spelman's *History of Sacrilege* does not give a pleasant idea of life in those days!

I have mentioned the Estrella Gardens, in which our children generally walked. The dome of the church and convent to which these formerly belonged is handsome. It was founded in 1779 by Queen Maria, in fulfilment of a vow by which she sought to bear a son to the throne. It cost an enormous sum of money; and the Portuguese charge against it the filth which, till lately, disgraced their city in the eyes of all strangers: the money, which had been destined for the drainage of Lisbon, was taken to build this church.

But, to see the lovely scenery of Lisbon to the greatest advantage, you must climb the peaks of the same chain of hills to the eastward—peaks that are crowned by the churches of N. S. do Monte, N. S. da Graça, and N. S. da Penha di França. On the terrace of this last-named church, in particular, pause and let your eyes drink in the scenery beneath and around, with the assurance that, live they ever so long, they can nowhere, except perhaps at Naples and Constantinople, enjoy a prospect so glorious and beautiful. Beneath, on one side, is the city, bathed by the waters of the broad Tagus as it comes down from the Spanish mountains, through the spreading Cova da Piedade and stretches away past Belem Castle to the broad Atlantic: on the other side are the pointed peaks of Cintra and the heights of Torres Vedras: the whole scenery is broken up and diversified more than any other equal space of ground—the city by the old heroic castle of S. George and the hills of Buenos Ayres and Estrella, and by gardens yellow with orange groves interspersed amongst them all: the country both on this and the other side of the Tagus diversified by cultivation and wastes, by villas and dark pine forests :—I know not if, apart from classical associations, anything in Naples is more beautiful. And be it remembered that the historic associations of modern Lusitania are far grander and more heroic than any classical dreams appertaining to Southern Italy.

Little worth recording beyond the landscape beneath them is to be seen from these three churches. Murray will describe this little, and will show his own small wit by sneering at some very ugly and taudrily dressed figures intended to represent the Blessed Virgin—forgetting that one very ugly and ill-painted likeness of his own relative, which he has so gorgeously framed, and which he looks at with such affection as it hangs over his own chimney-piece! An Englishman once came to me at Lisbon with a complaint that my English butler had knocked him down. I inquired into the case, and then said to the complainant—

"It seems you had been disputing about religious matters?"

He assented.

"If Stevens," I continued, "had spoken of your

mother in the terms in which he says you spoke of the Blessed Virgin"——

"I would have knocked him down, sir!" exclaimed the man.

"Then perhaps you will forgive his having knocked you down because you spoke in such a manner of her whom you believe to be the mother of your Saviour."

My complainant withdrew without another word. However, I do not approve of the knocking down argument; and to prove that I bore no malice against poor Mr. Murray's author, I inquired for the wondrous lizard, which he tells us must be seen if we would not be laughed at by the Portuguese as one "que foi á Penha e não vio o lagarto —who had been at the Penha and had not seen the lizard." The sacristan smiled when I asked for the beast, and wondered why strangers inquired for it. He showed us, in an ante-room, the figure of a small crocodile, or some such animal, about four feet long, which was dried and stuffed, and hanging to a hook in the wall. Mr. Murray says "a pilgrim on his way to pay his devotions here, slept by the road-side. A huge lizard appeared to devour him; but by the timely appearance of our Lady, the pilgrim awoke and the reptile was killed."

The poor sacristan did not know so much about it. He had only heard that this church being peculiarly frequented by sailors, the captain of a vessel, in days gone by, had brought back this dried animal from foreign parts and had made a present of it to his brother, who was a monk in the convent; and that it had hung on that nail ever since. A great many so-called Catholic legends are fabricated by Protestant tourists. "*Se non son vere, son ben trovate*—if they are not true, they are well imagined."

But the most interesting and beautiful of all the ecclesiastical buildings in Lisbon is the church and monastery of Belem; and of this Mr. Murray speaks well. This magnificent structure, he says, was intended as an expression of gratitude for the successful result of the experiment of Vasco da Gama. The site was selected as being the place whence that hero embarked, July 8, 1497, on his adventurous expedition; and to which he returned 29 July, 1499, after discovering the Indies. Here had stood a small eremida, founded by the Infante Dom Henrique, the great promoter of maritime discovery, for the convenience of mariners. In this chapel,

Vasco da Gama and his companions passed the night previous to their embarkation in prayer. On the successful return of the expedition, King Manoel the Fortunate founded this pile, and lies buried in a sarcophagus near the altar. We have seen many a worse inscription than that upon this tomb :—

> Littore ab occiduo qui primi ad limina solis
> Extendit cultum notitiamque Dei,
> Tot reges domiti cui submisere thiaras,
> Conditor hoc tumulo Maximus Emmanuel.

The principal entrance to the church is by a side door, or double porch, richly carved and ornamented with thirty statues. The church itself is of an unusual height—its apparently almost flat roof resting upon the loftiest and slenderest pillars of white marble. So impossible did it seem that these slight shafts should support such a roof, that all the wise ones of the day predicted that it must fall so soon as the scaffolding should be removed; and the poor Italian architect, Potassi, fled and hid himself from the shame that was to cover him. The king ordered that the scaffolding should be removed by malefactors already condemned to death—in olden times they had always plenty of such on hand—and promised a free pardon to all such as should not be crushed by the falling building.

The scaffolding was removed. The roof did not fall. The architect crept out of his hiding place. The church stood, and still continues to stand, notwithstanding the three centuries and a half that have passed over it; and notwithstanding the shocks of the great earthquake.

Our butler, to whom I have alluded, was a very curious character. He had been with us for some years. In the opening pages of this book, I wrote of a Mr. Andrews, the radical coachbuilder and Mayor of Southampton. Mr. Andrews had entered the town early in life as a journeyman forgeman with his bride; and casting up their joint worldly goods, had found, he said, that they amounted to seven shillings and fourpence. However, by honesty, and cleverness, and politics, he had worked his way upwards, and had established a very large coachbuilding business of his own. I said that he partly owed his success to his cleverness, and of this I will give an instance. We had the Royal Agricultural Society's meeting at Southampton, and beds were let at a guinea a night. "A guinea a night, sir," said Mr. Andrews to me; "I had a good many rooms here in my house, and

I wrote to several gents that my beds were quite at their service. I had always a good luncheon on the table and a hamper of champagne for them in the corner of the dining room. They were naturally obliged to make me some return; and, before the show was over, I had orders for three thousand pounds worth of carriages. Did not that pay me a vast deal better than letting my beds at a guinea a head would have done?" . . . .

However, to return. In commemoration of his start in life, Mr. Andrews was in the habit of giving a grand annual dinner to all his workmen and such liberal big wigs as he could get together. Having an eye to the borough, of course I was invited, and went. He gave us capital dinners and lots of champagne. I had driven myself over one year in an open phaeton with Stevens, that he might wait on me at dinner. On our return, Stevens began talking to me about his religious scruples. He spoke very thick, and I told him we would talk on the subject next day. Neither next day, nor during the year did he allude to it; but on that day twelvemonth, we were again driving to Botleigh Grange, after Mr. Andrews' festival, when said Stevens, speaking again as thick as on the former anniversary,—

"This time last year, sir," he said, "we were coming home, just as we may be doing now, and I told you I wished to become a Catholic. You have never said one word to me on the subject since that time. Now, all the sins that I have committed from that night till now are on your conscience, sir, not mine. What's religion good for but to prevent one committing sins? Well now, I thought your religion would have kept me from sin; but as you never instructed me, I think that all I have done wrong is on your conscience, not mine." I again postponed our conversation till next morning; and this time, it was followed up, and Stevens became a Catholic, and knocked down the fellow at Lisbon for speaking irreverently of the Blessed Virgin. He had always had some proper feelings of religion. I had learned that, between our two dinners at Mr. Andrews, he had built himself a cottage at Bittern, and had fixed a little stone cross over the door.

"I wish you would take that away," said Dr. Hatherall, the burly rector, whose sermons were said to be written by his wife.

"Why, sir, what harm can it do?" asked Stevens.

"Well; people pass this way a good deal as

they go to church, and they may think it strange. I wish you would take it away."

"No, sir, I shan't. If people notice it as they pass, and if it makes them think as how their Saviour died for them, I don't see as how that can do them any harm. I think it must do them good."

And he did not take it away; and Dr. Hatherall went on his way repining. I had wished to put a headstone with a cross carved on it over the grave of an Irish nurse of mine who lay buried in his churchyard; but the burly rector wrote to me that the cross and the name of poor nurse Cowley would remind people of her religion; that he should have people praying for her soul; and that, in short, he would never allow any stone or any inscription on any slab over the grave of any of my household. He would have nothing that could tempt people to pray for the dead.

Nota Bene: He had made the widow of the founder pay £60 for permission to put up in the church a piece of sculpture to the memory of her husband. Sixty pounds for permission to erect a monument (by the sculptor Bayly, R.A., and which would be an ornament to any church) to James Barlow Hoy, the founder of the church, of which this fellow, Hatherall, was then the rector! The memory of this impertinent dictation—this *prepotenza* of the parsons, made one congratulate oneself on being in Portugal rather than embalmed in the country life of England. Members of a corporation, with personal and corporate interests different from those of general society, there is no sympathy between country gentry and country parsons. The gossip of their wives, their daughters, and their connexions:—the favour which the state shows to their monopoly, and which fashion and timidity compel the family-man to bow before:—the dislike which they know to be felt by all, and the scarce-covert sneers of the independent few:—the encroaching opposition of dissent—these triumphs and tribulations generate in the rural clergy, a spirit of backbiting, bumptiousness, bullying, and bitterness, which makes it collectively the nuisance of all country society. The exceptions are—the single men, good fellows who write their own sermons—the liberal-minded men, who are looked upon as black sheep by their brethren; and the gentlemen—the men of the world whose position in society does not derive from their being parsons.

CHAPTER IX.

THE GREAT EARTHQUAKE.

Prognostics.—Present dread.—The Minister, De Pombal.—Attack on the King.—Funny Conspiracy.—Uncertainties.

IF it were possible that any one should arrive at Lisbon without having heard of the great earthquake and of the Minister Pombal, he would, after a very short stay, be better informed. He would hear of the effects of the earthquake on every public building he went to visit; and he would observe, in every private house in course of construction, walls of wooden frame-work filled with lath and plaster raised inside the main stone walls, and jointly with them supporting the roof; so that, in case of an earthquake, the whole structure should rather incline to one side than topple down upon the in-dwellers. Strong must be the fear which prompts such precautions, and such risk of impending ruin to guard against the possible recurrence of an event which smote the city one hundred years ago!

On the first of November, 1755, Loch Lomond and Loch Ness in Scotland were strangely agitated; till, at length, a huge wave rose out of the latter and overflowed its beach to the extent of thirty feet. At that time, the waters of the hot wells at Bristol became red as blood, and those of another well perfectly black; while the retiring tide of the pretty Avon River suddenly turned back towards the land.

That same first of November had dawned upon Lisbon through a dense fog; but the bright autumn sun soon scattered the unusual visitor; and under a clear and glowing sky, the multitude sought the churches to celebrate the festival of All Saints. How many of them were doomed not to leave those churches alive! At thirty-five minutes past nine, a low rumbling underground noise was heard, which all knew to be the forerunner of an earthquake; for they had felt several during late years. They prayed somewhat the more devoutly, for no great harm had ever come from these shocks. The noise, however, this time increased; it came nearer, and yet more near; at length it rose as loud as the roar of artillery. Crash! above and around, 'shook the churches; staggered the buildings. Down, instantly, went the upper stories of the loftier houses. Their inmates had no time to escape; those passing in the streets below, had no time or space to avoid the falling roofs. From the houses, they dashed themselves through the windows into the streets to avoid the ruin within, and were crushed by the falling walls. Without, all was darkness; the bright sun had disappeared; and through a murky atmosphere, and on a rolling, unsteady, earth, they groped and staggered to the more open spaces of the city. Happy those who were able to effect what all had wished—their escape to the river quay.

Here thousands had congregated; and congratulated themselves that they were safe, let what would happen elsewhere. They leapt into the small boats which lined the beach; they crowded the grand new quay that had lately been built of solid stone far into the river. Another shock! and they saw the church of S. Catherine fall suddenly to the ground, crushing those who had fled for safety to the open and lofty space beside it. They saw .... but, heavens! look to seaward!

The river—it rises! it rushes onwards, upwards, as if loaded with all the waters of the Atlantic: it yawns; it opens; the boats fastened to the beach, the new stone quay—all—all disappear, with the multitudes that throng them. The big ships in the new stream are dashed upon one another, or swallowed down, or cast far upon the ruins where had stood the city. The captain of one vessel, who escaped, declared that the earth at the bottom of the river had surged up with his own anchor higher than the bulwarks of his vessel.

Down, however, again suddenly down, went the Tagus, doing fearful damage to the little shipping that had escaped. A third time the earth reeled, and more of the city toppled down. Less, however, less violent, less and less frequent, became the shocks. But a new horror arose. From several and various quarters of the city, from churches that had been illuminated for the morning worship, from private dwellings, and from public kitchens burst forth innumerable flames. Widely they spread. Fiercely they raged. For six days and nights, they devoured whatever the earthquake had spared; and sad was the scene of desolation when, at length, they were got under.

Out of 20,000 dwelling-houses, hardly three thousand remained standing. Beneath the ruins, or swallowed up in the sea, upwards of twenty-four thousand inhabitants had disappeared. Lisbon had been one of the richest cities in Europe. One million sterling was lost in coined money; four millions in jewels and precious stones; two millions in diamonds belonging to the crown. The whole property destroyed was calculated to be of the value of £536,360,000. Of this loss, seven and a half millions sterling fell upon British subjects; but, to the honour of England, be it recorded, that, so soon as the calamity was known, the King called upon Parliament to assist the sufferers, and nobly and generously was the appeal responded to, out of the public purse and from private liberality.

But as London was purified by its great fire, so all the beautiful streets and squares, intersecting each other at right angles, that we now admire in Lisbon arose after the earthquake, under the presiding genius of the world-famed minister, De Pombal—world-famed for his talents and the iniquitous use he made of them. Enriched by the wealth that Brazil and its other colonies continued to pour into Lisbon, the government of this powerful favourite of the weak king Joseph I. was soon able to repair all material damage. But while the world was admiring the energy of the minister, it was startled by the frequent rumours that told of his darker deeds. Of no very illustrious family himself, as he had won the favour of his sovereign, so he had aroused the jealousy of the older gentry; and on these and on the clergy who would not abet his views, he resolved to avenge himself. About three years after the earthquake, the king, who, with the royal family, had fled from the palace but a few seconds before it fell, was attacked by unknown desperadoes as he was riding through a solitary lane near Belem, and did not escape without a wound. Here was a glorious opportunity for a minister who was said to rule by the discovery of pretended conspiracies! Pombal immediately hatched a sort of Titus Oates plot, and involved in it every noble family who had not cringed to him or whose lands he coveted. The king believed it all; and without a semblance of real evidence, the prisons were filled and the scaffolds reeked with blood. The rack and the headsman did their work on the quay of Belem. The bodies of the victims were burned, and their ashes thrown into the Tagus. All of the illustrious house of Aveiro were extipated. One, of the other great house of Tavora, who had refused to intermarry with the De Pombals, was stripped of lands and titles, and left to beg his bread in the streets of Lisbon.

"Funny conspiracy!" exclaims Voltaire: "in the history of the world, there had never been such a one in any country. A conspiracy hatched at the same time by monks, by nobles, by merchants, by soldiers, by bishops, by Jesuits at Goa, at the Brazils, and at Lisbon, by Germans, by Poles, by Hungarians, by Portuguese. As there never was invented a more atrocious and a more bloody lie, so there never was a more gross and ridiculous one."

However, it answered the minister's purpose. He degraded the nobles, enriched himself, and banished the Jesuits from Portugal. After the death of his weak sovereign, a solemn inquest was held on the alleged conspiracy, and all the victims were declared to have been innocent. Eight hundred persons were alone found alive in the prisons, out of the nine thousand whom he had incarcerated. And, amid the national execration, he was banished twenty miles from the court by a weak queen, who would not bear too hard upon her father's memory, and was allowed to die in peace, and in the enjoyment of his ill-gotten wealth.

The family of De Pombal still exists. I had the pleasure of knowing many of them well—as noted now for their virtues as their progenitor had been for his scoundrelism. The Duke of Saldanha is one of the clan; and boasted to me that, when the supposed bones of the great minister were lately removed from the church, where they had remained for upwards of half a century unburied, more than forty of his kin had followed the solemn procession.

It was, however, as doubtful whose or what were the bones so honoured, as it is doubtful over whom is raised the monument, lately inscribed, in the cemetery of Lisbon, to the English novelist, Henry Fielding.

CHAPTER X.

NEIGHBOURHOOD OF LISBON.

Climate.—Flowers.—H.R.H. the Infanta Isabel.—Quinta of Lumiar; of Oeiras —The Grape Disease.—Oranges.—Horse Races.—Mafra.—Another Horse.—Cintra.—The Royal Palace.—D. Sebastian.—The Duke of Wellington and the King.—The Pena.—D. John de Castro.—Mr. Beckford.—The Cork Convent.—The Pinch of Snuff and Prince Torlonia.

But winter—if there be any season of the year that can be called winter in this delicious climate—had now passed away. The thermometer had generally stood at from 60 to 65 Fahr. During one fortnight at the end of January and beginning of February, it had gone below 60, and even as low as 54. There had generally been about ten degrees difference between midday and midnight. There was a fire-place in one room in our house—a room to the north—and this we had sometimes lighted; but spring was come and we had felt no winter. Baron Kessler, the German physician of King Ferdinand, had indeed often visited our invalid, and had every time made her draw a deep breath, which produced a cough, and then the Baron had looked wise, and had exclaimed :—

"Il y a quelque chose—there is a something!" and had ordered a syrup; but he had never been able to decide what the "quelque chose" was; and now we were all enjoying the contemplation of the bright pink blossom that covered the judas trees, that studded the gardens beneath our windows down to the Tagus edge.

The flowers in Lisbon and its neighbourhood are very beautiful. There is a small public walk, in the lower part of the town, the tropical trees and flowers in which much interested me. The new garden of the Estrella I have already spoken of. Then there were villas in the neighbourhood, in which the natives showed a love of flowers and of gardening rare amongst residents on the continent. The gardens of the Marquez Fronteira at Bemfica were almost as interesting by day as his house had been at the grand ball he had given soon after our arrival.

To that same village of Bemfica, we were taken to be presented to H.R.H. the Infante Isabel, who had governed the kingdom as Regent for her brother, the Emperor of Brazil, with much prudence and popularity. We found her a kindly-mannered, benevolent old lady, who showed us the magnificent magnolia trees in her garden, as large as large elms, and interested herself very much in our family.

The Quinta of Lumiar was a much grander place—beautifully laid out on ground that afforded every facility for landscape gardening. Here were the most lovely flowers and flowering shrubs, greenhouses, and parterres; and, amid secluded groves, were small paddocks fenced in for Southdown sheep and deer!

But grander than any of them, though not so well kept up, were the palace and gardens of Oeiras, a few miles down the Tagus—one of the many seats of the great Marquez de Pombal. We walked ourselves half to death in these extensive grounds, under the guidance of one of the family; and admired the magnificent cellars, in which were some scores of casks for wine, each, apparently, as large as the big tun at Heidelberg, but which had remained perfectly empty since the infliction of the grape disease. A hard tussel, indeed, had this and many other wealthy families to maintain themselves without this chief source of income; but the De Pombal gave us a plentiful and excellent luncheon in his Quinta, which was most acceptable after our long walk.

This allusion to the grape disease gives me an occasion to mention that it had shown itself in Portugal three centuries before, to such an extent that it had been provided, in leases still extant, that tenants should be entitled to a proportionate reduction, or even a total return, of their rental in the provinces in which it appeared. At this time, people were fearing a somewhat similar disease which threatened the oranges, and which must have been a grievous loss to many in Portugal. For example, I was one day talking agriculture with one of the largest landed proprietors in the peninsula, the Marquez de Ficalho, son and heir of the Dowager Duchess of Ficalho (I do not know why he did not assume her title), when he replied to a question of mine—

"Oranges! I grow little but oranges. I leave you English to grow corn, and the French and Italians to grow wine and oil: my land and climate will grow oranges, which are more valuable than anything else; so I no more grow corn than an Englishman would grow oats or a Lucchese apples."

The advance of spring had also been greeted by horse races, to witness which we had driven out to

Campo Grande. This, however, was only a first effort to get up hurdle races; and after all the horses had vainly attempted to leap a fence two feet nine inches high, the attempt was abandoned as impracticable, and we all returned merrily to Lisbon.

But now, before the summer should be further advanced, I would make more distant excursions into the country—with our own "caroagem" and horses, as the newspaper editor had foretold I should travel. We started on the 5th of May. The road I followed was disagreeable—hot and dusty; but it was wide and well-made; and after a five hours drive, we looked down upon that immense pile of stone, the spires of which we had beheld far out at sea, some months before, as we had approached the mouth of the Tagus. I drove down to the poor unpaved village of Mafra; took possession of rooms and stable, and ordered supper at the decent little inn; and then went to see the mighty palace.

Mighty in its massive ugliness: majestic in its massiveness, rises the great church with dome and towers, and the great palace joined to it on either side. From the hot sandy common, unpaved, undecorated, unenclosed, the huge building of ruddy sandstone rises in unmeaning grandeur, a parallelogram, of which the longest sides measure 770 feet, and are four storeys high. This is its history :—

The magnanimous king Don John V, who built that rich chapel we have described, had no son and heir, but vowed that if one were born to him, he would change the poorest monastery in Portugal into the richest one. Don Joseph came into the world—and so did Mafra; for in a hut on this spot, were found to dwell twelve monks of the poorest order in Portugal. Straightway 15,000 persons were set to work for thirteen years, under the direction of the architect Ludovici, a German: and at a cost supposed to exceed 19,000,000 dollars, uprose, upon the desert plain, the huge fabric, containing a glorious church, a magnificent monastery, a palace for the king, one similar to it for the queen; the whole adjoining, but lighted from nine inner courtyards, and covered by a flat roof, on which ten thousand men might be reviewed. Above this roof, rise four domes, one at each angle; the great dome of the centre church; and, on each side of it, one of the two spires containing the wondrous clocks and chimes of bells. These were made in Holland; and when the

Dutch manufacturers of whom they had been ordered declined the costly job, because they feared the little kingdom of Portugal could not bear the expense, Don John replied that his agents had made a mistake; that the machinery was to be twice as costly as they had ordered; and he sent the money in advance to pay for it. Truly, Don John the Magnanimous was a magnificent fellow!

These bells are said to have cost near three millions of dollars. We went up to them and saw a maze of wheels within wheels, and of little cogs and great cogs, much like those in a cotton factory. The keeper moved a plug and they played a remarkably sweet and pretty tune— much as a Geneva musical box would have done— and we gave the keeper one thousand three hundred reis, with which he was very well satisfied. So were we. We returned to supper at our inn.

You know not, gentle reader, what it has cost me to come to this lame and impotent conclusion. It required an effort ere I could consent to leave the palace without saying more about it: without telling that, in all the nine hundred rooms it contains, there is not one really large and handsome hall; and without describing the architectural riches of the really beautiful church. But these descriptions are they not written by Beckford, and by my friend Dr. Illsley, in his excellent *Lisbon Guide*, and by Murray's *Handbook*, which quotes from him? It was all very well for the author of *Vathek* to describe them in his earlier days, when these guide-books existed not; but now, no one going to Portugal would go without them; and I see not why I should poach upon their manor. I profess to give only personal impressions of what I see; if the reader judges from what I say that the country is worth seeing, let him buy professed guide-books and go and see it. I shall not give architectural descriptions until other matter fails me; and until I know not how else to fill my volumes.

One of the disadvantages of travelling with one's own "caroagem" and horses is, that one is tempted to take short cuts. Such an one led from Mafra to Cintra. By the bye, I have never told the reader that I had been able to replace my poor horse that had been killed by the P. and O. Company; that I had replaced him at Lisbon. My very obliging banker, Mr. Krus, had found out for me that Count Farrobo had a fine iron-grey English horse, the fellow of which had died in

Lisbon. This was a tolerable match for the survivor of mine, although rather too weedy in the legs; and this I had bought for two hundred and forty thousand reis—which meant, I forget how much. With these horses, therefore, and our English britzska, I branched off from the weary road from Mafra to Lisbon across one that led direct to Cintra. It was an awful track; but English horses will always do their work, whatever it may be; and I had ever held it a maxim that I could drive wherever wheels had passed before. At last, therefore, we arrived at the Hotel Victor in Cintra, and gazed on the two enormous piles, like chimneys of vast factories, that rose at no great distance.

Let poets say what they will of Cintra, these are the most striking objects there; and the Frenchman who said that the kitchen was always "*la pièce la plus intéressante de la maison*" would have spoken indisputable truth had he applied the sentence to these mighty conical chimneys of the kitchen of the royal palace, that enclose under their roof the fireplaces and ranges, like the giant cover of an Irish stew.

Everything about this palace denotes that it was founded when the Moorish kings ruled at

Lisbon, though their Christian conquerors have since occupied it. The consequent anachronisms and mixture of the architecture are very curious. The ornaments of the windows are quite Arabic. The paintings of the rooms are quite of Christian chivalry. The legend connected with the ceiling and frieze of the Hall of the Magpies, for example, reminds one of the days which first heard "*Honi soit qui mal y pense.*" King John of Portugal, once upon a time, was caught by his fiery queen, Philippa of Lancaster, paying some questionable attention to one of her maids of honour. " Por bem !—for good ;" or " all right !" exclaimed the king. And he forthwith had this room decorated with magpies, to denote the tattling qualities of his courtiers ; while each magpie, by a legend coming out of its mouth, repeated the " Por bem !" which the king took as his motto.

In another room, are painted the escutcheons of twenty-four of the oldest families of Portugal ; the arms of the family of Tavora and Aveiro, whom De Pombal ruined for their pretended conspiracy against the king, having been erased by the revengeful minister. Here is the wretched apartment in which Affonso VI was confined for fifteen years, with the tracks of his daily walk worn deep in the brick pavement as he paced it to and fro; and here, too, is the room in which the brave young King Sebastian held his last audience, and in which the royal crown is said to have fallen from his head—a sad omen of what was to follow. For the chivalric young king having determined, as every reader knows, to carry the war against the Moors into Africa, crossed the seas with the very flower of his powerful and wealthy kingdom; but was so utterly defeated at Alcacer Quibir, that only fifty Portuguese are said to have survived. The body of the king could never be found, and a regent was appointed in his stead; then, when, failing the direct line, the hated Spaniard succeeded to the rule, a belief in the continued life and future return of Sebastian was sustained by patriots, and became almost a national creed. Different claimants appeared and were disposed of; but so strong had become the popular faith in the return of Don Sebastian, that even after the "sixty years captivity," after the Spaniards were expelled by the gallant Dukes of Bragança, people still looked forward to the return of this unfortunate youth, as of a Messiah miraculously preserved for the good of his country.

We are told of one personage who appeared at

Venice, twenty years after the lost battle, and who really did give evidence that he was the missing king. Some negative evidence to the truth of his story might be suspected, from the fact that he as suddenly disappeared or was made away with, after he had shown such marks on his person as Don Sebastian was known to have had; after he had described all the crown jewels in Portugal; and after he had told of certain signs engraved on the reverse of a ring which Don Sebastian had really given to the Marqueza Medina Cœli.

This anecdote of the ring reminds me of another, more interesting to English people. The first Duke of Wellington, meeting Mrs. Dawson Damer at a dinner party, was observed to look intently at a ring worn by that lady. After dinner, he accosted her and requested to be allowed to see it, as the children say, " in his own hands."

" Where did you get this ring ?" said F. M. the Duke.

" It belonged to the late Mrs. Fitzherbert."

" Yes. Do you know the trick of it ? Have you opened it ?"

" Opened it ! I know of no trick !" exclaimed the lady.

The Duke touched a spring, and showed behind the ring a tiny miniature of the Regent in his best days. "There were two of these rings," explained the Duke. "They were exactly alike—so my attention was drawn to yours. The fellow ring to this differed from it in that it enclosed the likeness of Mrs. Fitzherbert. The king gave that one to me before he died, and ordered me to place it on his breast before the coffin was closed down. I did so."

Return we to Cintra where—

"The horrid crags by toppling convent crown'd,
The cork trees hoar that clothe the shaggy steep,
The mountain moss by scorching skies embrown'd,
The sunken glen whose sunless shrubs must weep,
The tender azure of the unruffled deep,
The orange tints that gild the greenest bough,
The torrents that from cliff to valley leap,
The vine on high, the willow branch below,
Mix'd in one mighty scene with varied beauty glow."

So mouths Byron—a boyish style he left with *Childe Harold*. "The horrid crag by toppling convent crowned," is the most striking feature of Cintra from a distance, as the Moorish chimneys are from the town. The Convent of the Pena, however, no longer exists as such, having been suppressed with other religious houses. Bought by a private person who could not keep it up, it was since purchased by King Fernando, and restored with that taste which he so greatly possesses. A wide carriage road now winds up the hitherto rugged ascent, and leads to a drawbridge and castle gateway, over which are carved the arms of Portugal and Saxony. Turrets and towers rise beside native pinnacles of rocks, and amid cloistered courts and hanging woods. No spot on earth is more romantic; no gardens more wonderfully placed; no view more magnificent than the view beheld from this lofty embattled tower. The great heath plain on one side dotted with cultivated oases of vines, and broken by the lonely pile of Mafra; the blue Atlantic stretching on the other sides, and seen through the broken pinnacles of rock; and the tufted cork-tree covered hills of this glorious headland of Cintra. Let us remember too, although the boyish petulance of *Childe Harold* thinks such trash as leads him to exclaim—

> Poor paltry slaves! yet born midst noblest scenes—
> Why, Nature, waste thy wonders on such men?"

let us remember that to this giddy height, on which he had founded the convent of the Pena, King Emanuel constantly toiled up in the hope of descrying the fleet of Vasco da Gama returning from the discovery of India; and that he himself on 29th of July, 1499, was in fact the first to descry the pilot vessel of the successful adventurers re-entering across the bar of the Tagus. "Poor paltry slaves," indeed! Find me a sovereign now-a-days who would care sufficiently for science and progress to undergo such personal toil for its sake. Show me a people who would follow up the spirit of magnificent adventure more eagerly than did the gallant Portuguese.

Through the lovely gardens of the Pena, a path conducts to the ruins of the castle of the Moors that crown another rocky peak. These possess no great interest beyond a large Moorish swimming-bath, about fifty feet long, which is constantly supplied with the clearest water by some of those unseen springs which rise in the ridge of Cintra, and produce that freshness of vegetation, and that cool atmosphere, which entice the Lisbonians to spend the two hottest months of the year amid its pleasant hills.

After breakfast, next morning, our carriage came to the door, and I drove past the Quinta of Marquez Loulé, on the open space in front of which is the fashionable evening lounge of the inhabitants of Cintra, during the season of villeggiatura. It was now deserted; and I note the place only as being the house in which the disgraceful convention was signed between Sir H. Dalrymple and Junot, the convention at which folks in office "fain would blush, if blush they could, for shame." Then I drove on to the villa and grounds of Penha Verde, once the residence of the great Don João de Castro, and still belonging to his descendants; we lingered long in the shady walks of these neglected grounds, and gathered some leaves from the six trees growing on the rock which this great hero and, during twenty years, Viceroy of the Indies— through whose hands the fabulous wealth of that newly discovered world had passed to his country —from the six trees and rock which he had asked to have added to his garden in sole requital of all his toils and conquests. The prayer was granted; and, after swearing to the truth of a declaration that he had spent his whole income in providing for the wants of his fellow soldiers, and did not possess coin enough to buy him a meal or a change of linen, this great pious man expired in the arms of St. Francis Xavier, the apostle of the Indies, as he himself had been its ruler. On a beautiful mound, overshaded with ancient cork-trees, is a small chapel with some nice inscriptions, intimating that it had been founded in compliance with a vow made to imprecate a safe voyage out and a safe return.

Unwillingly we drove away from this classic spot to one more popularly known to English people, unknown to universal or nobler fame :— We reached Monserrat, the villa founded by Mr. Beckford, the author of *Vathek*. Like Fonthill Abbey, it is almost a ruin. " Quid feci ? ubi lapsus sum ?" exclaims the motto of the once heroic Courtenays.

The little town of Collares did not justify the enthusiastic descriptions I had read of its scenery; and, turning homewards, I left my carriage at the side of a bleak volcanic waste, and cut across the country for a couple of miles to the Capuchos, the last convent founded by D. João de Castro, for twenty Franciscan monks. It is a curious place ! Recollecting that penance and mortification have been taught by the founders of all religions — Pagan, Jewish, and Christian — we must admit that here the rite can be practised to perfection ! Here are a church, sacristy, chapter house, and about twenty cells, partly dug out of the earth, partly built of stone, but all lined with cork to keep out the damp. Each cell is about five feet square ; each is entered by a door so low that one has to bend nearly double to pass; no windows; the doors fastened with sticks; the convent bell pulled by a vine withe. Never, elsewhere, did human beings live in such wretched holes! Nay, even the hole or cave of Honorius, which is shown in the convent garden, is preferable. I crawled into it, and by drawing up my legs, it was long enough to cover me, and I could sit upright on the ground in one spot. But here, at least, was seclusion and quiet, and comparatively fresh air; and, not having the monastic spirit upon me, I felt that I would rather live here, as the hermit Honorius did, for the last sixteen years of his life, than have been doomed to the close community of the cork cells. This holy monk joined his brethren in their church services and in the labours of the day; but chose this hole as his own cell, and here he died at the age of 95, in the year 1596. Lord Byron says of him :—

"Deep in yon cave Honorius long did dwell,
In hope to merit heaven by making earth a hell."

Murray's *Handbook* quotes the inscription on a stone in front of the cave :—

"Hic Honorius vitam finivit,
Et ideo cum Deo in cœlis revivit."
"Here Honorius ended his life,
And, therefore, lives with God in heaven."

And Murray adds, "these are lines which some may prefer to Lord Byron's sneer on the same subject."

The *Lisbon Guide* also quotes the two inscriptions, and bids the reader to disembody his mind, and ask himself, when passing into a future state, whether he would rather have been Byron or Honorius.

Verily, the noble Childe's "philosophy" has not met with the applause he anticipated!

We returned to Cintra, lunched, baited the horses, paid our bill (15,420 Reis—about £3 : 8 : 0 for 6 people and 2 horses), and, in the cool of the evening, drove past the once royal villa of Ramalhaon—now the property of the tobacco contractor Guedez, with whom I was destined to fall out—and returned to Lisbon.

One often does fall out with these tobacco contractors. My son, of the Brompton Oratory, before starting to go to Rome for the great centenary gathering of 1867, desired his usual tobacconist in Bond Street to fill his box with choice snuff that he might have a good pinch to offer to the big wigs he should meet.

"Beware what you do, sir," said the tradesman. "A customer of mine had just the same fancy a few years ago, and being at a party at Prince Torlonia's offered him his box. 'Capital snuff!' exclaimed the Prince; 'where could you have got it?' 'I brought two or three pounds with me,' replied the Englishman; 'and, as you seem to like it so much, if you will send your snuff-box to my lodgings to-morrow morning, I will fill it for you.'"

Prince Torlonia was the tobacco contractor; and, next morning, instead of the snuff-box, appeared to the astonished traveller, two gens-d'armes to sequestrate those two or three pounds of snuff from which it was to have been filled.

Hospitable, wasn't it?

CHAPTER XI.

INTERIOR OF PORTUGAL.

A Portuguese Railroad.—Caldas.—An Innkeeper's Bill.—Battle of Aljubarrota.—Batalha.—Monastery of Alcobaça.—Don Pedro and Inez de Castro.—Portuguese Inns.

WHEN we arrived at the railway station on the morning of the 25th May, we found the Saldanhas, Lavradios, and a large merry party of mutual friends, who were starting to spend the day at one of the Farrobo country houses. We were received with most gratifying acclamations, and were urged to change our plans and join their party. It was impossible to do so, as we had sent forward our French coachman to the point where we should have to leave the railroad. Away steamed the train along the banks of the Tagus, which soon opened into the wide marshy lake known to English sailors as Jackass Bay. We passed through Alhandra and Villa Franca, where ended our famous lines of Torres Vedras, and found our carriage at a miserable station called Caregado. Here we left the river, and drove through a pretty country to Cercel. We dined on an omelet, and the horses baited; and we then proceeded to sleep at Caldas.

Now Caldas, be it known, is a clean well-paved town of 1600 inhabitants. It is celebrated for its mineral waters, and is on the high road from Porto to Lisbon. As a matter of course, we had calculated upon finding here good entertainment for man and horse. We were in the interior of Portugal; and, as this is the only occasion I shall have of speaking of Portuguese inns, I will mention that, at the Nova Hospederia of Caldas, no meat and no milk could be found; and that next day the bill showed what entertainment we had enjoyed, as follows:—I say bill; but, on reflection, I really think that they had not arrived at such a height of civilisation:—I paid, however, as follows:—

For three beds (for self, wife, and coachman)	680
Wine and omelet, and bread; (they could get nothing else)	740
Breakfasts; (we had carried our own tea)	320
Coachman's food	480

Horse corn	900
Straw	720
	3840

About 18s. We visited the hot baths, which seem very commodious and well managed. The temperature of the water is 92 Fahr.; and the hospital, maintained by the government, contained 600 poor patients.

It seemed to be settled rainy weather, and we drove on through an uninteresting country, my predominating remembrance of which is as of open heaths. The road was good—newly-made or improved. With straining eyes, but without halting, we passed the monastic pile of Alcobaça and the great battle-field of Aljubarrota—the one the largest in the world, the other as important as ever patriot valour won. For in 1383, D. Ferdinand I. had died, leaving only one daughter, who was married to the Spanish King of Castile. Portugal would never succumb to Spain; and in its general Cortes, unanimously elected for its sovereign an illegitimate son left by the father of the late king. This valiant one, Don John I., collected what forces he could; and, having defeated detached bodies of the Spaniards in two engagements, came up with the main body of their army on the fields of Batalha and Aljubarrota. He had but 6,500 men. The King of Spain had a host, the numbers of which are reported variously from 33,000 to 90,000; he had also the first artillery ever seen in Portugal. The Archbishop of Braga rode along the Portuguese lines, and blessed the eager troops in the name of the true Pope, Urban VI. A Spanish Bishop blessed the Spanish host in the name of the Antipope, Clement VI. A cannon was fired by them, and two brothers in the Portuguese army fell dead. Never had the troops heard such implements, killing from such a distance. A panic seized them.

"I know for a certainty," exclaimed a ready-witted patriot soldier, "that they were two base scoundrels and traitors, whom Heaven deemed unworthy to share our glory!" and onwards Don John's little army rushed. The Spanish tent was stormed and all its furniture taken. The great standard of Castile was taken, and the invading Spaniard, ill of the ague, leapt upon his horse and never drew bridle till he reached the friendly garrison of Santarem. The great cauldrons used for cooking the beans of the Spanish soldiers were taken; and when, two centuries later, during the sixty years captivity, an abbot of Alcobaça was so poor a courtier as to show one of them to the Spanish Sovereign then reigning in Portugal, and proposed making it into a bell, "Let it alone," said Philip II, "if it made so much noise in the world as a cauldron, who could endure it as a bell!"

All this we thought of as, through the rain, we drove over this historic ground and passed the old bakehouse, the oven peel of which, wielded by the brave baker's wife, killed seven Spanish soldiers during the gallant fight.

"*Endiabrada como a padeira d' Aljubarrota*—as bedevilled as the bakeress of Aljubarrota," is still a popular saying.

But soon we entered the little valley where, in consequence of King John's vow if he won the great battle, soon uprose, and still towers in its magnificence, the monastery and church of Batalha. Shall I attempt to describe this world-famed pile? —its cloisters, which nothing in Europe can rival—its "unfinished chapel," which nothing in Europe can surpass! Such pinnacles, such flying buttresses, such battlements, such spires, such carved stone, nowhere else can meet the wondering gaze in such harmonious confusion. With honest national pride, I saw the arms of England impaled with those of Portugal over the tombs of the gallant King John and his Queen Philippa, of Lancaster, who was consulted on the plan of the building, and suggested some modification of English Gothic to its wondrous architect; and, with honest hatred of all that is mean and barbarous, we cursed the memory of those French savages who had broken and defaced all they could deface and break in their rapid marches through Portugal. It would have taken months to study, as they deserve to be studied, the endless beauties of this glorious pile. With a feeling of unsatiated wonder that such should be found in this retired valley, similar to that which oppresses the mind after viewing the temples of Pæstum, we eat our bread and omelet at the poor little inn, and drove back to Alcobaça.

The ancient Cistercian monastery of Alcobaça is the largest in the world. A Portuguese saying declared that its cloisters were cities, its sacristy a church, and its church a basilica, or, as Mr. Kinsey translates it, "a basilisk." It contained one thousand monks, less one. The convent was enormously rich, but most generous and judicious in the distribution of its wealth. The poor fed at its gates; the more intelligent were educated by it; and, like all the other great monastic houses in Portugal, it always paid thirty per cent. of its yearly income to the service of the State. The church is very grand — after Batalha, the grandest building in the kingdom. The kitchen is even more remarkable for its size; its fire-place is in proportion — twenty-eight feet long and eleven feet deep. The whole building was much injured by the French in their flight, Massena himself having ordered it to be burned down. That which has been rebuilt is in no way worthy of that which was destroyed. This convent, like other religious houses since the suppression, is falling into ruin. A great part of it is used as barracks.

But the church of Alcobaça derives an interest unequalled by any other church, in that it contains the monuments of the wretched Don Pedro and Inez de Castro. Who has not mourned over the recital of the loves of the hereditary Prince of Portugal and the beautiful Inez! of their secret marriage, and of the murder of the poor bride by order of her brutal father-in-law, King Alfonso? Who has not felt with the bereaved husband in his anger against his father, and in the steady revenge with which he sought out her three murderers? Two only was he able to secure; and we must hope that a certain amount of madness prompted his subsequent proceedings. He caused the heart of one to be cut out through his breast; that of the other to be torn through his back; and, while their bodies were being burned to ashes, he sat and dined by the light of the flames. He caused the body of his beloved wife to be unburied, clothed it in royal robes, and seated it on a throne; and compelled all the nobles of his kingdom to pay homage to the horrid pageant. Then, with unknown pomp, it was conveyed from Coimbra to this mighty church, and placed in a tomb, the chiselled art of which has excited the admiration of five hundred years. Nothing, indeed, can be more beautiful than the bas-reliefs that surround this high sarcophagus, on the top of which lies—larger than life—the noble figure of the murdered queen. It is supposed to be, and doubtless is, a true likeness, since it was carved under the superintendence of her widower. The nose was broken off by one of the French barbarians of Massena's army; but there are traces of great beauty in all of the statue that is uninjured. At the bottom of this, and turned feet to feet, in order that, on the day of resurrection, his Inez might be the first object to meet his eyes, is the fellow-sarcophagus of her husband. Like the first, it is all of the whitest marble, of the most excellent workmanship ever perfected, after that of the queen; and is surmounted by the large reclining figure, with the handsome face and stern features, of Don Pedro "the Severe."

It was thoroughly wet weather. We slept at the poor little inn here; baited next day at Cercel, and slept at Caldas. I was much pleased with the behaviour of the people at these places. The inns, it is true, were poor as poor could be, and were quite unprepared to receive gentlefolk travellers. But the people were most willing and civil; they were modest and kind; and their rooms and bedding quite clean. They contrasted very favourably with some of the blustering landlords of France and Italy, who know not how to charge enough for the dirt and discomfort of their miserable pothouses. We took the railroad at Villa Franca and returned to Lisbon.

CHAPTER XII.

A LOCATION IN LISBON.

The Minister of Finances.—House-hunting.—The Tobacco Contractor and Lady O'Shaunessy.—A Brazilian Speculator "stumped."—Another Minister of Finances.—The House of Peers and the Author.—The English Minister afraid.

It must, by this time, be sufficiently evident to the Reader that we liked Portugal, liked the climate, liked the Portuguese, and felt grateful to them for the really friendly manner in which they had received us into their society. To back up and give active results to this feeling, was the doubt whether our invalid daughter would ever be strong enough to spend her winters in England; and the dread that, on her account, some other Dr. Latham might, every autumn, send us winter-wanderers over the earth. Would it not be wiser, safer, pleasanter to secure a residence at Lisbon, to which we might retreat from Northern regions, and in which we might find ourselves, at once, really at home and amongst friends? Such was the advice constantly urged upon us by these friends of a few weeks' standing; and I looked out for a house.

But we had left England thinking only of a few months' absence; and, though we had brought one carriage with us, for leave to use which I had deposited, with the Custom House, more than it was worth, I did not like to sink this money and as much more on any other carriage we might send for, or to pass our winters amid a gay society without having any china and plate for our own comfort (and the admiration of our friends!), or any jewelry with which to deck my wife and daughters. My readers of the *Wabash* know how this same plate and jewelry had before bothered me. I therefore signed a request, which some good friend drew up for me in Portuguese, to Senhor Silva Sanches, the Minister of Finances, that he would admit these objects duty-free for my own personal use; and, in the letter which accompanied my application, I stated that I would not definitively engage any house until I had his answer and unless that answer were favourable. My application was taken to the Minister by Marshalls the Duke of Saldanha and the Duke of Terceira; and, two days afterwards, I received an order to the Director of the Custom House to admit the effects duty-free.

Armed with this, I went to work; and, after an ineffectual attempt to deal for one which we familiarly called the Orange Grove—rather than pronounce the unpronounceable names of the owner—we fixed upon a large house in the Campo S. Anna. We were told that no one was in treaty for it; and a price was named to our lawyer, with a promise to wait twenty-four hours for our answer. He was sent back immediately, to say that we would give the money. Two days afterwards, I was informed that the proprietors had sold the house to M. Guedez, the rich tobacco contractor before alluded to, for the same amount, and that the law empowered vendors to retract any bargain within sixty days. M. Guedez assured me that he had been long in treaty for the house, and had offered considerably less for it; that, having received a message informing him of the amount I was willing to give, with an intimation that he should say instantly yes or no, he had immediately closed the bargain. He wrote that he was desolated to find that I was the purchaser from whom he had taken the house; that there must have been some misunderstanding, as the vendors were recognised to be the soul of honour; that he would gladly surrender his purchase to me, but that Mme. Guedez liked it, and that her wishes had always had great weight with him; and that, in her delicate state of health, he could not even mention the subject to her, &c., &c., &c.

I thought of the innkeeper, whom the Lord Lieutenant had knighted during a drunken frolic, who would willingly have forgone the honour but that Lady O'Shaunessy, his wife, would be displeased.

I looked further, and fixed on a grand house of Duke Terceira, on the edge of the Tagus; but a Brazilian heard that I had been about it, and bought it for a price I had refused to give, on the speculation that he would sell it to me again at a still higher price. He was disappointed.

At last, I found a beautiful uninhabited house of Marquez de Pombal in the Via Formosa. On the other side, its own grounds sloped away in terraces, covered with orange groves, down towards the broad Tagus, which they seemed to reach; although there was a strip of the city concealed between the gardens and the river. It was a beautiful house, beautifully situated. The family could not sell it; and, after a long treaty, I engaged to rent it on a twenty years lease.

All this, as may be supposed, had been a matter of interest to society at large; and even the King, his father, and the Duke of Oporto, now King Luiz, all condescended to ask me one evening at the Palace if we had found a house. His Majesty himself knew of the matter because I had been instructed that I ought to thank him personally for the portaria, or order to admit my goods, which his Minister had issued. Judge, then, of our surprise when I received notice that the Minister of Finances having been changed, the new man, Sig. d'Avila, had revoked the order issued in my favour by his predecessor, on the plea that it was illegal!

But, although I was much annoyed at the time, I am not going to make a serious matter of it now; and I hope the reader may be as amused as I am by reading over old papers at this distance of time, and seeing what an excitement I unhappily caused in the restricted society and parliament of Portugal.

In the *Jornal do Commercio* of the 13th May, 1857, I find a leading article in which the editor calls attention to a letter I had addressed to him;

and admits that the disagreement between two Ministers of Finance, the one repealing what the other had granted, gave me just cause of complaint. It is very true, the editor says, that diplomatic ministers are alone entitled to receive goods for their own use duty free, and that I am not of that number; but that as the favour had been occasionally allowed, the "severidade de fiscal è excessiva," upsetting all my domestic arrangements, and preventing strangers, in similar circumstances, from coming to reside temporarily amongst them. My letter was, however, as follows :—I translate from the French, in which I wrote :

"Sir,—Last December, you announced my arrival in Lisbon in terms far too flattering. The truth is, I did not come to Portugal to travel, but in search of health. Your beautiful climate has agreed with us so well that we had planned to spend here all our winters. But, before I took any decided step, I explained, to the Minister of Finances, that, unless he granted me a *portaria* to receive, duty free, certain comforts from my home in England, such as plate, china, and some of my books . . . The Minister, M. G. da Silva Sanches, granted my request; and I engaged the

Marquis de Pombal's house, No. 17 Via Formosa, on a twenty years lease.

"There was a change of ministry; and, after all my arrangements were made, M. D'Avila, successor of M. Gomes Sanches, has revoked the *portaria* to which I had trusted.

"M. D'Avila asserts that such a favour would not have been granted to a stranger in England: that might have been a motive for refusing it in Portugal, but not for withdrawing it after it had been granted. England, however, would have preferred that its custom-house should lose a few thousand francs rather than that one of its Secretaries of State should break word with a foreigner.

"M. D'Avila pretends that the *portaria* was illegal. I, as a foreigner, knew nothing of that. I compromised myself on the faith of the Minister of Finances. Some years ago, certain states in America, which had borrowed largely from foreigners, made a similar discovery, and repudiated their debts. Foreigners are now giving their money towards the formation of railways in Portugal; perhaps the Minister will discover that such loans are illegal and will repudiate them?

"This conduct of the Minister, who has acted

upon his own responsibility, has been so much discussed in Lisbon that I must pray you to publish this letter in order to explain the facts of the case."

Two days afterwards, the same paper gave a short report of a discussion on the subject that had been raised, in the House of Peers, by the Marquez de Vallada; and the best of the joke was that I misapprehended the short statement, and wrote and thanked the Marquez Vallada for coming forward (although I had not the honour of his acquaintance) to compel a vain and obstinate and upstart Minister to behave fairly towards a foreigner! I afterwards found out how the matter really stood, as will appear from this other letter to the *Jornal do Commercio.*

"29th May, 1857. On my return from Batalha I find, in the *Diario do Governo* of the 25th, the *procès verbal* of what took place in the House of Peers on the 16th :—When your railroads are completed, the *Diario* will move quicker. They discussed, I see, the letter that I had written to you two days before; and the present Minister of Finances and the Marquez Vallada congratulated one another that the former had prevented an Englishman from coming to spend his money at

Lisbon. For one column and a half of the official Diary, they insisted that the letter of the law should be followed in Custom House matters, without the least respect either for precedents or for the honour of the Government." * * *

But, enough of my letter. The Minister, who had granted the permission, manfully defended in Parliament what he had done; and the matter was discussed long and acrimoniously.* The

* Forgive my vanity, which prompts me to preserve the following speech in its original Portuguese. It will, at all events, prove that I have not misrepresented the position which our kind friends had given us in the society of Lisbon. The government paper thus reports from the debate in the House of Peers the speech of the late Minister of Finances—" O Sr. Julio Gomes. Não me recordo agora quando mas creio ter sidos nos ultimos dias que tive a honra de ser Ministro, que se me appresentou um requerimento do cavalheiro a que alludio o Digno Par o Sr. Marquez de Vallada, pedindo que se lhe concedesse a entrada livre de dereitos, de objectos do seu proprio uso como eram pratas e loucas com a sua firma. Este cavalheiro desejava muito residir em Portugal, para vêr se conseguia restabelecer a saude de uma pessoa da sua familia; não vinha estabelecer aqui a sua residencia, se lhe não concedessem, livre de dereitos, a entrada dos objectos de que se falla. Constoume per informacões de cavalheiros digno de toda fó, que o referido individuo era um perfeito cavalheiro, que não vinha introduzir em Portugal objecto nenhum de commercio; e declarando elle que eram objectos de seu uso, vendo-se em todos a sua firma; e sendo certo que alguns precedentes havia a tal respeito: pareceu-me que para fim tão justo, como o querer residir n'um paiz, cujo clima julgava proprio para o restabelecimento da saude de uma pessoa da familia, não deveria eu deixar de seguir esses precedentes. A concessão foi feita: porém com as precaucões necessarias, como a da condicão expressa de que, vindo a sair de Portugal, seria obrigado a reexportar os mesmos objectos, ou a pagar os direitos

withdrawal had, in fact, been one incident in a Ministerial intrigue, the object of which was to offend Saldanha, Loulé, and others, and to make way for a complete " Cabrallista" Cabinet, an intrigue into which it was very amusing but very disgusting to see a stranger drawn.

But how did our own people behave in this matter? How did the representatives of England, who are paid so many thousands a year to protect the interests of the supposed "Roman," who is not to be "whipped" in any part of the world,—how did they behave? I was told by everybody that a material, tangible wrong having been done to me, it was the clear duty of our legation to have it redressed; and the representatives of France laughed at the bare suggestion of a doubt whether they would permit a Frenchman to be so wronged. I had brought a letter of introduction to our Minister, Mr. Henry Howard, when I came to Lisbon, and had been on terms of

que na entrada se exigiriam, se por ventura não houvesse tal concessão. Em taes termos foi que eu intendi fazar, e que fiz a concessão. Veio, porem, o meu illustre successor, e julgou que devia revogar aquella determinação. Não lhe levo a mal a sua resolução: mas tambem me parece que não se devera levar a mal a que eu havia tomado, pois nas circumstancias que ponderei, e adoptadas as precauções que já referi, não julgo se possa dizer que eu estava inhibido de seguir os precedentes que encontrei."

intimacy with his family ever since. I reported the case to him and asked for his interference. He expressed his disgust; but said he did not think he ought to interfere officially. Mr. Smith, our British Consul-General, considering it somewhat of a commercial matter, asked Howard to permit him, as Consul, to remonstrate with d'Avila, because he wished, at the same time, to charge him with his "dirty trick to Mr. Stoddart," who, having paid duty on an English piano, had been encouraged to change it for another by d'Avila's promise that the second should be admitted duty free,—which duty he had made him pay again nevertheless. Mr. Howard desired the Consul not to move in the matter. My friend Marshall Duke of Terceira, took an apologetic message to Mr. Howard from d'Avila; a message purporting that the latter only wished for some explanations from me, and would then issue another permission. Mr. Howard replied that he did not intend to interfere in any way officially; and consequently, when I sent the required explanation, d'Avila wrote to me in reply, that he should now adhere to his first decision. Mr. Howard called upon me and warned me that, happen what would in the matter, he would not move; and gave a large party, at which d'Avila was present, but to which we were not invited—the first omission since we had been at Lisbon. This is the way our English Ministers abroad back their countrymen! Who would care; what foreign Government would care for any opinion expressed by a man of the intellectual calibre of poor Mr. Howard, and of most of our foreign Ministers, when he had abdicated his official position and so deprived himself of the weight that might attach to his opinion if given as that of the English Minister?

These gentry are always above or beneath their position, from pride or imbecility. It is high time the country should enquire what salaries they draw for the fulfilment of duties which they neglect.

I reported the matter between me and the Portuguese Government to Lord Clarendon, and received an assurance from the Foreign Office that "his lordship had called the attention of Mr. Howard to my complaint, and had instructed him to take such steps as he might consider the facts of the case to justify, with a view to procure for me redress."

I had left Lisbon without waiting for this letter, which reached me elsewhere. For the Marquez de Pombal had behaved most handsomely. Knowing the conditions on which I had rented his palace, and hearing of d'Avila's misconduct, he did not convoke his *conseille de famille* to ratify the proposed lease; and agreed to my suggestion that we should each put our copy of the agreement into the fire, or into whatever is supposed to represent such a consummation at Lisbon towards the end of the month of May.

The weather was getting very hot; and we enjoyed the cool breezes of the Atlantic, which some think to disqualify Lisbon as a refuge for pulmonary invalids. I do not share their opinion. The winds of the Atlantic are, at all events, preferable to the icy north and east winds that scourge the Mediterranean shores of Italy.

"Padre," said an Italian in confession, "I have to accuse myself, father, that I swore at the wind."

"Beware, my son," said the priest. "Swear not at all—least of all at the works of God. But what wind was it that you cursed?"

"It was the east wind, padre."

"Ah! it was very wrong. But I own that that cursed east wind does very much try my own temper."

CHAPTER XIII.

SPAIN.

Difficulty of going to Spain.—*L'Helvétie*.—The Medical Lecturer.—Cadiz.— A Spanish family.—Gibraltar.— Malaga.—A Bull-fight.

It may be remembered that, when advised by Dr. Latham to take our daughter to a warmer climate for the winter, I had selected to go to Lisbon because it was not on the road to anywhere else—because we should be obliged to return to England after the winter. The awful passage we had experienced in the Bay of Biscay on our voyage out, made us, however, shudder at the thought of returning by the same route; and a friend in Lisbon — the Condessa Lavradio — so strongly recommended the mineral waters of the Pyrenees for lung complaints, that we resolved to cut the Bay of Biscay and go home southwards. Our butler—Stevens—and our Swiss nursery maid could not master the geography of our intended tour, and begged to be sent to England direct. There remained only our English lady's-maid and French coachman, and those troublesome horses and carriage, which I so repented having brought with me.

For I did not at all relish the idea of coasting the whole of Spain; but, wished to reach Cadiz and Malaga from sea, to go from thence to Grenada, which Washington Irving had endeared to me, and thence visit Madrid, and follow a high road to the French frontier. But

"Surgit amari aliquid,—the toll."

I found that I should be required, on entering Spain, to leave a very heavy deposit at the Custom House, equal to the total value of the horses and carriage, but that an authorisation would be given me to claim back my money on presenting the receipt at the opposite frontier by which I should go out of the country. "Well, no great harm in that!" I exclaimed to a warning friend. "It is what I have often done in France."

"Aye," he replied; "but do not flatter yourself that you will have to deal with French custom-house officers. The Don will take your deposit with the greatest politeness, and will give you a receipt in due form; but, when you present it at the northern frontier and ask for your money, his brother Don will shrug his shoulders, and say, no doubt truly enough, that he has not any; and, if you remonstrate, he will swear at you and order you to drive on!"

I inquired of several—even at the Spanish Legation in Lisbon—and was assured that such would probably be the course of proceeding. As the reader knows, I had been corresponding with Ministers of Finance lately: my hand was in and my blood was up: and I wrote to Lord Howden, our Minister at Madrid, requesting him to obtain from the Spanish Government an authorisation for me to take my horses and carriage into Spain and across the country without paying either deposit or duty. My proposition seems to have surprised his lordship; for, after informing me that he had made my application to the Spanish Government, his private secretary adds, " Lord Howden further desires me to state to you that he cannot answer for the result of this application, as the Spanish Minister of Finances may, not unnaturally, think himself offended by the suspicion involved in it."

Not a bit of it! My friends knew Spain better

than our Minister. Within a month, I had the honour of receiving from his lordship the formal notification from the Primera Secretaria de Estado that the Minister of Finances authorised me to keep my horses and carriage for forty days in Spain without let or hindrance. This would give me time to travel across the country.

But though issued with great expedition for a State paper, it had not suited my purpose to wait for it. I was also led to prefer a sea voyage by finding a vessel that much pleased me. This was the screw steamer "*L'Helvétie*," afterwards celebrated in Garibaldi's expedition. It belonged to a French mercantile company, and was one of a fleet sailing between Havre and Marseilles. It was a large vessel—too large for that service—else it could not have been changed into an important member of the armed navy of Italy two years later; and I willingly closed with its terms, and paid down 2,600 francs for our places. Our children—their number increased by the arrival of Constable, whom I had sent for from England and placed in the English College at Lisbon, when we had thought of passing all our winters there—our three boys and three girls—were deposited by me in their berths on the evening of the 2nd of

June, and I went to take leave of many kind friends who had gathered at one of the pleasant reunions that were collected by the American Minister—Mr. O'Sullivan—and his charming family.

At half after ten o'clock on the following morning, the 3rd of June, it was not without a feeling of regret that we steamed down the beautiful Tagus, and passed Belem Castle; and that the towers of Lisbon disappeared from our view. The vessel turned to the left hand, and we were again on the broad Atlantic. We had a noble vessel, incomparably superior to the old tub, *Tagus*, which had brought us out; and here our horses were in boxes well suited to their size, and were in no danger of being murdered as poor Norfolk had been by the P. and O. Company. M. le Capitaine Martin, the skipper of the *Helvétie*, was a very civil and pleasantly-conversible person. His surgeon, too, was a clever little fellow; although he had been plucked at the Medical College of Montpellier; and, in revenge, he loved to tell how the lecturer there, the most celebrated physician in France, used to conclude his course of lectures by saying to his class, " Gentlemen, I have told what you ought to do, according to the rules of art, in every illness; but my conscience obliges me to add, that I believe human life would be much longer and happier if there were no doctors in the world."

There was little else to entertain us, as the vessel held her way out of sight of land, than conversation and cookery; our *cuisine* and fare were good. We passed Cape S. Vincent during the night and in a high gale of wind. Next morning, we were steaming eastward, under a beautiful sky. Twenty-five vessels were in sight. The sea seemed made of dolphins, so thickly were they strewed over it, as they tumbled about and showed their glittering backs. A pilot came on board. He had just before led out the Spanish fleet bound for Mexico, and had led it on the rocks of Trocadero, by which some of the vessels had been damaged! We anchored in the excellent harbour of Cadiz.

I could not go on shore that afternoon, for my hat had been blown away during the gale; and there was a difficulty in getting from the town a *sombrero*, as, I suppose, I ought to call a hat bought in Spain. Next morning, we took boat and landed; and I own that the verses in *Don Juan* were jingling in my head:—

> "I said that Juan had been sent to Cadiz—
>   A pretty town, I recollect it well—
> 'Tis there the mart of the colonial trade is,
>   Or was, before Peru learned to rebel:
> And such sweet girls—I mean such graceful ladies,
>   Their very walk would make your bosom swell:
> I can't describe it, though so much it strike,
>   Nor liken it—I never saw the like."

Now really there is little else to say of Cadiz. Its political history of late years had only connected it with Ferdinand VII and the holy alliance. The weather was disgustingly hot; the glare of the houses painfully white; no grand buildings; no imposing monuments; a fortified town amid tame scenery; its streets drawn out very much at right angles, tolerably clean, but every wall so glaring with whitewash that I turned for relief into a caffe. Lemonade and oranges were brought, apparently as a matter of course. We went to the cathedral and the church of N. S. de Carmel, and heard Mass. These were fine buildings; their floors were covered with matting, on which various females knelt, or, rather, sat upon their heels, half concealed by their black veils. It was certainly a becoming dress; and their walk, as they tripped along the streets fan in hand, was more elegant than the tread of other women. They did not show the soles of their feet, as most English women do, to those who walked behind them.

We returned on board to dinner, and set sail at sunset. Our party was increased. Hitherto we had enjoyed the whole of the passenger-room on the *Helvétie* to ourselves; but we now found amongst us an old Spanish lady, with her two grown-up sons, their chaplain, and several servants. We dreaded annoyance; but soon learned to congratulate ourselves on finding pleasant people, our intimacy with whom lasted long afterwards, and whom I should always meet again with pleasure. The mother was going to Montpelier for her health. Don Juan Ponce de Leon y Gordon (there is a name for you, reader! he quartered the arms of Castille and Leon, and of the English, or rather the Scotch, ducal house of Gordon) was going to Rome with his younger brother, who was studying for the church, and their chaplain. We should meet again.

At half-past four next morning, I was on deck. The rock of Gibraltar was before me; Ceuta on the right.

"Why are we not in?" I asked of an officer.

"Look at the deck; the sea washed over it for three hours."

We were becoming good sailors, for we had not been aware of the storm. At half-past six, we cast anchor. I sought out the camp of a Highland regiment, and found a cousin of mine on the sandy plain. With this officer, we spent the day. Under his guidance, we saw all that could be seen; passed through the wondrous galleries; drank lots of iced ginger beer; then walked to the Alameda above the Victoria Battery. Ape's Hill was in front—seen above the Tower of Rosea. The view was beautiful. The bay—or what seemed to be a bay—was more beautiful than that seen from Naples. I was very much delighted. And, although I was not pleased to see the fox-hounds kennelled close to the cemetery, I should have liked a day's sport amongst the partridges on the rock of the apes.

We all returned and dined on board; and again the ship steamed forth at sunset.

Next morning before sunrise, we were anchored off Malaga. It was Sunday morning; and as the mercantile pursuits of the *Helvétic* would cause us to spend all to-morrow here also, I had anticipated pleasure in becoming acquainted with a place to which so many of our consumptive countrypeople are sent to die. The prospect, however, was not inviting. The town rose prettily enough from the water's edge, as all towns do; but it afforded but a poor subject for a sketch. The hills behind it were rather bold; but perfectly bare. They seemed to be made of ruddy brick-dust. There was nothing to tempt an artist either to sketch or to walk. I did sketch the place, however; and we all went on shore, and to mass at the Cathedral. The interior of this building is magnificent. Its choir is beautifully finished in chiselled marbles. But the heat was scorching in the streets, and the air seemed full of dust; which, they told me, it always was, owing to the sand mountains abounding in the neighbourhood. We returned on board ship; but not until I had purchased, for four francs, a ticket to the amphitheatre, that I might witness a grand bull-fight, which was to take place that afternoon. I even then planned to write these pages. It was the only opportunity I should ever have of seeing a real Spanish bullfight. I doubted not that it would be the last I should ever wish to see.

I took my place in the fashionable circle of a large amphitheatre. It was thronged from the bottom to the top with people of all classes; but fashionable people were there; fine ladies; gentle, pretty-looking girls; in fact, the cream of the population of a city containing forty-five thousand inhabitants. Let us see what was the amusement which allured them. I noted down the whole in a species of shorthand at the time; and I now transcribe from the copy I made of my notes on the following day. Thank Heaven, gentle reader, if you are disgusted. I must not tone down a sickening and despicable picture in deference to your sensibilities. Let the Spaniard read a literal description of the sport in which he delights; and do you, more gentle reader, pray Heaven that even he may be as much disgusted as you are.

The arena of the amphitheatre was fenced in by a high palisade; inside this, was a passage, beyond and above which ran the tiers of seats and of spectators. At one end of the oval, arose the state box of the civil governor; at the other end, but on the arena and in the palisade, were two large folding doors. They opened precisely at four o'clock; and a number of riders cantered into the pit, as well as their wretched horses would do it; for, truth to say, the horses were wretched animals, fit only for the knacker's yard—or a Spanish amphitheatre. The riders sat in high peaked saddles, their feet encased in stirrups made like slippers; on their thighs and legs, were strapped strong greaves of wood to protect them from the horns of the bull; in their hands, were heavy spears. Such were the six caballeros who awaited the onset. The folding doors opened, and in rushed :—I quote from my notes:

No. 1—A black bull: stared about him; then rushed at one horse after another. The riders never attempted to ward off the attack, but turned the flank of the horse to receive the horns of the bull. He gored all the six horses, disembowelling some. The riders spurred the horses at him again. They limped up, dragging their guts on the ground, and treading on them with their hind feet. The bull was stupid. Laid him down. They stuck darts into his neck as in Portugal, and roused him to his feet. Then entered the matadore in gay attire. With one arm, he distracted the bull's attention; with the other, he pushed the darts aside, and stuck a short sword into the neck-bone of the bull. It fell dead. The band of musicians was heard triumphant. The folding doors opened. Some gaily caparisoned mules entered. Their traces were put round the neck of the bull, and of five dead or dying horses, and, at a canter, they dragged them from the arena.

Should this be called act the first or first round? The company chatted, flirted, smoked, and ate oranges.

No. 2—Black and white bull. Gored and killed three horses. Two other gored horses hobbled out. Matadore entered and tried to kill the bull. He struck many blows, missing the vital part. The bull ran round with three swords sticking in its neck before it fell.

No. 3—Red and white bull. One horse fell gored. Its rider forced it up. One of its fore legs was broken. Its guts were dragging on the ground. He beat it across the pit and out. The bull was struck by the matadore twice. It staggered to the side of the arena and fell.

No. 4—Black bull. It gored a horse. The rider dismounted. The horse ran without its rider all round the pit. Bull gored it again as it passed. *(Applause!)* Rider caught it. Its guts were out, but he got on it again. *(Thundering cheers!)* He flogged it up to the bull, but the bull would not touch it. Rider dismounted. Then, bull up to horse again; gored it again; horse fell; rider came and took off its saddle and bridle; bull gored it again, and it died. One other gutted horse was led away. Another was gutted, but the rider kept his seat while the bull turned away and made an onslaught on the first dead horse; goring it three times more. This bull fell dead at the first blow of the matadore.

No. 5—Black and white bull. The horse gutted by the last bull stayed on to receive this one, but could not bear up its rider. He dismounted. The horse was dragged towards the gate, and placed so as to be gored. It received the horns again, but was not killed, and was led away. A fresh horse and man were attacked, and both fell at once; man seemed bruised and limped away, while the horse staggered up and kicked at the bull. The bull turned away and gored another, then came back to this one and gored it down. With more spirit than the others had shown, the wounded horse got on its legs again, all its guts dragging on the ground. Thunders of applause uprose! It was gored again and died. Meanwhile, a grey horse, better than most, was bearing its rider beside the paling; the bull rushed forward; the rider turned the side of the horse to the bull, whose horns seemed to pin it to the pales. The rider scrambled off and over the paling, while the horse was gored again and again. Cheers from the people! Another brown horse gutted, was lying on the ground with its head erect; it looked at the bull as it passed, and the bull looked at it, but did not touch it. Next time the bull trotted past its head was lying flat on the sand; the bull stopped and gored it again and again. This bull itself fell dead at the second blow of the matadore. The brown horse, before mentioned, was still alive and looked up. They flogged it, and tried to make it rise and go out of the arena. It could not rise; so they put a noose round its neck, and the richly-caparisoned mules dragged it away at a gallop. They then drew away, more leisurely, four others that were lying dead.

No. 6—Black and white bull. Three horses and riders only were in the ring. A scarcity of horses was apparent; and cries from the spectators arose for "more horses!" The bull gored two of these in succession. Thunders of applause arose, when the riders got up again, the horses' guts dragging on the ground. One was gored again and obliged to go off. The other was gored again, but still kept the ring. One of the three was not touched at all—horses were scarce. Then the matadore came in. The sword was twice stuck in the bull's neck, and twice fell out of it. After two more stabs it fell.

No. 7—White and black bull. Only three horses were in the ring. The bull quickly gored two of them, then leaped over the palisade. Its hind hoof, however, hung in the top woodwork long enough for the people in the passage to scramble off, amid much dread and shouting. At last, the bull was got over. Doors into the circus were opened, and it was turned again into the ring. But it would not face the horses. The first matadore came in to provoke it; he jeered it; he stuck darts into it; he struck its nose with his handkerchief; he stuck two darts beside its tail; at length he gave the fatal wound in the neck and fled, leaving the sword in the vertebræ. The bull staggered and fell dead. This matadore was said to be named Cuistard, of Madrid. The bull was given to him by the Civil Governor. He cut off one of its ears and threw it up in the air, trying to catch it, as it fell, on the point of his sword, but failed to do so.

No. 8—Red bull. But there seemed to be no more horses. The same three only were in the ring. One of these was already gutted. Its rider flogged it up to the bull, striking its head with the butt end of his spear. It was gored twice, and the man got off. The bull then gored the other two, knocking off their riders. They all mounted again. The bull attacked the white horse, and shoved off the rider; he regained his seat; the horse was again gored, and he again got off. Here were great cheers! The other horse, overtired, gored, and unable to bear its rider, was led out; but the white horse, left standing in the circus, was gored again and again. Then the matadores came in. They wounded the bull only, and the people rushed into the pit cheering and jeering at their awkwardness. But, suddenly, the bull seemed inclined to show fight against them, and they all fled away. At last, it fell dead. From a window, I saw the dead horses lying together. I was told with pride that twenty-eight had been killed. Sunday, 7th June, 1857, Malaga, in Spain, thank God!

So end my notes. And so, thanking God, not that such deeds are done in Spain, but that they are not done anywhere else, I leave this disgusting butchery. For, be it remarked, it is a misnomer to call this a bull-fight; here is no fighting. The flanks of the horses are turned by the riders purposely to receive the horns of the bull; and the more the poor horse is mangled, the more are the spectators delighted. This is evident from the whole description I have given. They would not even lessen the torture of the horse by having a knife drawn across its throat before its mangled carcase is drawn from the arena.

The delight of the spectators was derived from the suffering of the horses—from the sight of their entrails draggling the ground and pulled out of their bodies by their own hind feet, as they trod upon them.

Faugh!

CHAPTER XIV.

THE CALCUTTA.

The Coast of Africa.—A Dream.—Second Sight.—Shipwreck.

At five o'clock on the following afternoon we set sail for the coast of Africa.

"Where did this event you are speaking of take place?" I lately asked a lady.

" On the coast of Africa."

" But, my dear madam, the coast of Africa is a very indefinite description. Was it in the waters of the Mediterranean or of Madagascar?"

" On the coast of Africa," she repeated.

And the *Helvétie* was carrying us to the coast of Africa. I shudder at the thought as I write; and must account for my shudder by narrating the event of which we had been speaking.

In the house of Charles, afterwards Sir Charles, D'Oyly, at Dacca, in the East Indies, his wife

Marian said one morning to the wife of Shearman Bird, who with her husband was staying with the D'Oylys, "I wish, Louisa, you would go down and make breakfast for Charles and Shearman; I have been upset by a sad dream, and will come down later."

The friend did as requested; and, after breakfast, returned to the room of her hostess, who had not appeared.

"Dearest Marian, you seem more distressed than you were before I went down. What is it that has so upset you?"

"I cannot get over it, Louie. I had such a vivid dream, in which I saw the *Calcutta* in distress and my sister Julia floating on the sea waves. All her beautiful auburn hair was spread out round her shoulders in the water, and seemed like a net bearing her up. It has made a strong impression on me; but now I have told you, I dare say I shall be better; so let us say no more about it."

The friends went down together, and the matter was not again alluded to.

Some while afterwards, Mrs. Shearman Bird, joining the party before dinner, found them very grave and discussing a letter just received, which stated that anxiety was felt for the *Calcutta*, which had been passed at sea in distress, but had not been heard of, though due for some time at the Cape.

"But let us say nothing of it to Marian, as she is already alarmed about her sister," cautioned Mr. D'Oyly; and, in expectation of her entrance, they changed the conversation and began talking on other matters.

Mrs. D'Oyly entered the room. She looked at them and listened for a few moments in silence, then exclaimed:—"You think yourselves very clever, good people; but your forced liveliness does not deceive me. You have had bad news of the *Calcutta*."

In truth, the *Calcutta* never came to port.

Many many years afterwards, a ship's crew, landing on the coast of Africa, found amongst the natives several women and children whose looks proclaimed them to be Europeans, and who were proved, by a broken language they spoke, to be of English origin at least. An anxious inquiry was instituted amongst them; and it appeared, beyond a doubt, that they were remains of the crew and passengers of the ill-fated *Calcutta*—wrecked upon that shore. Every offer was made to convey them to Europe or to India; but these were positively declined. The unfortunate ladies said that they had formed ties, and had borne children in the wild country on which they had been cast; that affection bound them to these, even if they had not dreaded to seek again their proper place in the society of Europeans.

But where did all this happen?

"On the coast of Africa," replied the daughter of the Louisa Bird of the story. "It is evident," she said, "that Julia Arnott was washed overboard, or in some way drowned; and that the *Calcutta* went ashore on the coast of Africa."

CHAPTER XV.

AFRICA.

Oran.—Variety of Costumes.—Mount Atlas.—"Isidora."—Walter Scott.—Future Fame.—Old Vidal.—Lord Exmouth's Bombardment.—The French Consul and the Dey.—Algiers.—The Arab Quarter.—An Arab Mansion.—The Kasbah.—Amount of Booty.

At five o'clock on the following afternoon, we set sail from Malaga for the coast of Africa. It had been a great inducement to me to take passage by the *Helvétie* that she was bound to pass a day at Cadiz, Gibraltar, and Malaga; and then to cross over to Oran and Algiers, on her way to Marseilles. So should I have an opportunity of seeing something new, and of taking a glimpse at a new quarter of the globe.

It was a beautiful evening; the sea as smooth as ice; a bright starlight night. The following morning was as lovely. Fine hills of Africa uprose before us. Desert rocky islands were in the foreground. At one o'clock after midday, we cast anchor in the little harbour of Oran. At five miles distance, is the beautiful natural and fortified harbour of Messel Kebir, in which the largest vessels can ride at safe anchor. A small town built up the two sides of a steep ravine, some fortifications, an old castle, the lofty and beautiful tower of a mosque—such is the aspect of Oran from the sea. I saw this, and gave directions that my carriage horses should be landed, that they might stretch their legs in a gallop and walk, while the *Helvétie* carried out her mercantile pursuits. Remembering the brutality of the first lieutenant of the *Tagus*, when I landed my dying grey at Vigo, I was much gratified by the willing exertions of Captain Martin and all the crew, who had them put on shore, with my French coachman, without the slightest difficulty.

I was very much interested in Oran. Never, not even in the streets of Vienna, had I seen such a motley mixture of different nations and tribes. The French, in uniform of course, divided the population with the natives; but these were of many different tribes, of many different garbs. Arabians and Jews, people from not distant Morocco, followers of the heroic Abd-el-Kader or robbers of Beni-Amer—Moors and Turks—all mingled together and showed their different costumes—gorgeous, dirty, and picturesque in the variety of their shape and of the colour. Englishmen also must have been there, then or heretofore; for a little shoeblacking urchin, that emblem of civilisation whom the French carry with them wherever they go, lifted his little box, and, coming towards me, exclaimed, " Mousu ! black your shoes ?"

We walked on the outskirts of the town and then through some gardens to the grand mosque. The vegetation was wonderful. Even after Portugal, we were surprised at the luxuriance of the flowers and foliage. The mosque was a most interesting monument; and we returned on board highly delighted that we had taken Africa on our road from Southampton to the Pyrenees.

On the second day, our horses were brought back on board, and we steamed away from the little harbour of Oran, leaving our pilot and his man swimming in the still waters, into which they had been thrown by the upsetting of their boat. It was nothing doubted but that they would right both themselves and it.

On the next morning, we were cutting through

a waveless sea—the coast of Africa at no great distance on our right—over which towered bold mountains, covered with snow — doubtless the eastern extension of the once mighty Atlas; the range of the lesser Atlas broke up the country before it. Soon after midday we were at anchor in the harbour of Algiers.

To me, of all people, this anchorage was most interesting. No European could be indifferent to the beauty of the spot; but it had historic and romantic interests to me, which it could possess to no other. For were not the concluding scenes laid here of my most interesting novel, in three volumes, entitled, " Isidora, or the Adventures of a Neapolitan?" Had I not introduced upon the scene Barbarossa, the then dreaded Dey of Algiers, and the glorious expedition of Charles V against him? Had I not identified myself with the times and the locality as those ever must do who write descriptions of such spirit-stirring events? Poor Isidora! How I loved her! And how the book was admired and bepraised by reviewers, who had more sense than readers of these latter days, who prefer any trashy, sensational, or fashionable novel—any compound of unnatural sentiment, impossible adventure, and tedious prosiness, to the most stirring scenes of real life. Well for him that Walter Scott wrote when he did! Had he published in these times, he would, like me, have been praised by men of intellect and taste; would have sold his few hundred copies; and would have been forgotten until some future age again brought to light and fame that which was too good for his contemporaries. What a consolation it is to think all this! What a popularity I shall have with some future generations! I once knew an old rogue named Robert Studley Vidal, of Cornborough, in North Devon, whose delight for some years, was in thinking what a fine fellow he should be—what a dash he would cut after his death, when I should have taken his name, and, with his little property added to my own, should rattle, four in hand, through the streets of Bideford. Having persuaded me to change my residence and purchase in his neighbourhood in order to round off his estate, he altered his mind and left his property to others; but clogged with conditions which necessarily prevented all gratitude, such as that they should ever bear his only name and his little arms, under penalty of forfeiture to S. John's College, Cambridge. Perhaps I ought not to allude to this iniquity. There is a silly old saying which declares " de mortuis nil nisi bonum," the absurdity of which some one demonstrated by translating it—"When bad men die, let all bemoan 'em."

What, however, if future ages should be ungrateful for the bequest I make them of my "*Isidora*"? I shall have bequeathed as well as have expected in vain an inheritance. But I shall not have taken any one in.

Then I, who was old enough to remember back to any period, however remote, bethought me, as I lay in the harbour of Algiers, of our own grand expedition against the Dey, when Lord Exmouth had bombarded his pretty town. It was a dreadful massacre, but did not efface the disgrace that weighed upon all Christendom for having so long permitted the existence of such a nest of pirates. Even the treaty with Lord Exmouth, by which the Algerians agreed never more to make slaves of Christian captives, only scotched the snake; did not kill it. Fortunately for the cause of civilisation, the barbarians took liberties with France, which no powerful government could forgive; and when, after many squabbles, outrages, threats and partial submission, the French Consul at Algiers went to pay his customary respects to the Dey on the 30th April, 1827, his Deyship most opportunely boxed the consul's ears.

So the world was told! Perhaps it was not quite so bad! Hussein Pacha was then Dey of Algiers. He had been educated as an artillery officer in the service of the Porte; but, in consequence of some ebullition of his obstinate and violent temper, had gone and joined the troops of Algiers. His superior education and intelligence secured to him quick promotion. He was made prime minister; and after the death of the sovereign, was elected Dey in his place without bloodshed or opposition. Such an election had never been known in Algeria. He shut himself up in the fortress of Kasbah with a guard of Zouaves, instead of the hitherto all-powerful Janissaries; was moderate in the exactions by which he increased his treasure; and had reigned twelve years prosperously before his unlucky quarrel with the French consul.

"But I did not box M. Deval's ears," he said. "I liked him: he was gay and insinuating, and I thought he was attached to me. We were very familiar, and I treated him like a friend. When he came to pay me his usual official visit at the end of Ramadan, I complained to him that I had received no answer to four letters I had written to the King of France; and, would you believe it? he replied 'The King of France has something else to do than to write to such an one as you.'

"I was surprised," continued Hussein Pacha; "my friendship gave him no right to be rude. I was an old man, and was to be treated with respect; moreover I was Dey. I told Deval that he was forgetting himself. He continued to talk in a very unbecoming manner, and I exclaimed, 'Wretch, leave the hall!'

"He would not stir; but looked at me so insolently that, mad with anger, and, as a mark of contempt, I struck his face with my *chasse-mouche*—my fly-fan. That is the real truth."

Here then we are in the port of Algiers—every fortress surmounted by the tricolor-flag of France, which had so avenged the affront to its consul. From a wide basis on the sea-shore, the town, embedded in the verdure of a pretty country, rises, terrace above terrace, and white as a chalk quarry, to the summit of the hill crowned by the Kasbah. The flat roofs, the Roman pines, the few spreading date trees, the luxuriant vegetation, the pinnacled mosques, and the torrid heat, all show that we are no longer in Europe. But when we land, the throng of French soldiers and officers about the streets, the companies drawn out to exercise in the square of Bab-el-Oued, the straight streets drawn at right angles to one another, and built of uniform architecture, over arcades like those of the Rue de Rivoli—make us doubt whether we are not really on the northern side of the Mediterranean, and in a garrison town of France. All the lower part of Algiers has, in truth, been destroyed; cleared away to make room for French architecture and wide streets. Here are French shops, French cafés, French people—everything French; except that Moorish woman in her picturesque, many-coloured, many-folded dress with flowing veil over her shoulders, and kerchief carefully drawn over her mouth and the lower part of her face; and except many a tall, dirty Arabian of the male sex, looking as one may imagine a conquered Arab to look in the altered streets of his once impregnable town.

The Arab quarter, as it is yet called, still rose, however, beyond the modernised lower streets; and this quarter I hastened to clamber over, although warned that a walk there would not be unattended with danger. A very labyrinth of lanes twisted about and crossed one another in every direction; so narrow that four persons could scarcely walk abreast through them; while they were, in many places, arched over at the top, so that the houses seemed all to touch each other, and to form one mass of ruin, through which and amongst which the wretched inhabitants burrowed, rejoicing that they were, at all events, shaded from the heat of the sun. The road of the Kasbah was the only one that seemed somewhat less irregular; but from this, every now and then, steps descended on either side into some gloomy ravine, or what would have been a gloomy ravine but for the whitewash so liberally bestowed upon every wall twice a year; and which, by the bye, must be a great check to fevers and infectious diseases.

And yet, every now and then, a half open door into what seemed, from without, to be a tall ruinous barn or warehouse, showed a luxurious mansion amid this mass of ruins. Within the door, was an arched gateway with a stone seat on each side where, I was told, the head of the establishment sat and transacted business with strangers. "Her husband is honourable in the gates, when he sitteth among the senators of the land."—*Prov.* xxx. I went beyond this porch in more than one instance, and there I found an open court paved with marble or coloured stones, and around which ran a colonnade of slim pillars of white marble, on which the first floor rested, and above which was another open gallery resting on similar pillars. The windows, that were missing in the dirty streets, looked into these pretty courts, and a curtain, stretched across at the top, kept off the burning rays of the sun.

I was told that the inner apartments in general are very large—long, but not wide:—that one of these is the general living room of the family; that at one end of most of the rooms, is the trelliced gallery of cages raised four or five feet from the floor, in which the Arabs place their beds.— N.B. I have described them in poor *Isidora!* Nothing, however, can exceed the richness of these rooms. The walls are hung with damask silk; the brick floors are covered with the richest carpets, and the ceilings are of carved wood, beautifully painted. The roofs of the houses being flat, are often surrounded with trellice work, and covered with creeping plants and flowers, so as to form a private but airy garden for the Algerian ladies—who, poor things! never go out shopping.

I went up to the Kasbah; by the same long, winding, steep, irregular street, up which the French had dragged their artillery after the capitulation of Algiers—knocking down a bit of

wall here, or a buttress there, as the carriages
struck against either side. A colonel with a small
detachment had gone ahead while the ruins were
being cleared away. His approach was seen from
the Kasbah, and the Dey precipitately withdrew;
his slaves and servants followed his example—
carrying away whatever they could lay their hands
on in their fright, and which was afterwards
picked up by the Jews. There was no disturbance
to the troops as they went along, for a convention
had been drawn up by the conquerors, and carried
and proposed to the Dey by a brave *parlementaire*
who, however, died of the fright and danger to which
he had thereby exposed himself;—died in the
hospital, neglected and unrewarded by his government. The troops had not been molested in their
advance through the town; the shops, indeed, were
shut, but the traders sat quietly in front of them,
as if waiting till they could open them again. The
Turks and Moors went about with more appearance of indifference than of fear. Mussulman
women peeped through their lattices; Jewesses,
who are the handsomest race in Algeria, thronged
their terraces and looked down on the soldiers.
Not a native soldier or sentinel was seen; those
who had families had gone to their homes; those

who had not, had retired to their barracks. They had all fought bravely against overwhelming odds, and now submitted with Turkish fatalism to the decrees of Providence.

The Kasbah in which the Dey had resided, and where the French commander-in-chief took up his quarters, was neither a palace nor a fortress. It was an irregular pile of buildings enclosed by a high wall; castellated, Moorish fashion, and showing wondrous long cannon, with muzzles painted red, from many a porthole and embrasure. The French debouched from the narrow road and found themselves before its main entrance. This was a heavy gateway without other ornament than that which would be ever most prized in such a climate—a marble fountain which threw water beautifully clear and cool into a gracefully-sculptured vase. A narrow passage beside the stables led to the principal court of the divan; by the bye, does the phrase "going to court" imply that our sovereigns formerly received in such? This court of the divan was large; was paved with marble, and surrounded by a covered piazza or arcade, that rested on Moorish columns of white marble.

In the court was a magnificent citron-tree and a little fountain from which sprung a thin *jet d'eau*.

One side of the covered arcade was more ornamented than the others, and glittered with mirrors of every shape and country. A raised seat or bench ran from one end to the other; and, at one part, was covered with scarlet cloth richly fringed. Here it was that the Dey used to hold his divan, distribute justice, receive foreign consuls or merchants; and here it was that occurred the famous scene of the fly-flicker. In all this arcade, there was no other furniture, if we except some Smyrna carpets, a clock set in a gilt bronze frame, a little writing table, in the drawers of which was a Koran, some boxes of perfumery, and an almanac, or roll of parchment four feet long by about three inches wide, on which, in Arabian letters, were written the months of the Hegira with apposite verses of the Koran, and the whole surrounded with beautiful arabesques in gold and the brightest colours. There was also in the gallery a mahogany table which bore an English barometer. At the further end of the gallery, was an iron door with enormous locks, which led to the treasury. This was composed of three corridors divided into bins without windows, and in which were heaped up coins of every country, from the boudjou of Algiers to the grand four-dollar piece of Mexico.

All around this principal court of the divan, were the other dependencies of the palace—halls and warehouses, stables, and little gardens stocked with ostriches; a kiosk; a mosque; an armoury; a menagerie with some lions and tigers; a large powder magazine, the domed roof of which was made bomb-proof by a double covering of bales of wool: piles, too, of shot and shell were there—the whole being enclosed by a wall some forty feet high, behind the parapet of which were nearly two hundred pieces of artillery, carefully painted green and red, the colours of the Dey, and one half of which pointed to the country, while the other half domineered the town itself, and gently hinted submission and obedience.

One brutal French general, after taking possession of the Kasbah, found his amusement in plucking alive all the many ostriches which, as I have said, had lived, petted, in those little shady gardens; and to others who were shocked at the piteous cries which the poor animals sent forth as he skinned them, the home-sick general always exclaimed "My little Anaïs will be pleased with these!" The anecdote was so well known that it became a catch-word in the army when any one plundered or did any particularly inhuman act:—

"My little Anais will be pleased with this!" said the soldier.

The apartments of the Dey and his harem were on the second floor, and the western side of the Kasbah. A little wooden staircase, painted red and green, like all the woodwork about the palace, led to a gallery, with large Turkish windows looking into the court of the divan, and opening into three large rooms, in which he lived; and, at the end, into a little kiosk, in which Hussein used to take his coffee and smoke his pipe after giving public audience. Under the kiosk, was a low door leading to the harem: this consisted of two courts around which were chambers and baths, and all the requisites for the comfort of the ladies. These rooms, however, had no windows towards any public part of the palace; what they had were all barred, and overlooked the private garden only; while a few narrow long slits in the walls, like shot-holes, gave glimpses of the distant sea and country. The furniture of the harem was more sumptuous than elegant. It had neither the taste of the French nor the cleanliness and propriety of the English; but piles of the richest carpets were thrown in heaps about the brick floors; gold and silver tissues of every variety:

cushions of every shape and every size, in velvet and in cloth enriched with Arabian embroidery; looking glasses without end; heavy mahogany tables, loaded with ornaments of gilt bronze; beds surrounded with Indian muslin gnat-nets embroidered with gold flowers; sofas and divans everywhere; and the whole overlaid by an atmosphere heavy with perfumes of rose, jessamine, musk, and aloes. In these rooms of the harem, were numerous toilette-tables; little boxes and dressing-cases of precious Asiatic woods, adorned with mother of pearl, amber, ivory, and ebony; vases of China and Japan beyond all price; and an incredible quantity of little comical bits of furniture, of which the new French owners could not imagine the use, but which they supposed to have been made to satisfy the ennui and childish fancies of the voluptuous and fantastic inmates.

The apartments of the Dey himself were much more simple, and had bare whitewashed walls. Carpets and divans were the only furniture; pipes, arms, English clocks, and marine telescopes were all that the conquerors found in them. But the arms were of an inestimable price. Some of the officers of the staff divided amongst themselves muskets enriched with pearls and coral; sabres with gold and silver scabbards. But what of that? Had not their predecessors of the empire gathered memorials of victory from Lombardy and Tuscany; from the Cathedrals of Toledo, Grenada, Burgos, and Valencia; from Swabia, Bavaria, Saxony, and Bohemia?

Thus, then, were the head-quarters of the French established in the scarcely-evacuated home of the deys; and, as the new comers saw all the rich barbaric civilisation around, they congratulated themselves that they had shown some moderation in their treaty with Hussein, who was known to be less inclined to surrender than to fight to the last and then blow up the Kasbah with all its treasures (as he had already done with Fort Sultan-Kalessi), and to cut his way through the French force with the remainder of his own brave troops.

Great was the delight of the French on finding one hundred and sixteen thousand kilograms of gold and silver in the Kasbah; and in calculating that the value of this, and of the artillery and goods warehoused in the palace, paid all the expenses of the war, and left them a balance in hand of about three hundred thousand pounds sterling. While the historian will smile at a calculation so like one that might have justified to the dey himself one of his own piratical expeditions, the moralist will rejoice that, on whatever terms, a nest of robbers has been smoked out, and the north of Africa restored to civilisation.

I returned at night-fall from the Arab quarter without having experienced, from the poor brokenhearted and gypsy-looking population, any of that molestation to which I had been told that I exposed myself.

CHAPTER XVI.

THE SOUTH OF FRANCE.

The Great Mosque.—Shopping.—Climate of Algiers.—The Balearic Islands.—Marseilles and old acquaintance.—Prosperity of France.—Aix.—Eating and Washing.—La Crau.—The new Archbishop.—Arles.—The Giant Bones.—The Man Market.—Nimes.—The Wisdom of Doctors.—Montpellier.—The Pig Market.—Silly Bees of Narbonne.—Cheap tea.—Street Processions.—Cafés et Billards.—Battle of Muret.—Approach to the Pyrenees.

I SPENT little time on board during the two days that the *Helvétie* lay in the harbour of Algiers. All was new and attractive and interesting on shore. We wandered long in the gardens; delighted with the glorious vegetation, which was even more splendid here than at Lisbon or Oran. Shade, to be sure, was not to be had in sufficient extent; but this could always be secured when we turned our steps back towards the town; and, even here, we could not but prefer the narrow cool alleys of the old Arab masters, to the wide handsome streets made by the French—flaring and scorching with sun, and reflection, and refraction. The great mosque was beautifully cool. This is a very large hall supported by numerous massive pillars, at the foot of which, here and there, solitary Mussulman devotees crouched upon their carpets. We went through it silently and unobtrusively—having thrust our feet into slippers provided at the door—and were rewarded by the thankful looks of the worshippers. "Salum Aleikum," exclaimed an Arab woman to us as we came out. Very different were the looks and manners that greeted two Frenchmen who stalked about the mosque with all the insolence of victorious vulgarity; talking loud and spurning the noiseless slippers that were offered to them.

I was much interested, too, in a Court of Justice which I found open, and where a cause was being heard in the native language, and with ceremonial judiciously combined from the habits of the conquered and of the conquering race. Indeed whatever acts of barbarity (such as the roasting and stifling a whole tribe in a cavern, as was done by Colonel, now Maréchal, Pélissier) the French may have committed, they have been most anxious to conciliate the Algerians, and to make their rule beneficial to the country.*

* Let us give the Colonel's own version. A tribe of Arabs, routed

But more interesting than all, to my wife and daughters, were the frequent visits they paid to the little native shops and booths, laid out with glittering Arabian necklaces and ear-rings, and bracelets of coral intermixed with little Turkish coins of gold or seeming gold; or of rosaries made in a similar style, for those who would blend such nicnackery with their piety. The French had built, for their new subjects, a bazaar in their own style; where the Moorish salesmen sat cross-legged in their stalls, surrounded by glittering trinkets and hanging benouzes, haïks, and sarmahs.

The principal mosque, converted into a Catholic cathedral, is still a handsome building; and here we all attended divine service on the Sunday morning. The congregation was, of course, well

in the open plain, had fled, as always, to wide natural caverns. As troops could not venture within, he fired faggots at the mouth of the cave: then offered to let the fugitives go free, if they would leave arms and horses. They refused. More faggots were fired. A great tumult was heard underground: some clamouring to surrender, others preferring to die. Again they were urged to come out. They refused. Some women would have done so and fled: they were shot down by the tribe. The Colonel sent a French envoy. They fired at him. Faggots and more faggots were then thrown on. The smoke drifted inwards towards the shrieks and the moans of the fugitives. Then all was silent.

Five hundred dead bodies were found in the caverns. The whole Dahara submitted. Patriot Arabs never again fled to caverns, whence they had always set Turks and French at defiance.

dressed and of the more well-to-do classes, as poor Frenchmen do not emigrate. The heat was intense, as we threaded our way through the crowd; nine o'clock in the morning and three after midday being the hottest periods at Algiers. The thermometer stood at 24 Reaumur—84 Fahrenheit—in the shade; where I now write, in Tuscany, it marks 100 in the shade and 80 at midnight. What may one not come to at last! How I hate hot weather! The heat, however, does not last long at Algiers. The north wind from the Mediterranean, or the west wind blowing from the snowy ridge of Mount Atlas, much refreshes panting existence; and the winters are so mild that Algiers is becoming much frequented by invalids from more northern climates. The attraction for many is, also, the character of the town—a little military capital, perfectly French, and with every convenience and, perhaps, better society than could be found in the *bise*-blown towns of the south of France.

Before midday, we weighed anchor and steamed away from these pretty hills. Two Russian frigates were alongside of us, and these had contributed much to the gaiety of Algiers; as the French military bands had played every evening, instead of three times a week, since their arrival. The French were then bent upon making themselves agreeable to Russia. We steamed onwards with a good breeze; and I found that Capitaine Martin had secured a cargo of nine hundred sheep, which he had engaged to deliver at Marseilles for five francs per head—no bad payment. This was to be the longest stretch of water we had passed over since Lisbon; but even this was diversified. At sunrise next morning, we were off Port Mahon. A fine outline of rocks rose on our left hand—the highlands of the Balearic Islands, Minorca, Majorca, and Ivea. Again we were quite at sea—out of sight of all land. But these usually-boisterous waters were placid to us; and at four o'clock in the morning of the second day after leaving Algiers, we were in the harbour of Marseilles.

It was not the first time that I had landed at Marseilles; and even the Custom House people were amused at seeing the same carriage landed from Africa, which, little more than two years before, they had received from Italy. The Commissionaire greeted me as an old acquaintance; asked eighty francs for passing it, but took only twenty; while the examiners of the douane opened only one of our many boxes. All these I consigned to a *portage* company to be conveyed to Toulouse; here, too, they had asked me twenty francs for one hundred kilos, but were satisfied to take seven. We had a friendly parting with the skipper of the *Helvétie*; on whose excellent boat we had passed fourteen very pleasant days. My wife and daughters got into our britska, the three boys and a servant into a cab, and away I drove from the filthy port of the Juliette to one of the nasty hotels of the town.

"If Paris had our Rue de la Canabière, it would be a little Marseilles," say the conceited inhabitants of the latter splendid city. Splendid, but disagreeable. I hate all commercial cities, where everybody else has something to do and one feels quite out of place. So, after eating a bad breakfast and doing a little shopping, and sending off my three boys and servant by diligence to Aix, I again took whip in hand and drove out in the same direction.

But what a flourishing country this France had become since I had known it years ago—before the second Empire! Flourishing, at all events, in appearance. The passing traveller could not tell by what state, parochial, or personal indebtedness the appearance of prosperity was brought to public buildings, fields, or roads. It was a pleasant trip, that afternoon drive to Aix; and 1 gladly saw again the cloud of steam, hovering over the fountain of hot water that rises in the centre alley of the promenade, that had delighted my boyhood.

We staid three days at Aix to repose; and if the reader be human, he will also understand that it was requisite to have the family linen washed. It is said, and truly, that Walter Scott never omits recording that his personages took their meals. I do not remember that he ever mentions that they were detained by the requirements of the laundress. I have always liked Aix—a well-built nice quiet town in a pretty country—well suited, I should say, to English who seek a good climate and economy. It was the octave of Corpus Christi; and although the Festival itself, like other festivals of the church, is kept, in France and in Piedmont, and in countries where time is of value, on the Sunday succeeding, yet pretty processions were organised by the different parishes and schools during these pleasant summer afternoons. Popular *Cantiques* were sung; and the ears of green corn, vine branches, and flowers, which were sometimes carried around the Blessed

Host, poetically showed the faith, hope, and gratitude of the people.

Between Aix and Arles, lies the miserable stony flat called La Crau—perfectly desert and apparently uncultivatable—although 40,000 sheep are said to find a wretched existence amid its forty square leagues of pebbles. I do not believe it; because it requires something like decent pasturage to maintain half a sheep to the acre.

The new Archbishop was making his first public entrance into Arles, attended by the clergy of the diocese, troops, civil authorities, and everything that could add importance to a high dignitary of the Church and State. A silken canopy was upborne on eight gilt staves to shelter him from the sun; but, with a clever appreciation of the spirit of the people, he walked a couple of paces before it. "*Il ne va pas sous le daïs!*" I heard one woman exclaim to the other. "*C'est bon! Le bel homme!*—He does not walk under the canopy! That's right. What a handsome man!"

Everybody knows that Arles is one of the towns in the south of France, most interesting for its remains of Roman antiquities—although the more the Government have dug at these, the more ruined they appear. Here are theatre, amphitheatre, and catacombs; and here, too, under our Hotel du Nord, were catacombs or cellars, which, I confess, interested me more than the undoubtedly Roman remains. For what were these? The walls and vaulting were evidently Roman; but the piles of human bones, interspersed with strings or necklaces of ivory beads, whence could they have come? And the bones were declared to be, and appeared to be, above the size of modern mortality. I took away one ivory bead from amongst them, which I carried in my purse for many years as a *memento mori*. The bones are fast disappearing in the carpet bags of English travellers, who, the hotel-keeper told me, seldom leave without taking some away with them. Evidently, therefore, the bones are not those of Christian saints; or they would have been denounced and spurned as relics that could not be preserved without wickedness.

The square before the hotel, next Sunday morning, was as thickly crowded as the crowd could stand. I was told that it was the "Marché aux Hommes—the man market." That from break of day, here had congregated some two thousand labourers, about half of whom succeeded in hiring themselves out to farmers for three days' harvesting, at the wages of two to three and a half francs per day and their food. Good wages, had the hiring been for a longer period.

Over a bridge of boats and a suspension bridge, over Rhone and rail, and through clouds of dust and such wind as alone make this country undesirable, I drove to Nîmes, its beautiful capital:—beautiful in its public gardens, which seem as if laid out to receive the temples and remains of antiquity, some of which are unequalled in Italy—the Maison Carrée and the amphitheatre. That night, we slept at a waggoner's inn—the best in the large town of Lunel; and paid the bill, headed " Note de la famille Anglaise." The same uninteresting flat country continued until, on the following morning, we entered Montpellier.

When it had been decided at Lisbon that we should take our invalid daughter to the waters of the Pyrenees, we had been advised to consult some physician of the famous school of Montpellier, as to which of the many springs we should select. I therefore sent for a Dr. Combal, who had been highly recommended to me. He came to us that evening at the very excellent Hôtel du Midi; and manipulated, and thumped, and stethoscoped, and looked as wise as all doctors do. How the silliest of them acquire this trick of looking wise, I do not know. Dr. Combal, however, was really a sensible man. He said he must see his patient again next day; and did so twice. At his third visit, he recommended the waters of Cauterêts; and put into my hands a detailed account of her case, according to the habit of French physicians, for the guidance of the doctor at the baths. The people of Montpellier complained much that English people no longer frequented their town as of yore. Our countrymen have, indeed, found out that, however mild the climate may be, the cold winds of the bise and north-east are undesirable for pulmonary patients; and railroads have now opened up to them the more distant countries and worse climates of Italy, which they can reach with little fatigue. Montpellier, however, is an excellent town; and the Place du Peyrou and the view from its terrace is grander than any public walk I have ever seen. Imagine, however, the enjoyment of walking with the thermometer at 92 in the shade! It had only stood at 84 at Algiers.

We started on our journey to Cauterêts. The very unpicturesque and uninteresting surface of France became more diversified as we got nearer its confines, and, before reaching Béziers, our eyes were gladdened with the distant view of the snow-clad Pyrenees—grander than Mount Atlas, but not equal to the Alps.

There was a great pig market at Béziers, and the pigs were sold alive and by weight. Imagine, therefore, the harmony that filled the square in front of our hotel as the "black animals," as Italians call them, were hoisted, screeching and squeaking, into the scales and out again.

We passed the great canal du Midi, as they call the canal du Languedoc, and through more barren and then marshy ground, arrived at Narbonne. The name of some places impresses one with a pleasant idea, and I had fancied Narbonne in anticipation—I suppose because its honey is famous. What can have induced the foolish bees to settle themselves in such a nasty desert country as that around Narbonne, I do not imagine; and the town itself is a miserable old place. Its Hôtel de France is either tolerable, or rascally dear, as the humour of the day affects landlord and waiters. The cathedral is handsome; and, in trying to find anything else interesting, I hunted all over the town for some tea. At last, I was able to find a shop that sold me for 1fr. 60, five grammes or one sixth of an ounce—being at the rate of one hundred and forty shillings a pound. I gladly left Narbonne with my prize.

And so, on and on, we continued our journey, sometimes through tiresome flats, and sometimes over pretty hills—offshoots from the distant Pyrenees. We were at Carcassonne on Sunday morning; and I thought the people did not seem to like that, before the principal service at the cathedral, the clergy formed themselves into a procession and passed out of one door, through a street or two, and in at another door of the church. Religious processions in the streets are, very properly, forbidden by the laws in France; and it would be better if the friends of religion would conform to those laws and content themselves with worshipping inside their churches. Then, at night, the hills about Castelnauderie were lighted up with bonfires in honour of St. John and of the harvest-home. My little boys, with my coachman and servants, always travelled by railroad or diligence, and met me, who drove the carriage with my wife and daughters, every evening at our destined place of rest, so that the journey was pleasantly and easily done. We always slept at large towns, and found tolerable accommodation and civility at whatever half-way house we stopped to bait in the middle of the day. The only bad impression which was produced on me in this intimate acquaintance with country towns and villages of France, was produced by the number and increasing number of cafés and billiard tables in even the smallest villages. In the smallest towns, I have seen cafés fitted up with a dozen white marble tables for different guests, and two or three billiard tables; and every Frenchman with whom I spoke on the subject lamented this growing taste for what we should call pot-house life. A cup of coffee does not intoxicate and may not cost much; but a cup of coffee or of liqueurs, a cigar and a game of billiards, take no immaterial part of a labouring man's wages, and withdraw him from home. His wife and children may fare as they can; his pleasures, his society, are elsewhere.

I did not like Toulouse; no doubt it is a large handsome town, and will have fine boulevards when the trees are grown; but a large fair was going on. I had difficulty in finding accommodation at any hotel; and, in short, the town impressed me unfavourably; and I turned due south next day and went and slept at Muret. Who knows now of the great battle of Muret, when, encouraged by a prophecy of St. Domenic, Simon de Montfort issued from the little town with his twelve hundred followers, and totally routed the hundred thousand men led on by the Count of Toulouse and the King of Aragon, who remained, with fourteen thousand slain, on the field of battle? Other such victories are recorded in history as having occurred in other lands and in other centuries, and are deemed glorious feats; but the victory of Muret is sneered at because it was foretold by a saint, and because it was achieved over the Albigenses, as the Manichees of Languedoc were called; —modern Manichees, whom our good, ignorant fellow-countrymen think to have been Protestants. Like their eastern prototypes, they believed in a good and a bad Creator; a good and a bad Christ; denied the resurrection; and believed in the transmigration of souls. Funny Protestants, truly!

The weary road through the weary plain continues to St. Gaudens, where, at length, the country begins to be diversified. At Montrejean was one of those quiet inns—with their front to the street and their back to a garden, a hill side and, lower down, a stream — which one occasionally meets with in travelling; and to which commend me rather than to the most luxurious caravansaras in Paris or London; where your personal individuality merges into the number of your apartment, where *you* only think of number one, and the waiters only know you as number two or number two hundred. Bagnères de Bigorre came next, and here we were, at once, in a busy little watering-place, full of hotels, shops, stalls of nic-nackery, saddled donkeys, and English visitors. On the following morning, I drove to Lourdes, to the beautiful valley of Argelès, and there entered a Pyrenean defile; and on a road overhanging a brawling torrent, and itself overhung by toppling crags, clomb my way to Cauterêts, and pulled up at the Hôtel des Princes.

CHAPTER XVII.

CAUTERETS.

Drinking and Bathing.—La Raillère.—Modern French and the Queen of Navarre.—The Bad-Hole.—The Doctors and the Sore Throat.—The Doctor and the Lungs.—Progress of Medicine.—Lac de Gaube.—Pleasant Walks.—The Pic du Midi.—The Cagots.—The Republic of Luz, and its Finances.—Barèges.—Madame de Maintenon.

CAUTERETS is a scrambling little town of hotels and lodging-houses, built on each side of a narrow street near the head of a stony ravine, down which tumbles a noisy torrent of melted snow. The ravine is closed in, about three miles higher up, by a bare mountain, in the crevices of which some patches of snow still lingered, and, indeed, linger all the year round. I found a tolerable apartment in the little High street, the Rue de la Raillère, at thirty francs a day for the first month and twenty francs for the second; and we all began drinking the waters of La Raillère early in the morning; and our invalid began taking the hot baths under the direction of Dr. Bonnet de Malherbe. These she continued for some time, apparently getting worse; but we were told that such was the effect of all these baths—that it was necessary to get worse before you got better. After three weeks, Dr. Bonnet apparently thought her bad enough; and told us that the waters could do no more for her. He had paid six visits, and I sent him forty francs. He wrote and demanded forty francs more, which I sent him. The usual fee of a French provincial physician is three francs each visit. A girl also had offered herself as housemaid; and had asked five francs per day.

But to drink the waters of La Raillère was a more pleasant occupation than bathing. This spring is situated about one mile from the town, nearer the mountains. A good road leads to it; and eight omnibuses go backwards and forwards to carry the drinkers. Donkeys, also, are to be had in plenty; and, altogether, an animated scene is presented by the rush of visitors early in the morning around the healing tap.

But earlier still in the morning, the waters are served out in buckets to the stallions of the different royal haras in France, which are sent to a veterinary establishment here to recruit their strength, get fat, and lose their coughs. It is curious that the different guides and descriptions of the Pyrenees say nothing of this horse-doctoring.

It is needless to say that the vast majority of the frequenters of these baths are French people. English come occasionally; but the baths of the Rhine are easier for them to attain. The French have, of late years, come to think a few days at the seaside or at mineral springs necessary to restore their digestions and spirits; and they rush to the Pyrenees as abounding in sulphur springs and magnificent scenery. This fashion has been growing upon them since the time of Margaret, queen of Navarre and sister of Francis the First. That accomplished and learned Princess has left an account of one of her visits to Cauterêts, surrounded by the poets, minstrels, and ladies of her Court. She gave the name of *Fontaine d'Amour* to the spring she most preferred; and amused herself, from the first of September when, she says, "the waters of the Pyrenees attain their greatest virtue. At that time," she continues, "there were many people at Cauterêts from France, Spain, and elsewhere; some to drink the waters; some to bathe; the others to tramp in mud; all which produce such a wonderful effect, that invalids, given over by their doctors, return quite well. When our time for returning, however, arrived, it seemed as though the Almighty had forgotten the promise made to Noah—that the earth should not again be destroyed by water—for all the huts of Cauterêts were so inundated that it was impossible to live in them.

"The French lords and ladies, who thought that they could get back to Tarbes as easily as they had come, found the smallest streams so swollen that they could scarcely cross them. But when we had to pass the Gave of Bearn, which, as we went, had not been two feet deep, it was so increased that everyone dispersed to seek the bridges; and these, having been of wood, had been carried away by the flood. Some took to the mountains, and crossed to Aragon, Roussillon, and so to Narbonne. Others tried to pass through the woods, and were devoured by the bears. The Rector of St. Savin received us, and gave us shelter, and procured for us excellent horses, good Bearn cloaks, plenty to eat, and clever guides."

The royal blue stocking then goes on to describe their way of living while they waited for the waters to decrease; and how they spent their time between exercises of devotion, reading pious books, and telling indecent stories in the manner of Bocaccio.

There are many charming walks and excursions to be made in the neighbourhood of Cauterêts; and one can scarce follow any of the ravines coming down from the mountains, without being rewarded by the discovery of some pretty scenery or wild and romantic spot. There is a most picturesque cascade amid some rocks wildly tumbled together about a mile below Raillère; and, close to this, rises one of the most powerful springs of the country. Its efficacy is proved by the fact that the peasantry of the neighbourhood, and even from Spain, throng here to collect the water as it trickles from a slit in the rock. They are said to be efficacious in gastric complaints, as those of the Raillère are for the lungs. This wild spot is called "Mahourat," which, in the language of the country, means "bad hole." And yet it was to this bad hole, where there is scarce footing for two people, between the rock and the ravine, that a consultation of Paris physicians sent their dean of the Faculty, M. Orfila, to take baths!

The doctors of the Pyrenees were obliged to

admit that, in this one instance, they could not effect the prescribed cure. It was a mortifying admission, unwillingly made by gentlemen as ready to swear by their several springs as Dr. Quackleben was by St. Ronan's well. Each one, however, only swears by his own particular spring. A Frenchman, suffering from a throat complaint at Cauterêts, went to Dr. Bonnet de Malherbe:—
"Doctor, do you think your waters agree with me?"

"Perfectly," replied the doctor. "You need a gentle remedy; and our waters are the mildest and least sulphurous of any. Every part of your body needs to feel their influence; and, therefore, you take the baths besides drinking at the spring. So you must have come to the right place. The Eaux Bonnes, on the contrary, which are so much vaunted, would be too strong for you; and you yourself know that those of Luchon would never do."

The patient tried for another fortnight, and then went to the Eaux Bonnes.

"Doctor," he said to the man of science there, "Do you think your waters are good for my throat complaint?"

"My dear sir," replies the Esculapius, with a look of pity, "Everyone knows that. They are exactly the thing for you. Luchon would be too strong, and the Cauterêts spring too weak. Ours have precisely that amount of energy which is needed to remove the irritation you complain of."

Three weeks afterwards, the sick man, still ailing, went to Luchon. He told the doctor there of the two trials he had made.

"Cauterêts! Eaux Bonnes!" exclaimed the physician; "What business had you there? You deserve what you suffer! Baths for tourists, pleasure, dandies! Do they pretend to contain sulphur enough to cure anything? However, here you are; and I will treat you like an invalid, not like a fine lady shamming sickness. Three big glasses a day; a bath every day; and, every day, a douche!"

The poor Parisian, disgusted with his three doctors and the Pyrenean specifics, returned to drink the water of the Seine, which did him as much good as any of the others.

So an admirer of the Pyrenees tells the story.

If, instead of running from spring to spring, one remains at the same, the game is different. After drinking and bathing for a week, the patient thinks seriously of his ailment; he thumps his chest or he draws long breaths; and, after a careful examination, decides that he is just as he was. He tells the doctor of his discovery.

"How impatient you are!" he exclaims. "The beauty of these waters is that they act slowly. They do not disturb the system. Violent remedies are poison."

Next week the patient, either from having eaten too much or drunk too much wine, feels somewhat worse than before.

"All right!" exclaims the doctor. "You see our waters are beginning to act. You must be worse before you are better. Go on just as heretofore, and follow my prescriptions."

Next day, after a good night, the patient has lost his headache, and is obliged to declare that it was a mistake to fancy that he was getting worse or better. What is one to think of these wonderful waters?

"Think!" says the wise doctor, "That these are intermittent symptoms. I have seen a hundred such cases. The very fact that you feel neither better nor worse proves that you will soon be well."

Time passes. Some fine day the doctor meets the invalid in the public walk and rushes up triumphantly:—"You see," he cries, "the waters were right after all. You are quite another man. You are nearly well. It only needed a little patience. I was sure that we should set you up!"

The poor invalid does not know what to think. Well, yes; he is a little stronger; his appetite is a little better. But may not this be owing to the change of scene and air, and to the exercise? The doctor says the waters have done it all. . . The doctor says he is cured, and the doctor must know best. However, the tone of his voice shows that he is not quite convinced, as he says, "But, doctor," . . . .

"I cannot hear any buts," says the doctor triumphantly, "it will all come right when you get home. You carry away a germ of health. Our waters have done their duty. They have aroused your natural energies; if they had even made you worse for a time, the result would ultimately have been the same. But you, however, have been fortunate in everything."

The poor invalid takes his leave and returns home to boast how lucky he has been.

A celebrated professor exclaimed to his students, in one of his lectures, "Lose no time, gentlemen, in prescribing this remedy while it is efficacious, while its virtue lasts. In the time of

Francis the First, the Eaux Bonnes were good for wounds, and were called 'Arquibusade waters.' The wounded soldiers from the battle of Pavia were sent to them. Now-a-days, they only cure chest and throat complaints. In a hundred years hence, perhaps they will cure something else. Who shall say that medicine makes no progress!"

"Formerly," says Sganarelle, "the liver was on the right side and the heart on the left. We have changed all that."

But our pretty walk to the Mahourat has led us far out of the track that leads to the romantic Pont d'Espagne. This is a foot-bridge of rough firs thrown, at a great height, over a chasm down which boils the same torrent. The scenery around is wild and wooded; and continues so, amid these mountain tops, till, at length, it opens a small dreary expanse of water, called the Lac de Gaube. The bare snow-clad rocks on the one side; the dark firs on the other; the clearness of the water, which is nearly five hundred yards deep; the heat of the weather; and the sensation that one is about five thousand feet above the sea level—all this, joined with the solitude of the spot—gave a great charm to this singular lake. There was, however, a fisherman's hut, and, beside it, a little flat-bottomed boat floated on the water; but, close by, arose a sad monument that recorded how a young Englishman and his bride had both been drowned there some years before, while rowing in that little boat.

These walks up into the Pyrenees were frequently enlivened by meetings with long-limbed Spaniards, in green jerkins and short breeches, striding down towards the plains of France, and each one loaded with a swine skin filled with wine, like those poor Don Quixote made such bloody war on. Such meetings proved that we were on the confines of another kingdom and far away from every-day life.

Then there is the amphitheatre of Gavarnie, which, according to the descriptions of French travellers, and the opinion of Lord Bute, as they are fond of quoting it, is the finest thing in the world. It is some twenty miles from Cauterets, and I much regret that I did not go to see it. The guide-books tell me that it is an immense circus formed in the eternal granite, three stories high, or rising and widening by three immense steps. That the highest wall is some five hundred yards high, down which tumble cascades of melted snow, that wave and disperse themselves in rain. The southern wall of this amphitheatre, which is of no great thickness, is the boundary line between France and Spain; and popular tradition asserts that a mighty cleft in the side of it was made by the sword of Orlando or Roland, who rode up here in full armour, and tried to force his way into the southern kingdom.

I was saying that I had not been to the cirque de Gavarnie.

"Why, then, did you come to the Pyrenees?" asked an enthusiastic Frenchman.

"Must I then go to the top of the Pic du Midi?"

"Here is M. Bourgeois just come from it. Tell us what you saw, M. Bourgeois?"

"Nothing. You know there is generally a fog in the morning. But I did see something white moving about; and I heard the bleating of sheep."

"And then?"

"And then I saw something grey through the mist; and the guide said it was the lake d'Oncet; and then we turned a corner and kept going up for four hours."

"Was not the scenery magnificent?"

"Why, so so. The view was not extensive and had little variety. When the path was straight,

I saw the back of the guide and the tail of his horse; and when the path turned, I saw the flank of the horse and one leg of the guide. We went at foot's pace, one behind the other. There was another party following mine and they were more lucky; because they saw my guide almost as well as I did, and they saw moreover my own velvet jacket and white hat."

"And so you went on?"

"Yes: my guide was very chatty, and said it was a beautiful day for the excursion, and that we should have such a grand view at the top."

"Well?"

"Well now. I will be good-natured," said M. Bourgeois; "and put you in the way of seeing as much as I did, with much less trouble. Go to the baths of the Espagnol which your daughter prefers, and ask for the smallest bath-room, and tell the attendant to have the water made very hot. After a quarter of an hour, go into the room and put on those blue spectacles that are lying by you."

"To see the snow-capped ridges of the Pyrenees?"

"Patience!" said M. Bourgeois. "Put on those spectacles, turn your back to the window, and look hard, without wiping your glasses. At first, you will see nothing but steam. After a minute or two, look more steadily, and you will see more steam. Make another effort; look as hard as you possibly can, and you will enjoy the same unvaried view. That was what I saw at the top of the Pic du Midi."

I made one day a beautiful excursion with our own horses and large britzska;—it was not, therefore, towards the Pyrenees. We drove down the romantic gorge to Pierrefitte, and then, turning to the right, passed up the still wilder ravine towards Luz. Nothing can exceed the boldness of the engineering that has built a carriage road through, amid, and upon these terrific precipices. The rocks sometimes toppling above the road; the road sometimes following ledges overhanging the torrent, and sometimes crossing, from side to side, on bridges that are said to be of marble:—they may be so—Menai bridge is of marble, though no one would find it out except from the little bits that are polished and carried away as mementoes. At length, the ravine opened on the smiling valley of Luz, where green meadows, intersected by glittering streamlets, and shaded by long lines of poplar trees, lay, in tranquil beauty, amid the surrounding mountains.

Here is a large church, as much like a fortress as a church. In fact, it formerly belonged to the military Knights Templars, and is entered under a battlemented tower, and is surrounded by a battlemented wall. Here is the low door, retired apart from all others, by which the unhappy cagots were obliged to enter and leave the building. This unfortunate race was found in all these countries of the Pyrenees, resembling much the cretins and goitrous idiots of the Alps, and known by different names in different districts; in Navarre, they are called *caffos*; in Guyenne, *cahety*; in Annis, *calibeots*; in Brittany, *cocons*. Some antiquaries think them descended from the Spanish Goths; some from those christians who accompanied the disastrous retreat from Spain of Charlemagne and Roland, and took refuge in the Pyrenean mountains. Many believe that their imbecility is owing to the hardships of their race or tribes, and not to the waters of the valleys they inhabit. They were always considered infamous by law, and forbidden to carry arms, or to follow any except specific trades. In towns they were shut up in quarters of their own, like Jews in Italy. Sickness, infirmity, and misery followed, as a matter of course, these barbarous enactments.

Christianity would not exclude them from its worship; but was obliged to conform so far to the spirit of the times as to assign to them a separate entrance and portion of every church.

Luz was the chief town of a little republic which formerly existed in these surrounding valleys. The best men of the neighbouring villages met here and settled their laws and taxation. Of these latter, and of the state income, no other record was kept than tallies or notched sticks, which they called *totchoux*. A clever financier of France, at the end of the last century, ordered that all the ancient registers and accounts of the country should be brought to him. The order produced from Luz two cart-loads of sticks, which he found it difficult to analyse and file, but which proved dry and excellent fuel.

A good road through a country that becomes more and more wretched, leads, in about seven miles, to Barèges, the most celebrated and, probably, the most efficacious of all the springs of the Pyrenees. Here the Government maintains a military hospital for the cure of old wounds, skin diseases, and ulcers; and the patient has the comfort of knowing that they have always professed to cure these same complaints and have not changed with the changing year, nor undertaken to cure other diseases which, for the time, might be more in the fashion. This is some consolation.

And, if ever invalid stood in want of consolation, he must do so at this miserable place. It is I know not how many thousand feet above the sea; it consists of one street that climbs the side of a bleak mountain; the houses on one side of which are of wood, because avalanches so often fall on that part during the winter, that it is deemed advisable to pack them up and carry them away before the snow collects. On the other side, are buildings of stone which might be equally whelmed but that an old beech wood grows on the mountain side above, and stops the falling avalanche. In grateful acknowledgment of this service an ancient law protects the sacred wood by decreeing the punishment of death to anyone who should carry an axe into it. In fact, the whole village is deserted at the beginning of October; the houses are shut up; the inhabitants go down to the plains; and a few mountaineers take charge of Barèges until the following spring.

But the state of the bathing establishment here is a disgrace to whoever has authority in the country. Here are sixteen wretched holes for the accommodation of an average number of one thousand invalids, besides those of the military hospital. There are, indeed, three large piscinas or open baths, in which people can crowd together; there is the bath for civilians and the military bath, both of which are supplied with the water that has been already used in the private baths; and there is the bath for the poor which is supplied by the refuse that has washed the sores of the civilians and of the soldiers. Dark, dirty, vapoury holes they all are. One must have a deal of health to stand such a remedy!

Madame de Maintenon was no better pleased with Barèges when she brought thither the little Duc du Maine and wrote those letters to Louis XIV, which first captivated the licentious king and imposed her rule on France. "You see, I keep up my spirits," she wrote, "in a place more frightful than you can imagine; and to increase our misery, we are freezing on this 30th of June. The company here is very bad. They treat us with respect, and bore us. All the women are always ailing; they are Parisian idiots who were surprised to find how big the world was when they had travelled thirty miles, as far as Etampes."

I remember a country bumpkin, from the flats

of Bridgwater, who clambered up to the top of Castle Hill at Nether Stowey. Looking around with wonderment, he exclaimed, " I didn't think the world had been so wide !"

We baited and breakfasted at Barèges; and gladly drove down the hill again. I turned off, however, at Luz, and clomb up the side of a beautiful wooded rock, not half a mile from it. Here, nestled amongst the trees and leaning against the precipice, is the charming little watering place of Saint Sauveur. All is pretty, neat, and romantic; for the waters of Saint Sauveur are good for nervous complaints; and only rich and fashionable people can afford to have nervous complaints.

CHAPTER XVIII.

THE PYRENEES.

Carriage and Horses seized for debt.—Lourdes and the Ages of Faith.—Legend of the Chateau de Benac.—Bagnères de Bigorre.—Bagnères de Luchon.—The old Guide.—Bear Hunting.—A Funny Story.—Isard Hunting.—A Sad Story.

We had been six weeks at Cauterets. Dr. Bonnet had declared that the waters could do no more for our daughter, and had exacted his fee. I desired Paul, our coachman, to have the carriage at the door on the following morning that it might be packed for Bagnères. He came to me, at eight o'clock, saying that a M. Lahore, keeper of the Hotel de Richelieu, asserted that the stables and coach-house were his property, and that the carriage and horses should not be removed until after the payment of one hundred and fifty francs for rent. I quietly went to the Commissaire of Police and told him that I knew nothing of the Hotel de Richelieu; for that, when I had arrived at Cauterets, I had been to the Hotel des Princes; that I had hired my apartments from a M. Bordenave who had told me that he could dispose of the stabling and coach-house which I had occupied, and which I supposed to belong to Bordenave, and that they were included in the rent I paid to the latter. The Commissaire forthwith ordered the Hotel de Richelieu to release my property and to appeal, if it so pleased, to a higher tribunal; and Paul drove up to our door in triumph. But the matter did not so end.

Our landlord, M. Bordenave, sent up his bill for rent of the apartment, breakages, &c., and added a note that this did not include rent of stable and coach-house. I wrote on the same bill that the latter rent was included, and that I paid the bill with this protest; and I sent the money to him by Paul. M. Bordenave refused to receive it; and we all took our seats and drove away with our money.

Once more, we drove down the wild ravine to Pierrefitte, and through the pretty valley of Argelès to the little town of Lourdes, to which history attaches some memories interesting to Englishmen. For, in the middle ages, this town belonged

to us; and Frenchmen tell, with pride, the story
of one who was faithful—even to England. This
was a certain Armand de Béarn, who had the com-
mand of the Castle of Lourdes for the king of
England. One day his suzerain lord, the Comte
de Foix, sent for him, and, in the presence of
many knights and squires, ordered him to deliver
up the fortress to the Duc d'Anjou. Armand was
astounded. At length, he said, "I owe you faith
and homage, for I am a poor knight of your clan
and of your country; but I will never give up the
castle intrusted to me—never. You have called
me here and can do with me as you will; but I
will not deliver it to any but to the king of
England."

The Comte de Foix drew out his dagger.
"Oh! oh! traitor!" he cried, "You will not, say
you?" and he struck him five times with his
dagger, while the barons and knights looked on,
but dared not move.

"Oh, monseigneur; you are not acting right!"
exclaimed the wounded man; and soon after he
expired.

Such deeds were done in what Kenelm Digby
extols as "The Ages of Faith."

We rested our horses; had luncheon; and proceeded on our way. The Chateau de Benac arose at some distance. What of that? asks the reader; the Chateau de Benac? Yes, of Bos de Benac. Listen.

Bos de Benac was a brave Christian knight who accompanied St. Lewis, king of France, in his crusade to Palestine. There, having much distinguished himself in battle with the heathen, his comrades saw him fall gloriously, and prayed for his soul. But Bos de Benac was not dead. He was carried prisoner into the interior; and held in slavery for seven years, subjected to all the outrages that Saracens could inflict upon him in hatred to the faith he constantly professed. Under the heat of the sun, he grew as black as the natives, while tending goats and camels in a lonely place.

One day, he was accosted by a little black man, who had two horns growing out of his forehead; and had feet like the hoofs of goats; while his look was more wicked than that of the most wicked Saracen. This was the devil, who cried out, "Ha! ha! Bos! Much you have got by fighting for the cross. Here you are a slave to my slaves. Your dogs at home are better treated than you. Do you know, at Benac they all believe you to be dead; and your wife is to be married to-morrow. Brave knight! Go and milk your goats. Ha! ha!"

Bos cast himself on the sand in despair and wept aloud. The devil seemed to take pity on him. "I am not so bad as folks say," he exclaimed. "This very night you shall be in your own country of Bigorre; only promise to give me a basket of nuts in exchange."

Bos hesitated; and the devil took advantage of his hesitation. He caught him by the hand, and away they went through the air. Bos saw, far beneath, a wide river winding, like a snake, through sandbanks; and then a city laid out upon the low shore. Onward they went; over the sea, dotted with black ships that looked like tadpoles; and then over a three-cornered island, from which arose a great hollow mountain full of fire and canopied with smoke. The devil looked askance, and hurried on over more sea; and the night fell, and the moon rose; and, at last, Bos looked down upon a long ridge of snowy pinnacles and joyfully recognised his own Pyrenees.

"Valiant knight! Go and seek your wife!" cried the devil, with a burst of laughter like the sound of an oak tree broken short off by the storm; and, as he disappeared, he left behind him a strong smell of sulphur. Bos saw that he was at the gate of his own Castle of Benac.

It was early morning; the air was raw; the earth was damp; and, after the sun of Egypt, Bos, clad in his sheep skin, trembled with the cold. A splendid cavalcade drew near. There were lords, knights, and ladies in brocades and cloth of gold and glittering armour. It was the lord of Angles coming to wed the lady of Benac. They all passed on before where he stood, and entered the wide gateway. Bos rushed forwards, but was driven back by the warders, who said, "Good man, return at midday, and you will receive you alms with the others."

The poor wanderer sat down on a rock. He heard the sounds of music and of rejoicing within his castle; he bethought him how another was about to take his wife and his property; and he grinded his teeth with thoughts of murder; but he had learned patience during his seven years of slavery; and, moreover, he was unarmed.

All the poor of the country began to collect in their rags and misery; but the rightful lord of the place was more ragged and miserable than they; and as he saw the reflection of his own wretched figure in the waters of the castle moat, his wild uncombed hair and beard, and the sheep-skin and rags over his otherwise naked body, and as he heard all around him invoke blessings on the newly married pair, revenge took possession of his heart.

They were all in the porch of the great hall; and through the open door, Bos saw the well-known festive room, hung round with armour, which he had often worn; with tusks of boar and antlers of deer that he himself had slain. He saw the lord of Angles seated beside his wife, and whispering soft words to which she listened smiling. In an uncontrollable fit of jealousy, he rushed into the hall, exclaiming: "Away, traitors! I alone am master here. I am Bos of Benac!"

"Lying beggar!" cried d'Angles, "I myself saw Bos fall dead on the sands of Egypt. Who art thou, wretch, who art as black as the Saracens themselves? If you are not one of them, the devil has suggested this lie, and brought you here. Loose the dogs on him, I say!"

But the pitying lady pleaded for the poor madman; and he was only hustled out of the merry crowd. With a feeling of rage and desperation, the poor wanderer fled into the surrounding forest.

But he fled not alone. At the sound of his voice, a huge greyhound had started from the feet of the lady, and, with a loud joyful bark had sprang through the crowd; whilst a favourite falcon that sat on her wrist, fluttered itself free of hood and jesses, and flew out at the open window of the hall. Poor Bos had cast himself in despair on the ground of the forest, when the greyhound bounded upon him, and, with many a yelp of joy, began to lick his hands and his face. The falcon perched upon his wrist, and with beak and arched neck and rustling feather, testified its joy in a manner well understood by its master. Tears of sensibility and of love came into the wanderer's eyes; and when, in the midst of this scene of recognition, the devil again appeared, and scoffingly exclaimed " How, Bos, are you not invited to your wife's wedding ? The Sieur d'Angles is just going to marry her," he cast himself on his knees and cried " Oh Lord, for whom I have fought, deliver me from temptation !"

The devil disappeared ; and the hands of the crusader, as he joined them by chance on his breast, touched the scapulary in which he had sown, for safety's sake, his wedding ring around his neck ; a ring which, in early days, he had taken from his bride's finger and placed upon his own. He started and cried "Thanks, oh Lord! Let me arrive in time?"

He ran; he sped; he flew. The greyhound bounded beside him. The falcon spread her wings above his head. The bridal procession was just entering the chapel; Bos was enabled to rush forward in the confusion occasioned by the barking of the dog and the cry of the falcon; and seizing the hand of the lady, he showed her the ring. She recognised it instantly; looked steadily at the recently despised beggar, and threw herself into his arms.

After a few moments, Bos de Benac turned to the wondering crowd: "I have suffered for Christ," he said. "I have been denied, like Christ. Men of Bigorre, who have denied me, and ill-treated me, be my friends as heretofore."

On the following day, says the legend, Bos took a basket of nuts and threw them down a deep cleft in the mountain which was said to be haunted by the devil; and having thus kept his promise like a knight, even to the Evil One, he set out like a Christian to confess the sin of having trafficked with him to the Pope. On his return, he retired to a hermitage in the depth of the forest, and his wife took the veil in a convent at Tarbes. The legend does not explain why they thus parted, after having so long mourned for each other, and I know no more about it than the legend.

It was the height of the season of Bagnères de Bigorre, on which account I was told that the Hotel de Paris had so much raised its prices since we had passed through early in July. In truth, these watering places have a short-lived harvest and may fairly gather in what they can while it lasts. In winter, they are desolate and cheap enough; and I never heard of any one except Lord Vaux of Harrowden, spending that season there. At this time, the little place looked lively enough, and the walk under its fine elm trees was crowded. It flattered itself that it was quite Parisian. Perhaps it was. I did not feel tempted to make acquaintance with its *beau monde*, or to accompany it to the heated assembly rooms, called Frascati, where the crowd played at cards and billiards, and danced in the month of August. It is a clean neat town, seated in a very pretty country, amid good roads and pleasant walks, and with these and some more distant excursions, I thought we could amuse ourselves for a fortnight.

On the last day of August, we drove out by the road of the mountains, and through fine scenery came to the little town of Arreau; thence through a beautiful forest of silver fir-trees, and over a very bleak pass, we reached a ridge of lofty mountain, from which we looked down into a smiling valley below. The road circled along the side of the hill, amid copsewood and cottages: night came on: lights began to twinkle from many a window: they formed an earthly constellation in one particular spot of the deep valley underneath: our horses trotted more freshly onwards: the sound of rushing waters uprose beside the road; and, at last, we emerged from the outer darkness amid the blazing light and crowded street, and brass bands and fiddles and pedler-stalls and glittering cafés and handsome hotels, that constitute the town of Bagnères de Luchon. We ended our thirty-five mile drive at the Hotel de Londres.

Bagnères de Luchon is, indeed, a remarkably pretty place: to be far preferred to any other spot in the Pyrenees by those who can choose their location there. Here is a fine boulevard, shaded by large trees, which runs up from the lower town—shops, houses, cafés and hotels on each side—and affording at all times an animated and umbrageous walk. This boulevard is the beauty of Luchon, though the mayor of the town who made it had to send for a troop of dragoons to protect himself from the people who would not mend their ways. Above this Cours d'Etigny, is a pretty English garden, with green turf, and benches, and clusters of trees around one of the mineral springs. The handsome establishment of the baths is lower down. I speak not of the medicinal properties of the waters. Let doctors decide on these. Barèges, Bigorre, and Luchon were all frequented by the Romans of old. Here was found an inscription to the god Lixon, from whence, we are told, the modern name, Luchon. The waters are all warm and sulphurous; and, in the vaults in which they are collected, are numberless serpents, drawn thither by the warm steam. These are perfectly harmless, and are the playthings of children, who make them swallow one another; and often a serpent that has been swallowed by one of its fellows, will crawl again out of the throat of the swallower, and swallow it in its turn.

Above the town of Luchon, the beautiful valley of the Lys leads on and on towards the snow-capped Pyrenees with ever-varying scenery. The weather was overpowering: so great was the heat that not even the dash of the waters could lead imagination to forget reality. We sat and walked, and sat again; and coveted, with an almost sinful desire, the two horses on which a lady and gentleman cantered past us. At length, we turned us again towards the plain; admiring the different openings into the further landscape, and the solitary tower of Castelviel which, almost everywhere, stands out as a picturesque object.

We were stopping to rest at one of these openings on the left, when I observed, seated in the shade of an overhanging bank covered with brushwood, an old man whose appearance was somewhat unusual. He was evidently neither a labourer nor a proprietor; but one whose clean limbs and tall slim figure shewed like a French "Leather stocking"—such as Cooper loved to describe his hunter of the prairies. As he saw that he was noticed, the old man rose; and leaning his still upright figure on an iron-shod staff, respectfully touched his bear-skin cap. I moved towards him and entered into conversation; desiring him to return to his seat in the shade.

"*Ma foi, monsieur*," he replied, "it is very hot; and the strangest thing of all is to think that, a few hours walk from here, people may freeze in the midst of snows that never melt."

"You mean on the Maladetta?" I asked, pointing to the ridge behind us.

"On the Maladetta, and everywhere in these mountains. And yet they are brave mountains, on which I have known many a happy day."

He sighed as he reseated himself.

"What, then, are you?" I asked. "What had you to do amid those snows?"

"I was a chasseur, Monsieur; a guide-chasseur to every part of these rocks. Neither valley, port, pic, nor glacier was unknown to Pierre Redonnet; not a stranger came to Luchon and wished to faire la chasse of bear or isard, but he sought out Pierre Redonnet."

"But are there so many isards and bears as really to afford sport?" I asked.

"Voyez-vous, Monsieur," said the old man with a cunning smile, "I have heard some say that there are more of both kinds in the Jardin des Plantes at Paris than in the Pyrenees; but it is not true. They are to be found by us of the trade, though the gentlefolks may not succeed, because they do not like the fatigue and the danger. Besides, *ça va avec trop de tapage.* A chasseur *d'isard* should go alone, or be posted alone; and wait for hours and hours in the snow until the chase is driven past him. See if a gentleman will do that! Neither isard nor bear will come up to be shot at by ten or twenty people who are out on a pleasure party, instead of on a matter of business."

"*Celà se conçoit*," I said; "but," I asked, to indulge the old man's evident love of talk, "is this *chasse d'ours* and *d'isard* so very dangerous?"

"How can it be otherwise," he replied, "to people unaccustomed to walk amid those rocks and on that snow and ice? And then sometimes *ils perdent la tête*—they lose their heads. I was once out with a party of young students from Montpellier, when we started a great she-bear that came straight down upon them. Four or five of the sportsmen forgot that they had come out on purpose to shoot bears; and, at sight of the little bright eyes of the beast, ran away behind trees and rocks. One of them, however, was more courageous than the rest, and fired. He did not hit the mark; and the bear came lumbering on. The hunter took to his heels; and, dropping his gun, slid down a precipice to save himself. He rolled to the bottom of a pit without much hurt; but, while he was rubbing his knees and elbows, he looked up and saw the bear sniffing round the top of the bank and seeking a safe place by which to get down. *Ma foi*, old chasseur as I am, it would not have been a pleasant tête-à-tête to have had to converse with the beast at the bottom of that quarry; and Madame l'Ours seemed resolved to begin the conversation. She found a place that suited her, and began stepping down backwards, holding on by the rocks and roots with the greatest care and a *sang froid admirable*. Luckily, I came up before she had reached the bottom, and I sent a ball through her which tumbled her down quicker than she had intended."

The old hunter laughed heartily at the remembrance of the exploit; and then, seeing that we had seated ourselves on a grassy bank in the shade, he evidently made up his mind for more talk; and blowing his nose with both hands, said, "That was *une aventure plaisante;* but sometimes we witness very sad accidents. Such was one that chanced to one of your compatriots when I was at the head of the guides-chasseurs of Luchon; it was in the year—let me see—yes, it was in the summer of the year 1843. Monsieur must have heard of that accident?" he asked.

I thought I knew to what he alluded; but begged him to recount the whole history, as he said that he had been of the party.

"Monsieur *m'excusera*. I was more than one of the party. I was the head guide; and my daughter was there too; for as the lady herself would go, she thought my Jeannette would be of more use to attend on her and her children than her own maid from England."

"Tell us all about it—beginning at the beginning," I said.

"Well, monsieur, then I must tell you what I heard from Jeannette, as well as what I saw myself. It was in the summer, as I have said, that this English gentleman arrived at Luchon with his family. There was a maid, and a valet, and two carriages; for there were no railroads in those times. It seems the gentleman had been very fond of the chase in his own country; and he often got into talk with me and the gentlemen here about the *malheureux isards*. At last, a large party was formed; and it was decided that we should go round the Maladetta and cross into the Spanish mountains. There was a M. de

Grammont, and a Comte de Nicolai, and our banker of Luchon, and one or two other gentlemen were to be of the company; and I was told to select eight or ten guides. We all wanted to start on Saturday, but the Englishman said he would not go out shooting on Sunday, and so we had to wait.

"Now, monsieur, I have to tell a curious thing. It seems that the wife of this Englishman, who was very young, and *belle comme un ange*, had a dream on the Saturday night which told her that something dreadful was to happen at a spot near a solitary house, with a tree and a tent and snow and mountains all about; and she had such influence with her husband that she persuaded him to take her and the two children with the hunting party. This was how my daughter was there, as I told you; for they had the judgment to take my Jeannette instead of the English femme de chambre.

"Ma foi, it was strange to see a lady like that ride out of Luchon at three o'clock on Monday morning, with two little girls in two baskets strung across the back of another mule; and all those gentlemen and guides laughing and talking around. We were, in truth, a jolly party! There were mules laden with provisions; and there were the lady and the babies and my daughter; and there were all the gentlemen thinking how triumphantly they would return laden with bears and isards; and there were all us guides, boasting and promising them such sport as was never yet carried from the Pyrenees.

"It was a moonlight night; and well I remember how bright and joyous everything looked, as, having turned off by that valley to the left, we rose to the top of Port du Portillion, and saw the Vallée de Burbe on one side and the rocks of Catalonia on the other. We descended amongst these, and marched bravely on up the Vallée d'Aran. About midday, we all reached the town of Viella, and dined on the provisions we had brought and on what the public-houses of this little frontier-town could supply. Having rested for three hours, we started again, and soon came amongst the snows that never melt in those mountains. Onwards, however, we bravely went. One of the little girls was tired, and began to cry; but we took her out of her pannier, and we and all the gentlemen, we took it in turns to carry her and to amuse her. It was quite dark when we crossed the ridge called the Port de Paillas and roused up the monk who kept the hospice or refuge house on the other side of the ridge. Here were three or four half-furnished rooms, two of which were placed at the disposal of the English gentleman and lady and Jeannette and the children. The other gentlemen and we guides took possession of the rest.

"As monsieur may suppose, the lady and children did not go any further. We left them asleep when we chasseurs started at day-break, in search of our game, on the following Tuesday morning. We went further into the mountains, scattering ourselves as we went; for the isard love the higher peaks so that they can find there the scanty grass on which they feed. The gentlemen used to place themselves in ambush in some wild ravine while we guides started off in search of them. When found, we were to drive them down the ravine, and the chasseurs were to fire as they passed.

"When we returned at night, we found that before the lady and the children arose in the morning, Jeannette and the monk and a peasant belonging to the place, had arranged a rude table under the spreading branches of an almost leafless tree that grew beside the solitary hospice; and had hung over the boughs some shawls and rugs that made a sort of tent and kept off the rays of the sun. She had thought to pleasure her mistress; but when the latter came forth and saw the arrangement, she turned deadly pale. Jeannette asked what was the matter.

"'My dream,' murmured the lady looking round; 'this is the very spot and the very tent I saw in that dream which impelled me to come up with my husband.'

"However, we were all very merry when we returned at night, though we had not killed anything. We promised ourselves better luck on the morrow.

"But our search was not successful. Day after day we used to start at daybreak, and returned home at nightfall without having done anything. Whether it was that the isards had got wind of so large a party being out against them, I know not; but so soon as we guides had caught sight of a herd browsing on some eminence with their little horns standing out against the blue sky, the one that was on watch always gave the alarm; and away they bounded in the opposite direction. At length, on the Friday, one of our gentlemen had the good luck to come across a bear, and shot it. How triumphantly we returned to the hospice and showed the shaggy brute to the lady and children! It chanced that some French and Spanish muleteers and contrabandists had met there that day; and they and we guides all began dancing to the sounds of a guitar and some castagnettes before the lady's tent; and boasted that, at all events, we should not return empty-handed to Luchon. Our return, on the contrary, would be the usual triumphant entry of those who have slain a bear. The prize would be carried before us; we should all discharge our guns in a feu de joie; the dogs would bark; the brats of the street would cheer and shriek; and all the company at the baths would run to their windows to applaud or envy us; and so we danced and sang and triumphed in anticipation. How different it was fated that our return should be!

"We started again at daybreak on the following Saturday morning; and Jeannette afterwards told me how her English mistress had congratulated herself with her that this was the last day of the week's hunt, and that they should return the next morning to Luchon without having met with any misfortune to justify the dread occasioned by her dream. We started at daybreak, and worked our way over the snow high above the sources of the

Garonne and the Hermitage de Montgarry. I know not whether our gentlemen had grown careless in their anxiety to kill something on this the last day, or from familiarity with the dangers of the spot, but certain it is that they slipped about a good deal; and one of them would have slid down a *crevasse* but that another, whom he caught hold of, had the presence of mind to throw himself on the snow and so save them both. At three o'clock after midday, however, we were all crossing a rocky glacier as uneven as all these are, when the foot of the husband of the English lady slipped, and he fell. His gun exploded; and the shot went through the flesh of his left arm. We all ran up, and congratulated ourselves that it was no worse. But here was an end of our sport. We tied up the wound as well as we could, and carried him back towards the hospice. It was a dreary walk. We had gone so much further than usual, that, delayed as we were by the wounded man, it was quite dark before we reached the hospice.

"I need not tell you of the misery of the poor wife as she came forward to meet us, and saw all her fears verified. We laid him on a bed and stripped him. It was a ghastly wound. The flesh was all blown away; and there were the arteries hanging down a quarter of a metre, and still pouring blood. While some hastened forward to summon the doctor from Viella, and one of the French gentlemen started to bring up a friend of his, a famous Paris surgeon who was taking the baths at Luchon, we tried to tie up these arteries; but we could not stop the blood. At length, his wife twisted them round her fingers and sat there, Jeannette said, the whole night without moving, as thus only could the bleeding be stayed. At ten o'clock next morning, the doctor from Viella arrived, and tied and bandaged all up properly, and did what was needed. But it was all too late. While the lady and my daughter were sitting beside his bed, his breathing gradually became less and less; and, without a struggle, he expired on that Sunday afternoon.

"With the early dawn next morning, we all commenced our sad procession. We met the doctor from Luchon, and he turned back with us. At Viella, we were, of course, delayed while the authorities drew up a *procès verbal* of the accident, and while a rude coffin was being made. This we all took it in turn to carry, slung to staves laid on the shoulders of four of us; and downwards, towards the valley, we slowly staggered. It was dark when we arrived at Luchon; there was a tremendous thunderstorm as we entered the town. This was not the triumphant return we had all promised ourselves!"

The old chasseur paused for a time.

"You see, I was right, monsieur," he continued, "in saying that this *chasse aux isards* is sometimes dangerous. Poor gentleman! His widow carried away the corpse; and I was told that she buried him in the Protestant cemetery at Toulouse. I do not remember what his name was; but it was a sad ending—to die in that desolate place, with that young wife and those two little girls."

"His name, my good friend," I said, "was James Barlow Hoy, of the Isle of Wight; he was long Member of Parliament for our town of Southampton."*

I pressed a bit of money on the good-hearted but garrulous old man; and, taking my wife's arm under mine, we returned thoughtfully to Luchon.

* This is the gentleman alluded to in a former chapter, p. 100, as the founder of the church of West End, in which his widow could not erect a memorial Sculpture without paying £60 to the Rector.

It is difficult to imagine scenery more beautiful than that in the neighbourhood of Cierp, which we passed next day on our drive homewards. Then came the little town of Saint Bertrand de Cominges, one of the most ancient and historic towns of Aquitaine, for which no one now cares. Its cathedral, however, stands out magnificently, and is very interesting; and none the less so because it was so pillaged and defaced by the barbarians of the French revolution of 1793.

CHAPTER XIX.

THE LAW-SUIT.

Character of the Béarnais.—Begging.—The Coat Button.—
The Picture.—The Asylum.—Henri IV.—Bernadotte.—
Arrested.—The President of Tribunals.—Denaturalised.—
The Trial.—Judgment.

BAGNERES de Bigorre is not in the old country of Béarn; but it, and the other districts of the Pyrenees I had visited, were so near to the confines of that province that the same national character obtains in them all. I regret to say that that character is not a pleasing one. The French proverb declares of the Béarnais—"civil and treacherous:"—I cannot say much of the civility, except when they are slavishly trying to overreach or to get something by begging or cunning. From four to fifteen years of age, the children are professional beggars. "None are ashamed of it," says a French writer. "Look at the smallest children sitting on their door-step and gnawing apples; they will toddle up and stretch out their little dirty hands. Look at a boy keeping his cows on the mountain side; he will leave them to ask for half a sou. Look at that big girl going home with a faggot of wood on her head; she will turn and ask for something. Look at that labourer mending the road, even he will say 'See what a fine road I am making for you; give me *quelque chose.*' Look at those brats playing at the end of the lane; as soon as they see you, they will catch hold of each other's hands and dance round in a ring till you are near enough to be asked to pay them for the show."

Somebody asked the maid of his lodgings to sow on a button on his coat. She brought it back with a shy and yet cunning look, and timidly said "It is one sou."

The sou was given; but so readily, that the girl thought she might try for more. She returned from the head of the stairs, and, taking up the coat, looked at the button she had sown on, "It is a very good button," she said; "a new one. I had not any in my box so I bought this at the grocer. It is one sou." She looked doubtful; but the owner of the coat, without saying a word, gave another sou.

Rose thought she had evidently lighted upon a mine of sous. She came back again after half a minute, and, with a degree of assurance unknown in the beginning, said " I forgot the thread. I had no thread and was obliged to buy it. It is very good thread and I sowed it strong so that it will not come off again. It is one sou." The stranger, without speaking, pushed another sou towards her.

Two hours afterwards, she was laying the cloth for dinner. She had been meditating all the while; and she now went through her work with a serious gravity of manner. At length, with cringing earnestness, she said, in the most gentle tone, " I ought not to lose by it. You would not wish me to be a loser. The cloth was very hard and I broke the point of my needle. I did not find it out before, but I see it is broken. It is one sou."

> " Ce peuple est innocent ; son ingénuité
> N'altère point la simple vérité."

The owner of the coat—and of the button—was a painter. He had been making a drawing of the parish church ; and wished, like Walter Scott, to hear a foolometer's opinion of his sketch.

" Do you know that, Rose ?" he asked, shewing it to her.

" Ah, monsieur ! Did you do that ?"

" Tell me: what have I copied there ?"

"Ah, monsieur! how pretty it is!"

"Yes, but what is it? Did you ever see anything like it?"

Rose took the paper and turned it about with a simpering stupid look.

"Is it a church or a windmill?" asked the artist.

"Well now!" exclaimed the girl.

"Is it the parish church?"

"Ah, it is very beautiful!" continued the girl; but she would not compromise herself by saying anything else.

"Treacherous and civil," says the proverb; and people from other parts of France doubt whether these Béarnais look upon them as their harvest or their prey. The result is much the same. Disinterestedness is not a mountain virtue. They are poor and clever; and they have to win their way in the world. So Henri IV, the Béarnais, won his way to the throne of France.

The people of the Pyrenees threw down stones on the rear guard of Charlemagne, retreating from the heathen after the death of Orlando, and then divided the spoil, the arms, and the clothes of those they had crushed. So they did with another body of troops sent by Louis le Pieux. But they enriched themselves. An old charter of 1221 provided that, if the lord were to arrest a native of Ossau while pillaging and ravaging his lands, he might detain him in the dungeons of his castle until he had compensated for the damage; but that if he could escape with his booty to his proper country of Ossau, he might return next day unarmed to the lordship he had ravaged and could never be touched, unless the lord, or, in his absence, the viscountess were to enter the lands of Ossau in person, in which case the Ossalais themselves were bound to assist in taking the robbers. This whole country, therefore, was an asylum of robbers and outlaws; since no one could be delivered up except on the personal appearance and demand of the suzerain.

Such a system ensured a spirit of insolence, daring, and enterprise. So, in the first crusade, the Count Gaston was, with Tancred, the first to assault the walls of Jerusalem, and built his "cows of Béarn," as he called his battering rams, on the top of a tower.

In those ages, the Counts of Béarn fought and allied themselves with everyone. They were conveniently placed on the skirts of Spain, England, and France; and passed from one to the other as either most valued their services. But they well earned their pay, and were always ready to fight or be killed for the love of blows or the love of money. And thus Henri IV, who was bred in a castle near here and left to run about the streets of his native village barefoot with the other brats, inherited that character which, on a wider field, made him a hero. After he had seated himself on the throne, he wrote, " I have scarcely a horse that can carry me in battle, nor a complete set of armour. My shirts are in rags, and my coat out at elbows; and, for the last two days, I have been dining with one and supping with the other, because my own purveyors say they can get no more on credit."

One month afterwards, when the Parliament of Rouen reported to him that their prisons of Normandy were so full of wretches charged with evading the salt-tax that one hundred and twenty had been taken out dead in one day, as from a pest house, his Majesty laughed; and said he could not afford to give up a tax which brought in so large an income.

This man turned out to be a hero—not only of Béarn but of France.

The last of these successful gentry from Béarn, of whom the world has heard, was born at No. 6,

Rue du Tran at Pau. In 1792 he was drummer in a French regiment; a few years later, he was King of Sweden. Henri IV became a Catholic for a crown. Bernadotte abjured his Catholicism for the same worthy object. It is to be presumed that neither one nor the other had ever any religion at all to abjure, or ever assumed any in exchange. In the same manner, German Lutherans, Calvinists, or Reformadoes become good Anglicans for a bit of English royalty, and *vice-versa*.

But I was not to arrive at Pau without paying my bill at Cauterets;—that bill, the amount of which I have stated, that M. Bordenave, the lodginghouse-keeper, had refused to receive because I protested that the stable and coach-house were included in the rent of the house. We had been living, for about a week, in a house I had hired by the day at Bagnères de Bigorre, when, returning one morning from a walk, I passed the Commissaire of Police, a huissier, and two gensd'armes who were loitering about the front door. Our servants told me in great alarm that they were come to arrest me. I took the matter more coolly. I put a rouleau of napoleons, which I had kept ready for the purpose in my pocket, and went out again by the stable yard door ; and took my way to the mairie, or town-hall. The armed force soon hastened after and overtook me, and the commissaire told me his errand.

"You may save yourself the trouble," I replied. "I am going to the hôtel-de-ville."

"To do what?" he asked.

"To do whatever the chief magistrate recommends. But why did you not arrest me as I entered the house just now?"

"We were told that monsieur wore moustaches, and you did not answer the description."

At the mairie, I was shown the warrant on which I had been arrested. In it, M. Eugene Bordenave declared to the President du Tribunal de Première Instance, that I, a foreigner, calling myself an Englishman, owed him for his apartment 1,225 francs ; for damage to furniture, breakages, wages to his porter, and to a housemaid whom he had kept for me, 143 francs more ; that I had left Cauterêts without paying him, having taken care previously to send away all my baggage ; that I was now likely, at any moment, to quit France in order to escape payment of what I owed ; and, therefore, he, Bordenave, prayed that I should be provisionally arrested : which thereupon the said

President had ordered. I deposited, in the hands of the court, the full amount claimed. The trial was then appointed to take place two days afterwards.

Matters being thus comfortably settled, I walked out to a pretty villa just outside the town, and paid a visit to Armant Joseph Lalanne, President of the Tribunal, and asked him what he meant by signing a warrant against me, and whether he thought it likely that a man and his wife, with five children and seven servants, a carriage and pair of horses, would run away from France to escape payment of sixty odd pounds? The poor old man was very much annoyed; begged a thousand pardons; said I was evidently quite a different person from what had been represented to him; and recommended me an avocat in whose hands I should place my defence. I asked what they could mean by saying that I "called" myself an Englishman: he said that a visiting card of mine, picked up in the lodgings at Cauterets, had been produced with the address "Rua do Sacramento, Buenos Ayres:"—that they all knew Buenos Ayres was in America, and thought me therefore a Brazilian. I made the old gentleman blush by telling him that such was the name of the quarter I had inhabited at Lisbon; and by asking him whether a Parisian, who had lived in the Rue d'Enfer, Luxembourg, was necessarily a citizen of Hell and Holland?

I went to call on Avocat Pailhé, and found an intelligent, pleasant man, in whose hands I placed my case.

On the appointed day, we met at the mairie before the juge de paix; and M. Pailhé made, I must say, a most excellent speech: he charged Bordenave with having "imposed upon the religion"—meaning "good faith," of the President; and wound up by demanding that I should be awarded six hundred francs damages for the affront put upon me. Thereupon, I declared that I could not accept any damages; but made over, to the poor of the town, whatever might be awarded to me. The old judge declared it to be a most unfortunate and improper proceeding on the part of Bordenave, and directed him to be summoned, and offered to hear the case privately in his own study on any day that would suit my convenience. This I refused to accede to—requiring that the trial should be as public as had been the affront: and, as I said that I had already taken a house at Pau for the winter, and could not delay my departure, the trial was appointed to come off next week on the 5th of September.

We again gathered at the town-hall: and after my coachman, poor Paul, dressed in his best crimson livery, had given excellent evidence, M. Bordenave was examined and admitted that, so far from having removed my baggage from his house secretly, I had asked him himself to recommend me a waggoner, and had sent it to Bagnères by the one he had named. He then lost his temper and became very violent; and the judge badgered him, and "diabled" him, and advised him to make it up with me. This Bordenave in his anger positively refused to do.

"Then," said the judge, "I am bound to give a written decision. I have made up my mind as to what that sentence will be, and will deliver it next Wednesday."

On the Wednesday, an argumentative judgment, as closely reasoned as such French documents always are, was delivered on fifty-two folio pages. In these, it was recapitulated that when the plaintiff had let me his apartment, he knew that I had been, for some days, at the Hôtel des Princes; that he must have known that I had carriage and horses, and was not very likely to have paid him so high a rent unless it had included stabling; that it was not very likely that I should have moved them from the Hôtel des Princes to the Hôtel Richelieu unless Bordenave had put the latter stables at my disposal; that he could not say I had sent away my goods secretly when he himself had provided the carrier; that he could not say that I had neglected to pay the rent when he had refused to open the money bag that Paul had taken to him; that he ought to have charged for the damages to furniture and breakages in the bill he had sent for rent, and not to have tacked on afterwards a charge for what might have been done by his own servants; that he ought, at the same time, to have charged the wages for attendance which I denied having received; and that for these and endless other reasons, I should simply and solely pay the rent of the lodging, without anything for stables, or for alleged breakages, or for service; and that Bordenave should pay all my expenses and one hundred and fifty francs damages—to be enforced, if he refused, by all the powers of all the gendarmerie of France.

CHAPTER XX.

PAU.

Betheram.—A legend.—Birthplace of Henry IV.—Chateau de Pau.—Abd-el-Kader.—Dearness of Pau. Unhealthiness of Pau.—Eaux Bonnes.—The Pass of Hourat.—The little statue of the B. V. M.—Talking Rocks.—Eaux Chaudes.—Temperature of Pau and London.

Not liking to take our invalid to face the winter in England, we had hired the first and third floors of an excellent house at the Basse Plante in Pau. The rent, until the 1st of the following June, was 4300 francs—an enormous rent for a distant provincial town; but the English had declared the climate of Pau to be super-excellent, and French and Russians followed thither in their wake.

On the 7th September, therefore, we left Bagnères de Bigorre, and, following a westward route to Lourdes, struck the Gave de Pau, and pulled up to bait at the busy village of Lestelle. I would not have delayed to mention this little place but for its vicinity to the celebrated church of pilgrimage and Calvary of Betheram. Nor, probably, should I have mentioned these further than to record the many stalls loaded with immense rosaries, which the pilgrims of Betheram choose to have as large as nuts, but for the enthusiastic description of the place given by Richard's *Guide des Pyrenées*, and the religious sentiment so unusually proclaimed in such works. "Betheram," it says, "unites those two touching sentiments of Catholicism, devotion to the Cross and to Mary. The origin of Betheram is buried in darkness, but it assuredly existed in the fifteenth century; and legends, which often speak as truly and more attractively than history, tell us how, in a very remote age, some children were tending sheep here when their attention was drawn by a sudden light on the rock, amid which they found a beautiful image of the Blessed Virgin. Priest and people poured out from the village. It was evident to the mind of all that heaven willed a chapel should be built on this spot; and as often as, deterred by the steepness of the rock, they attempted to build it on the adjacent level ground, marvels and disasters prevented the work; until, at last, they submitted to labour on the precise spot that heaven had chosen. "This," continues Richard, "is the legendary origin of Betheram. True it is that imagination may have added details which cannot be disproved; but ought this pretty legend to be at once disregarded because it tells us something extraordinary? Are not such incidents, on the contrary, very frequent in the history of religion? We, however, do not pretend to guarantee the truth of the story; but it is evident, from the very position of the chapel, that only the most serious motives could have caused such to be selected. The sides of the rock have been broken away at great expense, when, close at hand on either side, were two level spots that every one must have deemed far preferable. However blindly credulous we may think the people to have been, one cannot suppose that they undertook such a labour and such an expense without some motive."

There are some tolerable statues in the chapel: and some of those in the neighbouring Calvary are very fine.

The people of the provinces of Béarn, Basque, Bigorre, and Gascony, all look with piety towards the chapel of Betheram; and often come hither to pray with greater fervour.

Near this place, at Coarrage, are some picturesque ruins of the castle in which Henri IV was educated, as we have said. Over the gate, the Spanish motto still remains—*Lo que ha de ser, no puede fallar*—meaning "What has to happen cannot fail," or, more briefly, "What must be, must be."

But it was in the Chateau de Pau that this "Diable à quatre" was born. His mother travelled across France that she might be delivered in this old capital of Béarn; and sung a hymn of the country all the time she was in labour. His old grandfather came to see him cradled in the great tortoiseshell which is still shown; and having rubbed his lips with garlic and poured some wine of the country down his throat, wrapped the infant in his riding coat and carried it off; declaring that, as its parents had killed all their other children by their effeminate French ways, he himself would try what a real Béarnais education would do for this one. Away then went the brat; and, like Sam Weller, past through a course of education, bare-headed and bare-footed, in the streets of the village. He lived through it all; acquired an iron constitution; and at sixteen years, led a charge of cavalry at one of the many battles that then desolated France.

The Chateau de Pau is a most picturesque

building. Rising on a high ground from the midst of a clump of fine trees on the outskirts of the town, its pointed roofs and gables and irregular outline harmonise with and domineer in every landscape in which it appears. There are no grand rooms in it. It is a fortified palace of a little sovereign of the middle ages. They showed us the three wretched rooms in which the heroic Abd-el-Kader had been so long confined. A few chairs and sofas were their only furniture—"the savages eat upon the floor!" exclaimed the porter; little knowing that he was speaking of those whose ancestors were civilised and educated beings generations and centuries before the dissolute barbarian of whom he was so proud reigned over the then equally barbarous France—

"Et par droit de conquête et par droit de naissance."

The floor of the room was ruined by the frequent ablutions of the Emir, which threatened to rot the rafters and destroy the ceiling of the great eating hall below, when the prisoner was removed elsewhere and, at length, restored to freedom.

Pau is by no means a fine town; nor even an interesting town. Though formerly capital of the Kings of Navarre, it is inferior in its public buildings and general appearance to very many of the old provincial towns of France. The shops are poor; the houses, of which many are being built for the accommodation of visitors, are wretchedly ill-designed and outrageously dear. In their eagerness to fleece strangers, the good people of Pau are, I think, injuring themselves. Napoleon had lent the chateau to the Duke and Duchess of Hamilton a year or two before I was there; and I was told that when, after a residence of some months, the visitors left and the townsfolk expressed a hope to see them again during the following winter, the Duke replied that he could not afford to return to so expensive a place.

There is a fine walk and drive called the Park, well timbered with old trees, on a bank above the Gave; from hence and from many points, the view of the far-stretching Pyrenees, with the snow-capped Pic du Midi in the centre of the range, is very fine. In every other direction, the country is as uninteresting as a wide elevated plain, intersected by great straight high roads, bordered by poplar trees, must ever appear to any one but a Frenchman. Beyond, and especially to the west, are extensive marshy tracts which often carry fever and ague to Pau: so that, in truth, it must be considered as very far from a healthy place of residence. Our invalid daughter had here a more serious attack upon her lungs than she had ever known; and we should have left the place as soon as she was able so travel but were detained by a gastric fever, which long threatened the life of my penultimate son, Whittingham. At length we got away in the middle of November—gladly sacrificing six or eight months of the high rent paid for our house in order to escape from this disagreeable and unwholesome place.

But I would not leave the neighbourhood of the Pyrenees without having thoroughly "done" them —seen all the valleys, towns, and villages amid which issue those famous mineral springs. I had not yet visited Eaux Bonnes and Eaux Chaudes, which are as celebrated as any, and rise under the hills about twenty-five miles from Pau. We hired a light open carriage called an Americaine, and drove up the pretty valley and beside the river or Gave of Ossau. It was the beginning of November, and the women were busy ploughing and sowing their wheat: often with one horse, sometimes with a cow harnessed to the plough. The men were said to be tending their cattle in the distant mountains, or copse-cutting and making charcoal.

We baited at a decent inn at Louvai. A fog then came on, and we saw nothing more till we got to a comparatively level space containing about two acres. On the left hand was a row of tall houses looking as if they had walked out of a town and located themselves in the Pyrenees, with a wide foot-pavement before them; on the other side of the road, was a plot of wretched grass, for all the world like a bad goose green in an English village. We were told that this was the *Jardin Anglais*, and that this was the Eaux Bonnes : and that the road went no further; and that the whole was enveloped in similar fogs two days out of three. Disgusted with everything, we bade the driver turn his horses' heads and take us to the other celebrated Spa, called Eaux Chaudes.

We returned down the hills for about a couple of miles, and, regaining our former road, turned to the left and up towards the mountains. We entered the defile of Hourat : it will be remembered that, at Cauterets, one of the springs there was called " Malhourat—the bad hole". This defile of Hourat is, indeed, a fearful hole; through which, however, a magnificent road has been cut into the rocks overhanging the precipice and the river that brawls deep down below. The driver advised us to wrap ourselves well up; and we soon were met by a strong current of damp frozen air than which nothing could be more calculated to give the pulmonary complaints which the waters of Eaux Chaudes profess to cure. "At the end of the defile," writes the French author, M. Nisard, " the traveller stops and cries out "how beautifully horrible!" as if anything horrid could be beautiful. Here also the mountaineer, who knows all about these mountains, and who knows how weak man is against all their avalanches, their rains and their thunders, here he, also, stops; but it is to pray before a little stone statue of the Blessed Virgin, placed in a niche behind a grating, near which hang a faded garland and some glass beads. It is before this little statue that the Spaniards, going from Biscay to Pau, take off their pointed hats adorned with streamers; that the peasants of the vale of Ossau doff their caps of blue cloth. Civilisation alone does not unbonnet: it is afraid of catching cold; and instead of dropping a sou for the poor into the box beneath the niche, it bestows upon the little statue of the Blessed Virgin a self-satisfied reflection on the numbers of former worshippers and the fewness of those supplied by modern times.

Modern French writers are edifying. Let me quote a passage from the pretty work of M. Moreau :—

"Towards the end of the defile of Hourat, a little statue of the Virgin calls for your prayers. Happy you if you have nothing to ask of heaven; but, then, you owe it the more thanks; and to pray to God is to thank Him. But you, people of 'strong intellect,' beware how you cast a pitying smile on that gigantic Spaniard with iron limbs and wiry muscles who is kneeling there humbly before the Madonna. He cannot always, like you, select a fine day on which to cross the Hourat; often, when he has passed this defile to return to his wife and children and his poor home in Spain, storm and tempest have overtaken him in the snow-covered Pyrenees. Gladly, then, he has remembered that he had shown honour to the Blessed Virgin; and filled with faith in her power to protect him, he has asked her to pray to God to stay the avalanche; to turn the swollen torrent from his path; to appease the whirlwind; to stop the flooding rain; and to guide him safely to his sheltering cottage beyond. And saved, as he has been at these times of greatest danger, is he to forget his protectrice because the sun shines? Not so!

In sunshine and in rain, in the snows of winter and in the heats of summer, humble and grateful of heart, he repeats the same invocation—'Blessed Virgin, pray for me and protect me.'

"Traveller," concludes M. Moreau, "do you also pray; or else weep for the faith that you have lost."

There used to be some Latin inscriptions engraven in these rocks to record the passage of celebrated personages. To show the style of the sixteenth century, I quote one of them:—"Stop, traveller! Admire what you cannot behold, and behold what you must admire. We are only rocks yet we speak. Nature gave us being, and Catherine gave us voice. We have beheld Catherine reading what you read; we have heard Catherine speaking; we have upborn Catherine sitting. Happy rocks who have, without eyes, beheld her. Happy art thou, traveller, who having eyes dost not behold her. The sight of her gave life to us who were heretofore senseless stones: if thou hadst seen her, traveller, thou wouldst have been changed to stone. The Virgin Muses inscribed this to the Virgin Catherine, Princess of French Navarre, who passed this way A.D. 1591."

I do not think M. Moreau would bid us weep for the style of princely adulation that has been lost!

The Pic du Midi soon opened grandly before us, towering above the lower clouds and fog; and I rejoiced to find that the village of Eaux Chaudes retained some resemblance to a village, and was not merely a row or more of town lodging-houses. The thermal establishment is a fine building; more I should think than requisite for those who now frequent these springs. For at the time when the rocks spoke, as I have said above, and they were almost inaccessible, these springs were at the height of their fame, and drew votaries from far and near; now that an excellent road leads to them, and that every accommodation is provided for invalids, few comparatively frequent them. In truth, these are not lively places of residence. Instead of the poor consumptive frequenters of Eaux Bonnes, whose hectic cheek and hollow cough sadden one as they pass, here we have invalids hopping, and hobbling about on sticks and crutches, and drinking gallons of water believed to be antirheumatic.

In so far, Eaux Chaudes is more cheering than the former place; for whereas at Eaux Bonnes the fatal termination of the pulmonary disease is often accelerated by the waters, here, at all events, people do generally leave their crutches behind them. The people of the country, the mountaineers of the neighbouring districts, have, in fact, confidence in their antirheumatic virtues, and throng here in great numbers. This speaks more in their favour than any crowd of rich patients sent away by their town physicians when these latter could do nothing for them, and would not that they should die under their hands.

Doctors, however, declare that the waters of Eaux Bonnes are incontestably beneficial in the first stage of consumption, sometimes in the second; but that they are fatal in the third stage, and that Eaux Chaudes, as they are called, although less warm than most of the thermal springs of the Pyrenees, do cure rheumatisms and neuralgias, how, why, or wherefore, they cannot quite explain.

There are some beautiful walks and drives about Eaux Chaudes. The Pont d'Enfer is very romantic, and there are some picturesque cascades. We visited some of these on the following morning, lighted up by a bright sun; and as the fog had cleared off from the valley on our return to Pau, the scenery about Castets, below Laruns, impressed itself on my memory as being very beautiful.

The following table of temperature will enable the reader to judge whether it be worth while to go to the climate of Pau rather than remain in the South of England; since even the abominable climate of London is so little inferior to that of this much-vaunted Pyrenean city :—

Mean Temperature of Winter Months, Centigrade.

	Oct.	Nov.	Dec.	Jan.	Feb.	Mar	April.	May.
Near London	48.9	42.9	39.3	36	38	43.9	49.9	54
At Pau	53.6	46.6	41.5	41.1	43.9	48.1	52.8	56

And rushing, as we English do, from place to place in search of suitable climates, from our own that is better than most, it is truly wonderful how badly we select them. A clever doctor, seeing that his patient wishes to go to the shores of the Mediterranean, will generally recommend them; and the family and fellow travellers of the invalid approve— for they expect more pleasure there than elsewhere. I have known people go to Naples for sea-bathing and then marvel that it did not produce the same effect as bathing in the ocean! They and their doctor had all forgotten that the ocean is infinitely more salt than this inland sea : and that the water at Naples is so warm that a plunge into it can produce little shock and consequent revulsion of blood.

CHAPTER XXI.

FORBIDDEN BOOKS IN ROME.

From Pau to Rome.—Roman Turncoats.—The Temporal Power.

ARGUMENT.—Departure from Pau.—Lannemzan: no admission to the hotel because the cook was gone *pour faire des noces.*—Martres: hotel bill fifty-nine francs; quite satisfied with twenty-nine. —Toulouse: great, ugly town; narrow, crooked streets, brick houses, pavements of pointed stones; picture-gallery. The guidebook says the modern pictures are the best, because they carry one's thoughts at once to Paris. Once upon a time *The Hampshire Independent* newspaper, complaining that Government had spent the public money in buying three pictures by ancient masters, said, "if they will buy pictures, they might, at least, buy new paintings instead of old ones." Guidebook says also that Marshal Soult fought a battle here, and with twenty-five thousand men, routed three times as many English, Spaniards, and Portuguese, under Wellington. *Que roulez-vous?* The French are such brave, clever fellows!—Narbonne : Hôtel de France rascally dear.—Cette : great factory of foreign wines without ever a grape ; makes better Madeira than ever came from the island.—All the country about Montpellier under water. By express train, to Terrascon ; thence through beautiful country to Marseille. Waited for carriage and horses from Toulouse, and for chests of china and plate from England. They arrived by passenger-train ; cost eight hundred and ninety-eight francs. All on board the *Marie Antoinette* steamer. Had paid for passage and food to Civita Vecchia. They refused us the grub without extra payment. Agreed with other first-class passengers, and we all nicked them by going on shore at Genoa, and dining at Hotel de la Croix de Malte. Saw agent of the company ; he admitted our right to food ; said his principals were scoundrels, and referred us to them. No redress. Mem.—Never to go by *Marie Antoinette* again. *N.B.*—I believe she is gone to "Davy's Locker."—Leghorn harbour.—Beautiful night.—Landed at Civita Vecchia : best place to land at in the world ; tariff for everything; no cheating, no noise, no confusion.—Found *lascia passare* for my baggage. Custom House people said it would only clear through the gates of Rome what was on my carriage; that the rest must go to Custom House. So hired two carriages and seven horses, besides my own britzska, to take as much baggage as possible. Put a servant or two and child in each, and away. Paid five pauls to the guard who carried my passport to the gate of Civita Vecchia; five pauls to the guard who looked at the passport at the gate; five pauls to the one who did ditto at the gate of Rome; five pauls to the Custom House officers who brought out the *lascia passare;* three pauls to the porters at the gate, who bowed in obedience to it, and let us pass.

Now I ask the reader if this is not the pleasantest way of getting over the ground, both for himself and me? Here have I carried him a very long journey at more than speed of express-train; and here have I got into Rome, bag and baggage; greeted with obsequious civility by the medium of a few pauls which served to pay the wages of the Custom House officers whom the state was obliged to keep up against smugglers, which the banker, who had procured us the *lascia passare,* had assured it that we were not. Talk not of bribery and meanness! It was no such thing. They received their wages from me instead of from their own government, and I paid them for forbearance and civility. Those who are unwilling to pay for such, had better not travel.

We were in Rome safe and sound; but some carriages that had passed along the same road from Civita Vecchia, two hours after us, were stopped by brigands, and their inmates stripped of all they possessed. A foreign bishop amongst them was robbed of one thousand napoleons. I wonder whether he continued, as much as heretofore, to admire the exercise of the temporal power!

We were in Rome safe and sound; but we were not yet at an hotel. I was driving our own horses over that most fearful of all pavement,—it is made of lava so hard that no iron shoe of horse can take any hold of it (Romans generally drive their horses unshod as to their hinder feet, which they harden with some composition),—I was driving our horses, when down slipped one of them on that most detestable pavement. Our coachman, Paul, sprang from one of the other carriages, and ran up with the French footman whom I had brought from Pau. I flung the reins to them, helped my wife to descend from the driving-seat where she had sat beside me; and leaving them to raise the horse, started with her on foot towards the Hotel delle Minerva. I was puzzled in the darkness (for it was eight o'clock of the 3rd of December) in those narrow streets, and addressed myself to an elderly and most respectable-looking priest with an unusually large three-cornered hat. He insisted upon accompanying us, and I thus formed an acquaintance with one who, calling next morning to inquire how we were, devoted himself to our service with a constancy that was most useful and obliging.

With the help of this Don Filippo (such I discovered to be his designation), the Custom House authorities were induced to sign, without even opening the chests, a declaration that all my effects were used and personal to myself, and they were delivered up to me duty free; and I was enabled to rent the Palazzo Albani, at the Quattro Fontani, until the end of June, for 1,250 scudi, or £260.

Let not the reader fear that I am about to inflict Rome upon him. I have done it once systematically, years ago, in my *Transalpine Memoirs*, and incidentally in one of the cantos of my *Beggar's Coin*, and in that historical novel to which

Messrs. Hurst & Blackett persuaded me to give the name of *Modern Society in Rome*. If, then, the reader is not already acquainted with Rome, it is his own fault, not mine, and he must seek that knowledge in my other books. I shall here only take note of such personal, political, and social experiences as he could not find recorded elsewhere.

And first of all, of that same historical novel. I went to the Vatican to announce our return to Rome to our old friend Monsignore Talbot, one of the "Camerieri Segreti" of the Pope, when he surprised me by informing me that my book was forbidden in Rome.

"Forbidden!" I exclaimed. "What have you found in it against religion?"

"Not on theological grounds," he answered. "There is nothing in it that divines could object to; but forbidden by the police, in deference to an outcry raised against it by the Roman Princes."

"I have only recorded how they acted during the earlier days of the present Pope's reign: those whom I have brought forward were public political characters. If they have changed their opinions, it is not my fault."

"People do not like to have even that recorded.

But you have represented the Roman young men as fortune-hunters. It is very true they are so: your descriptions were so graphic that, as I read, I laughed till the tears ran down my cheeks; but people do not like this, either, to be said of them. And moreover," he said, more seriously, "you have given a personal description of the Secretary of State, Cardinal Antonelli: you have spoken of his lantern cheeks and nutcracker jaws" . . .

I had thought Cardinal Antonelli, in truth, too much occupied with cares of state and the interests of his own family to care what any one thought of his person; but I remembered that Lord Chesterfield wrote of a prime minister, the first politician of his age, who only loved to be complimented on his very inferior poetry; and I thought that perhaps Cardinal Antonelli set up for being a beauty.

I went to Piale's library, in the Piazza di Spagna, and asked him what he knew of the book. He knew that, whereas he had sent for three or four copies, which had cost him a guinea and a half apiece, they had all been seized by the police; whereat, of course, he was very angry with the author. Spithover, the other bookseller, told me that he had received a dozen copies from England, but that he had obtained permission to send them out of the Roman territories, and so had escaped confiscation. He had sent them, he said, to a correspondent at Florence, and one copy of them returned to Rome in every ambassador's bag. So anxious, indeed, were people to obtain the work, that I was told by a speculative gentleman that, if I could manage to introduce fifty copies for him, he would gladly pay me the publisher's price; because he knew that he could loan them all out to read at half-a-crown a volume!

And all this owing to the silly prohibition of the government! without which no one probably of the Romans would ever have heard of the work.

But I am forgetful. They would have heard of it. Princess Doria, daughter of the Earl of Shrewsbury, chanced to be in London at the time it was published. It made some little noise there. Marquis d'Azeglio, Minister of Sardinia, told me that he had immediately sent off a copy of it to poor Cavour; and I have heard, from one present, that it was discussed and my statements canvassed in the imperial circle at Compiègne; and so Princess Doria Pamphilj heard of it. She imagined that she herself was alluded to in it under a fictitious name; and her husband did not like any record of the liberal part he had played during the revolution, when he was minister of war under Mamiani. So he, too, joined in getting up the hue and cry against me. Perhaps he was mortified that I could not allude to the pretty little temple of white marble which he has since built in the grounds of his villa, in memory, as the inscription tells us, of the brave French soldiers who fell near that spot in one of the battles during that siege of Rome. Mark, oh reader! I pray thee, mark! This politician, who had been minister of war at the beginning of the revolution, and, as such, had, however unintentionally, led on his countrymen towards the Republic which these French invaders drowned in blood—this former minister of Rome raised a temple to the slaughterers of his own people; and engraved words to their praise and in their honour, without the slightest allusion to the Roman countrymen and umquhile followers of himself, whom those French invaders had slain!

And so a cry was got up against me for writing

contemporary history. It may, indeed, have been a mistake on my part to attempt to blend fiction and reality. But with such a plan, it was impossible to write the history of those times without introducing anecdotes that were known to everyone in Rome, and without pourtraying the characteristics of the different classes who looked on or took part in the revolution. I described classes : if individuals thought the cap fitted them and would put it on, that was not my fault. Many of the gentry now wished that their liberal tendencies should be forgotten ; and all sorts of absurd stories were imagined by strangers, who accused me of "making a bad return for the hospitality with which the Romans had received me three years before." This was an English version of the matter. Our countrymen knew not that hospitality, as it is understood in England, does not obtain and is not expected in Rome : —that Romans never make any return, in the English sense of the word, for the civilities they receive; and that the only way in which they showed their "hospitality" to me was by permitting me to feed and entertain them gratis.

That these are trivial personalities, we are all aware. But the would-be heroic Romans declare that nothing can be trivial at Rome. And, in sober sadness, I admit that what would be unimportant elsewhere is not so here, where it may reflect back, from these spiteful time-servers, to the scandal of religion itself—as we shall see.

I could, however, never distinctly ascertain how or by whose orders the volumes had, in reality, been prohibited. I had the pleasure of becoming acquainted with the learned and amiable theologian who examines most English publications; and asked him whether it really did contain any theological error, as Father Waterworth, the head of the Jesuits in London, had been prevented, by his superiors, from publishing a review which he himself had written in its favour: the Roman divine assured me that he had had no hand in the matter. I went to the Maestro dei Sacri Palazzi, who, I was informed, was the head inquisitor for the Index: the fine old monk received me courteously; and knowing nothing about it, but promising to inquire, requested me to call on him again. I did so; and he had then evidently learned something that he wished to conceal. He hesitated much in speaking; said that he was informed that there were "some inexact statements in the book that might produce wrong impressions in Rome";—that I "ought not to marvel at the prohibition because, out of one hundred books published in France, he did not allow ten to enter the Pontifical States"; —that "no satire was ever allowed to enter, because it was improper for one Christian to laugh at another Christian";—and that "Government was bound to forbid, not only everything that was opposed to morality and faith, but also to the kindly feeling of all to all."

One friend cut to the root of the matter, saying to me,—" The book was excluded by the private influence of some Romans with the police: you can easily acquire more influence than they in the same quarter, and make the police rescind their prohibition."

By bribery? I had no wish to try.

But some of the consequences of all this hubbub were curious: and I only dwell so much on it to show how they manage matters in Rome. Monsignore Talbot, before mentioned, dined with us— meeting a large party of English: he said that he had been so "called to account in high quarters" for having accepted the invitation, that he prayed us not to ask him again!

Was there not in the then state of Rome anything more worthy to occupy the mind of "high quarters"—of Cardinal Antonelli?

I called upon his Eminence, as I had often done during my former visit to Rome; and was told, by his gentleman, that he was "at home." I sent in my card, however; and soon after, the same gentleman rushed down to express his regret that he had made a mistake; for that the Cardinal had just gone into the garden.

"To avoid me," I said to some one. "As his Eminence lives on the third floor, I only hope he has broken his neck in jumping down into the garden; I shall so have been a benefactor to Rome and to religion."

But the old monk in white said that satire was very naughty: let us turn to what was more serious. Candlemas Day was approaching—that festival on which the parish priest in every church distributes wax tapers to the congregation in allegorical remembrance of the prophecy that the Infant Saviour should prove "a light to enlighten the Gentiles"; and which the Pope also distributes to those to whom he wishes to show favour and consideration. Three years before, during High Mass at St. Peter's, I had received from his hand one nearly as tall as myself. My wife now stated to Monsignor Talbot, who is the official intermediary between the English in Rome and the Pope for all such matters, that I should wish to be again admitted to receive a candle and the Pope's blessing on the Purification; and that she and her three daughters wished to be presented to His Holiness on his first reception. Monsignor Talbot advised that we had better not ask for either; that it would probably be refused; that I had offended the leading members of the Roman society, and that the Pope could not act in opposition to their feeling!

What say you to that, most devout approver of the temporal power? This was an official answer to a request made through the regular official channel, and I am therefore justified in publishing it. Here was a man whose father had made great sacrifices in joining the Catholic Church; who had himself founded chapels and written, in support of religion, works that had been approved by the highest ecclesiastical authorities in England and in America; who had converted many to the faith; and who now, with a convert wife and her daughter, was seeking a spiritual good—or what is delivered as a spiritual good—from the head of the church:—this man was repelled lest the gentry of Rome should be displeased. For, be it remembered, some spiritual good is supposed to follow the blessing of the Pope, whether delivered at a private audience or in St. Peter's with the candle:—that spiritual good was refused out of deference to some of the gentry of Rome!

Verily, although I had rejoiced at having been the cause that Cardinal Antonelli had risked breaking his neck by jumping out of a window, I was sorry to have occasioned poor good Pio Nono to forget his apostolic character in deference to laymen whom I knew that he himself despised from the bottom of his heart.

The character of chief pontiff is apparently incompatible with that of leader of the fashionable society of Rome.

My devotion to the temporal power of the Pope had received a rude shock.

It received another about this same time: Sir Moses Montefiore arrived in Rome to endeavour to restore the child Mortara to his Jewish parents. I called at his hotel, and introduced myself to the fine old man. I told him that I was an English

Catholic; but that I sympathised with him in the object of his journey; that I prayed him not to charge upon my religion an act which I reprobated as much as himself; and I placed myself at his disposal if he thought that I could be of any use in furthering the object that had brought him to Rome.

In fact, however, the Pope, as Pope, was perfectly right. No Christian priest *could* surrender a baptised child to be brought up as a Jew. But, as Sovereign, he was perfectly wrong. As Sovereign, he had no right to detain a child from the custody of its parents in deference to any religious preference whatever.

The character of Pope and the character of temporal Sovereign were, therefore, incompatible the one with the other.

In case these volumes should be also forbidden in Rome, in deference to the wishes of some whom I have named in this chapter, I hereby remind the reader that I have spoken of these people in their public official character and of the manner in which they performed those public duties which they were paid for transacting. I respect the domestic privacy even of these; but, in their public capacity, they are public property; and I have as much right to remark upon the way in which they transact the duties they have undertaken, as I have to criticise the incivility of any public servant who delays the delivery of a passport or neglects to answer a letter.

CHAPTER XXII.

ANTE-RAILROAD TRAVELLING.

Tailors at Court.—A J.P. in the Olden Times.—F.M. the Duke of Wellington.—Taking the Oath.—Journey from Spa.—Schaffhausen and Niagara.—Switzerland.—St. Gothard.—An American Traveller.—Lugano.—Blockade of the Ticino.—An Evening Drive.—An Austrian Corps de Garde.—San Salvadore.—The Frontier of Lombardy.—General Singer.—Again at Lugano.—Again at the Frontier.—The Cow and the Sword.—Away! away!

ALTHOUGH I was not to have a candle from His Holiness, and we were not to be presented to him, our daughters wished to see the public services and ceremonies; and we procured tickets of admission to the tribune erected in St. Peter's for the accommodation of ladies. I put on my deputy-lieutenant uniform, as enabling me to conduct them more easily through the crowd. A military uniform is very useful on the continent; where, as a friend once said to me, everybody believes that, if you are not a soldier, you must be a tailor. Not that being a tailor is always a drawback. Some years ago, at Florence, the late Sir Colin Halkett thought it his duty to intimate to the Grand Duke that one of the guests at Pitti Palace was his own snip in London.

"Qu'importe!" said the good-natured sovereign. "They are all welcome, if they come to spend at Florence what they have earned from you in London. You thus benefit us doubly."

And, on this principle, as somebody insists upon my having a full-length portrait of myself painted this winter, I will have myself represented as a deputy-lieutenant; for fear the painting should be doomed to remain in Italy.

That admission to the deputy-lieutenantship and county magistracy of England is altogether, however, a comical proceeding. I presume that both dignities are to be respected as "venerable institutions." My grandfather, who was lord of his own manor in Lincolnshire and prebendary of Lincoln Cathedral, as his forbears had been before him, named, "in the good old days of Adam and Eve," his son a county magistrate when he was five years old. The then lord-lieutenant, or, to give him his proper title, lord admiral of Lincolnshire, had written to my grandfather that he was about to name a new batch of magistrates, and asked if he would wish any friend of his to be put on the list. Amongst others, my grandfather proposed his son, whose age was well known to his correspondent: and so, at the age of fifty, he was able to surprise a meeting of brother magistrates in Lincolnshire, his seniors in age, by telling them that he had been in the commission about forty years longer than any of them. He had lived at his college in Oxford, and had then become a Catholic.

To be a Catholic in England was about as bad, in the eyes of the government of those days, as it was, in Rome, to write a book recording how Roman princes had turned their coats. I, myself, having been born a Catholic, could not aspire to the honours of the J. P. But, in 1829, after Catholic emancipation, our Lincolnshire agent wrote that he had sent in my name as a matter of course, and had had me put on the commission of the peace for the three divisions of Lindsey, Holland, and Kestevan. There the matter began and ended, for I had sought what was considered a more preferable "location"; and had taken up my residence in the south of Hampshire.

It was not, however, a matter of course that I should be in the commission of the peace in Hants.

"F.M. the Duke of Wellington," was our lord-lieutenant; and, although he had declared that the fear of civil war had induced him to propose Catholic emancipation, (which Sir R. Peel had helped to carry through, although he proclaimed that he did not consider it either necessary or expedient) yet the Duke had no fear that my co-religionists would take up arms to assert my individual pretensions. I was known to be an advanced liberal; and, therefore, at the very same time when he was making Mr. Lobb, a Tory agent and silk mercer in Southampton, a county magistrate and deputy lieutenant, he wrote to me that he considered that there was no lack of magistrates in the county; but that he would beg leave to call upon me in case of any Chartist riot, or similar emergency. This I objected to—telling his Grace that, if I were already named, I should, of course, do my duty; but that I would not be deprived of that to which I was now entitled, and have it thrust upon me, perhaps, hereafter, for the convenience of his government. What a characteristic answer the old boy wrote! F.M. the Duke of Wellington presented his compliments and begged to assure me that he would take care not " to call upon me under any emergency."

However, the conqueror at Waterloo was obliged to give in. His Tory ministry was at an end; the Whigs succeeded; and, although the Duke remained Lord Lieutenant of Hants, he was constrained to see me appointed by the Lord Chancellor. He submitted with a good grace, or, perhaps, he had forgotten all about it: for he afterwards made me one of his deputy lieutenants without any hesitation.

And thus it came to pass that I was entitled to put on an uniform in order the better to escort my wife and daughters to the crowded ceremonies at St. Peter's.

I must here be excused for mentioning a curious incident that occurred when I had had to qualify for the commission in the county of Devon. I went down to Exeter by appointment with the clerk of the peace; but, when about to take the oath, discovered that that functionary had omitted to procure the oath devised for Catholics, as he had been directed to do. He was in great distress and perplexity to excuse his negligence, when I said—

"If it is all the same to you, Mr. —, I will take the usual Protestant oath with the omission of only two words."

"Only two words, sir!" he exclaimed: "why

that would obviate every difficulty and delay! What are the words?"

"Or spiritual," I answered. "Let me omit these two words, and I will swear all the rest as willingly as Bishop Phillpotts himself."

The clerk of the peace was delighted at my suggestion, and I accordingly swore that "no foreign prince, potentate, or prelate hath or ought to have any power temporal within this realm."

After the word "temporal," I left out the words "or spiritual," not only because they asserted a lie —for I knew that the Pope had some spiritual power—but because I thought that he ought to have some in England.

The Exeter functionary, however, was overjoyed. He took his fees; and I daresay that I have administered justice in Devon as honestly as I should have done if I had taken the whole Catholic oath, or sworn the untruths contained in the Protestant declaration.

I have said that I went to St. Peter's in uniform. Let it not, however, be supposed that it used to be such an easy matter for those who were entitled to wear them to take a complete uniform into Rome. I had succeeded in doing so by the merest chance, and by rare good luck. In 1853, we had toiled up the hilly road that leads from Spa, past the mystic Sauvenière fountain; we had trotted over the dreary but much-bepraised Eisenberge; we had dipped down into the beautiful and secluded dell where slumbered the baths of Birtrich; we had crossed the pretty Moselle, in a ferry boat, at Alf; and had looked down upon the majestic Rhine at Bingen; for ten days, we had drank the pleasant waters and inhaled the foul smells of Schwalbach; we had loitered some hours in the pretty little world of Baden-Baden; at Offenberg, we had entered the wilds of the Black Forest, and had threaded its beautiful ravines to Freiberg, and down again on the opposite side; most expressive of all, we had exchanged Murray's handbook of North Germany for his diminutive twin-brother of Switzerland; and, at last, we had stood in the court of the gingerbread, Vauxhall-Gothic castle that usurps the left bank of the Rhinefalls at Schaffhausen, where Frau Bleuler, the dragon chatelaine of the castle, demanded one franc per head before she would allow us to catch a glimpse of the waterfall.

"If heaven permits such desecration," I observed, "what right have we to complain?"

"Monsieur," she replied, "the property is my

own; and I have a right to make what charge I please."

"When," I said, "the Saviour scourged the money changers and those who sold doves from the temple, it was not because they asked exorbitant prices; but the very fact of taking money in His house desecrated it into a den of thieves. This waterfall is the temple of the Lord of nature!"

She was somewhat abashed; took five francs for seven of us, and admitted us into her den.

But the memory of Niagara was fresh upon us. Before we had come in sight of the Rhinefalls, the span of the little river had proved that no great mass of water was there to be hurled below; these neighbouring banks seemed to contract still more under the thought of Niagara; and those of Niagara expanded, to our mind's eye, when we contemplated the utmost that Europe could accomplish. For it is here impossible to prevent the mind from drawing odious comparisons. The fall of Schaffhausen is so like that of Niagara on the American side—omitting altogether the great Horse Shoe fall—is so like, and yet so diminutive in its likeness—that one smiles at what appears to be an attempt at rivalry. In truth, the so-called cascade of Schaffhausen is not a cascade: it is a rapid, a slide, a shoot: it is not a tumble-down; it is not a waterfall.

Such, however, as it is, it is very grand; but let those who would see it to most advantage and judge of it most truly, avoid Frau Bleuler's puppet-show exhibition, and look at it from the beach beneath Webb's Hotel on the opposite side, or from the ferry boat that crosses the stream lower down.

We had slept at the great Hotel Bauer at Zurich, and regretted that it could give no view of the lake; we had crossed the bold ridge of the Albis, and had driven through magnificent scenery to the little town of Zug; we had circled one end of its pretty waters, and had seen the Righi and jagged Mount Pilate uprise as we approached the glorious shores of Lucerne; we had been drenched by rain in an open pleasure boat on lake Alpnach during a thunder-storm, when Mount Pilate overhead clamoured to Righi on the opposite side, and flashes of molten fire rushed from the unseen summits of the distant snow-capped Alps; we had again circled Righi and the shores of Zug; had passed the spot where Tell perpetrated what Mr. Murray daintily insinuates was a murder, and had driven over the town buried, not fifty years ago, under the wild earth avalanche of Goldau: we had longed to linger near the savage-looking little lake of Lowertz, and at the romantic, but unknown and secluded, baths of Sewen; we had slept amid the old walls of heroic Schwitz; had embarked on the steamer at Brunnen; and, beneath clouds low-hanging on the lake of Uri, had passed at the foot of those shelving crags, so steep that no road can be cut on their beetling sides, where the heroes of the Rutli could alone find footing, and where Tell sprang to land from the wave-tossed bark of the Austrian tyrant.

We had landed at Fluellen and, at his native town of Altdorf, had entered the great gorge of the Reuss; at Amsteg, we had harnessed two native *chevaux de renfort* before our English horses, that we dared not (although my poor Norfolk grey was one of them) trust further alone amid the wild scenery before us; slowly we had toiled up the ravine, over the foam-bespattered Devil's-bridge, through the hole of Uri, across the little meadow of Untersee; marking and marvelling how the science of modern engineers had not been able to improve upon that of the twelfth century, but had traced this new and marvellous road within a few yards of that which, in the year 1118, the Abbot of Einsiedeln had made across the Alp; not so wide, indeed, for wheel carriages then existed not; but answering the requirements of pack-horse traffic as perfectly as the modern road meets those of more bulky commerce. Above the village of Aspenthal, by zig-zag stretches, had we clomb the rounded side of S. Gothard itself; and through dense fogs, laboured on till our leaders stopped, of their own accord, beside a large building, of which the grey clouds prevented us from seeing the outline. They were detached; the Swiss postboys placed the drags under the wheels of our two carriages, and bade heaven speed us through the fog along the unknown road that led before us adown the precipitous Alps.

The clouds were soon left above; but then, indeed, our undertaking appeared more hazardous. How would horses accustomed only to the plains of Hampshire, how would a French coachman, untaught beyond the streets of Boulogne and Paris, descend in safety into the depth beneath?—how would my own brain, surcharged with anxiety for the risk to which I had exposed my family, meet scenery, and precipices, and waterfalls, such as I knew must lie before and beside me? The road began to circle, as does that of no other passage of the Alps; the angles were acute; no parapet protected them from the precipices; and while, at each turn, the heads of the horses protruded over the road side and above the brawling torrent that, tumbling from the higher cliffs, rushed, white with foam, some hundred feet beneath them, I could but commend my charge to Providence, and, stopping the horses I myself drove at the edge of a precipice, call back to the coachman to drive most gently round each angle of the road, lest the stumbling of a horse, or the breaking of a rein or of the drag, might precipitate his carriage into the abyss beneath.

Before sunset, we arrived at Airolo. Nothing of one drag and but little of the other remained to tell the tale of the service they had seen.

The following day was Sunday, and we made it a day of rest.

"Ma, signore," said the landlord of "I tre Re," —and what a pleasure it then was to hear Italian spoken again,—"Ma, signore, I understand that you are going to Lugano; but you will not be able to enter Lombardy at Como on account of the blockade."

"What blockade?" I asked.

"The blockade of Canton Ticino by the Austrians, which they have maintained since the beginning of February. They do not allow anything to pass in or out between Lombardy and Ticino. You had better put your carriage and horses on board the Piedmontese steamer at Magadisio, and land at the other end of the Lago Maggiore, so that it may appear as if you came from Piedmont."

"I guess that *we* shall have no difficulty at all in going through," observed, in a strong American accent, a lady who stood near us in the salle-à-manger of the little inn. "We always behave pleasant and conciliating to all the officers, and never find any difficulty. Anyhow, I have seen a great deal of Eurōpĕan travelling, and we always meet a great deal of good society. We knew Lady Wightman and her daughter at Lucerne—her husband is one of the British Queen's chancellors. And, last year, we met a lord on the Rhine. We calculate to go by Como, don't we?" she asked, turning to her daughter.

"No, mama; by Magadino and Arona on the Lago Maggiore," replied the girl.

"Good bye," said the mother, curtseying condescendingly to us. "I hope you will realise a great deal of pleasure, and meet with a great deal of good company. I am sure we shall!"

Thereupon, she scrambled into her little voiturier caleche; and, with many apologetic reasons why she had travelled this time without any servant, disappeared down the narrow lane of the village.

Thus, in a conversation into which this uneducated, vulgar American woman thrust herself—and I beg Europeans not to think I imply that vulgarity and want of education are essentially American—we became first acquainted with the blockade of the Ticino, and that we might experience some difficulty in passing from it to Lombardy. However, we could not cross back again over the St. Gothard; and, on the next morning, I drove gaily forwards.

The descent by the valley of the Ticino is like most drives through Alpine gorges; but the pass by Dazio Grande, where the valley narrowed itself over the torrent which cleaves its way and squeezes itself through the overhanging rocks, is more wonderful than the Devil's Bridge on the other side; and is equalled by no other pass that I remember. In fact, if we consider, as in strict geography we must, that the pass of St. Gothard begins with the Lake of Uri—that is to say, at the bottom of the ravine of the Rheuss, up which the lake of the Four Cantons forces itself—and ends at the romantic, castellated walls of Bellinzona, I believe that we shall all admit it to be unrivalled in magnificent scenery by any other Alpine road.

But below Bellinzona, another spur of the Alps still girt in the valley to the east, and we had to toil over the chestnut-covered ridge of Monte Cenere before we could descend into the pretty ravine that led us to the smiling town of Lugano, and to the lake that washes its arcaded streets.

The scenery of the Lake of Lugano is a commingling of the Swiss and of the Italian scenery that is very beautiful. The town lies at its northern end on a slope of hills covered with vines and mulberry trees. On the left hand, the lake branches off into the more barren recesses of the rocky Alps towards Como. On the right, the sugar-loaf peak of San Salvadore rises, a quarter of a mile from the town, and, covered with chestnut trees and evergreens, springs almost perpendicular to the height of two thousand feet from the lake. The mountains that encircle the lake are almost everywhere perpendicular—their peaks jagged and tinged with the ever-varying hues of an Italian sun; while their bases teem with the luxurious growth of the plains of Briante; and mulberries, vines, figs, and olive trees overhang fields of Indian corn, pumpkins, and blossoming buck wheat.

A magnificent-looking building recommended itself to us as the Albergo del Lago; and we secured a suite of handsome apartments overlooking the lake, and established ourselves for one week.

We were at tea that evening, when the waiter brought in some copies of the *Times* newspaper, sent for my perusal, he said, by a signore in the sala. When I carried them back to him, I found that he belonged to a party of English, Swiss, and Ticinese, who were engaged on the projected railroad through the bowels of the St. Gothard, which I had just passed over. Very delightful such railway travelling will be for those whose only object is to arrive at the end of their journey; and, good reader, if I had not foreseen that thou wouldst soon be in the number of those who will hurry forwards to reach places where they have nothing to do and where no one expects them, I would not have described to thee, even cursorily, the beautiful scenery we had passed since leaving Spa, and of which thou wilt gain but scant ideas in the railway carriages of modern times. Thou mayest, however, read this very book the while thou speedest forwards; and so learn something of the country thou hast skimmed over and under.

"But how do you mean to get through to Milan?" asked one of the company, alluding to the Austrian blockade.

I replied that I had not known of its existence until I had entered Ticino; but could not think it applied to foreigners travelling, as I was, with a foreign office passport *visé* at the Austrian Embassy in London.

"Can't say!" replied the Englishman. "I and my friend were examining the church at Bellinzona this morning, when an English lady came up to me in the greatest state of excitement, and claimed our protection as fellow subjects. 'Would you believe it,' she exclaimed; 'I was travelling quietly to Milan on the coupé of the diligence, and, last evening, when we were within a mile or two of Como, I was dragged out of my place; my luggage was taken down and put beside me on the road; I was surrounded by soldiers; and, amidst a jabbering of German and Italian that I could not understand, I was thrust into another diligence that came by, and brought back here to Bellinzona. What can they mean by such outrageous conduct?' I told her all about the blockade," continued my informant; "and advised her to go to Megadino, whence she could enter Lombardy by the Piemontese steamer on Lago Maggiore."

As far as I can understand it, the blockade was proclaimed after a mad attempt to get up an insurrection in Milan, in which some natives of the Ticino canton were supposed to be implicated; and it is now maintained by the Austrian government until it can obtain, either from the canton or from the general Swiss confederation, redress for certain grievances of which it complains.

On the afternoon of the following day, I ordered Paul to bring the britzska to the door at three o'clock. It was a beautiful afternoon, and away I drove—my wife beside me on the box and, in the inside, our three girls and two children. We turned up from the Lugano branch of our lake, crossed the ridge which joins the peninsular rock of San Salvadore to the highlands of the north; and passing another small lake on our right, descended again to the shores of Lago Lugano, which had come round to the opposite side of San Salvadore. We skirted our pretty lake for some miles, and then followed a brawling stream by which it outpoured itself into the Lago Maggiore, the level of which is two thousand feet lower. The people of the villages we passed stood in evident wonder—either at the sight of an English equipage or at the danger into which they thought we were rushing headlong. On the opposite side of the little river, we passed every now and then a sentinel in the Austrian uniform—white trousers and drab surcoat,—who handled his musket and glared at us as if he would like to use it. At length, the road shewed less signs of traffic; grass grew amongst its flints; and I was slowly following it up a steep sandbank, when an Austrian sentinel appeared at the top and hallooed out something. I knew not to whom he was calling—for I had forgotten the German I had learned twenty-five years before at Vienna and Dresden—and I drove on. He hugged his musket furiously; shook himself; ran from side to side, and sent forth redoubled shrieks—we could not tell whether of warning to others or of personal terror. Another hero with a musket, and then another appeared on the sandbank; while about a dozen soldiers in undress, clambered over the hedges and swarmed about us, apparently in as great confusion as ants when a heel has invaded their hillock. By this time, I had driven up to the top of the sandbank. Here was a bar made to be cast across the road. It was now open; but the soldiers, armed and unarmed, thronged about; and I reined in my horses. Paul jumped from the rumble; and trying to look grave, while his face showed the amiable feelings of every Frenchman towards an Austrian soldier, ran to the head of the horses. The sight of his crimson livery and cockade seemed to puzzle them still more; they all began talking at once; while, with a look of innocent ignorance, I asked what was the matter.

One in an undress came up, and said something about the "blocco."

"Oh, the blockade!" I exclaimed. "Is this the Austrian frontier?"

"Si, signore: and no one can pass."

"But I am not a Ticinese. I am an Englishman, and know nothing of your quarrels."

"Why do you come here?" he asked suspiciously.

"I am taking a drive with my family. We want to go to Luino to look at the Lago Maggiore and then return. Let me speak to the officer who commands this post."

"He has been sent for, and will be here in a moment."

An armistice being thus declared, the sentinels on the bank resumed their walk; the soldiers in undress threw themselves on the ground beside the road; two labourers from a field on the Ticino side came up to the hedge; and we all began a friendly conversation on the rigidity of the blocco.

A young officer in military undress soon came down to us, and politely expressed his inability to permit us to pass; his orders to maintain the blockade being most stringent: he himself had no power to grant passes; but he invited me back to his quarters, where he showed me a proclamation, by General Singer, Commandant at Como, which empowered the officers commanding on the roads to Varese and Milan to grant passes to travellers not being Ticinese. Luino, on the Lago Maggiore, was, he said, about a mile distant; and he did not seem to think we lost much by not being able to visit it.

When we returned to my carriage, I found that my family had been much amused by a Ticinese dog that had made frequent rushes across the frontier line, darting back instantly, and barking in triumph and delight at having defied the enemy.

A beautiful moon lighted us back to our hotel at eight o'clock.

The mountain of San Salvadore is the most

striking feature of the lake of Lugano. It rises, as I have said, almost perpendicular on three sides, to the height of two thousand feet above the lake; and would stand in the centre of it, but that, on the fourth side, it is joined by a low ridge to the further mountains. Vines, mulberries, and olive trees, with Indian corn and millet, clothe the base of it as of the other hills; and frequent farm-houses and church steeples peep out above them, and Italianise the scene. Higher up, woods of Spanish chestnut are rooted in the fissures of the rock and overhang the pathway that winds, round and round it, to the summit. There, on the highest pinnacle, a cottage and a chapel still stand, although unused and unoccupied. The view from hence is magnificent; the lake of Lugano at the base on three sides; a smaller lake on the fourth; Lago Maggiore glimmering between the peaks to the westward; the snow-topped ridges that gird in the lake of Como to the west; Monte Rosa, gloriously isolated and standing out from its Alpine ridge, on the north; and the wide plains of Lombardy and Piedmont, fading in mist, in the southern distance.

Fixed in the outer wall of the chapel is a monumental slab to a Polish exile, who, says an inscription, had found in Ticino the freedom he had sought in vain in his own country, and who had died one month too soon to rejoice in the blessed revolution of Warsaw — which the writer then, doubtless, thought enduring! Here is, also, a tomb, with a pretty simple inscription to a young English wife who had died in one of the villages near, and whose body had been carried hither at her own request. She was right;

> For never was holier hermitage given,
> Whence the soul might unfurl its young pinions for heaven.

We had intended to loiter away on the Italian lakes six weeks of the summer until the weather should be cool enough for us to travel more comfortably to Rome. The people of Lugano could not understand our lingering ten days on their lovely lake; and the banker, Airoldi (who had been recommended to me by Knorre et fils, of Lucerne, and who charged me two per cent. commission, and justified the charge by showing that Messrs. Knorre had made me pay the same, though they disguised half of it by calling it premium for gold on which, he said, none was payable), this honest banker came and seriously proposed to me to purchase the great hotel in which we were living, and to adopt it as my private residence.

It had been built by the Canton only eight years before as a government house; and as, by a change in the governmental system, it was now no longer wanted, they offered it to me for half the million of francs it had originally cost. I think we must carry about us some evidence of being citizens of the world; for, at Spa also, we had been strongly urged to purchase a residence; and some of the good people of Terre Haute, in Indiana, are fully persuaded that we shall return to end our days in the clearings of the Wabash.

At length, after ten days, having obtained our bill from the Donna del Lago, as we called our landlady, we took offence on finding that she had added a certain number of pennies per day to the charges on which we had before agreed; and declared that we would set off that very day. She smiled incredulously—deeming it impossible that all the loose things that occupied her rooms could be put into the boxes and the boxes stowed away under a month's time; but as the energies of English will and the capabilities of two English travelling carriages quickly developed themselves, she sent for the banker, and asked him to make terms with us. I told him it was too late; shook hands with him, and gallantly we drove away. Smartly we drove alongside the beautiful lake, and across the noble bridge that spans it from side to side. Smartly we drove along through the beautiful valley that widens amongst the lower hills. We passed Mendrisio; we passed Chiasso; we rattled on a few hundred yards further, and were brought to a standstill by a couple of Austrian sentries and by a score or so of soldiers who lay about the road. I dismounted from my coach-box, and was civilly conducted to the commissiario in a neighbouring building. He was a young Italian. He took my family passport, and the two passports of my coachman and butler; and said that he would send them immediately to the commandante at Como, and that we should probably have the permesso to enter in four hours.

"Four hours!" I exclaimed. "Why it is barely two miles distant."

"But the guard who carries the passports will have to walk there and back."

"Let me take him on the rumble of my carriage."

"Impossible to allow my signoria to pass without the permesso first obtained."

"Send him on horseback."

"I have no horse."

"Hire one from the inn at Chiasso: I will pay for it."

"I have no power to allow a Ticinese horse to pass."

We were fairly stumped; but were advised to go back the few hundred yards to Chiasso, while the commissario should draw up his report and send the passports. I also gave the messenger a letter for General Singer, in which I explained to him our position, and requested him to send the pass as quickly as possible in conformity with his own proclamation.

We went back to the inn; had a bad dinner, and waited four hours and a half. At eight o'clock, I was told that the messenger had found the office at Como shut, and that we could not have an answer until the next morning. Had we any feeling of irritation against Austria and Austrian rule? Oh no, of course not! No one has. We selected the least objectionable beds in the Albergo San Michele, unpacked our English travelling tea apparatus, drank tea, and went to bed. I had a horrid dream, in which some wicked spirit seemed to imprecate the expulsion of barbarians from Italy —Exoriare aliquis nostris ex ossibus ultor!

Morning came, and nine o'clock followed; but it

brought no reply from General Singer; ten o'clock —eleven o'clock—twelve o'clock came, and still, in the pot house of San Michele, we awaited the convenience of General Singer. Soon after mid-day, I received a message requesting my presence at the frontier office. I hastened thither. The answer had just arrived, and permission to enter Lombardy was refused. The commissario read me the document in which the refusal was couched. It was in Italian, and purported that we could not enter because my Foreign Office passport had not been visé at the Austrian Legation at Berne, and those of my two foreign servants, although visés by Austrian Consuls, were originally granted for the interior of France.

"But my passport is visé by the Austrian Legation in London," I said; "and I have not been within a hundred miles of Berne."

"So I explained to the Signor Commandante," replied the commissario.

"Then the visé of the Austrian Legation in London was a lie?"

"I can say nothing," replied the commissario.

"So the Austrian Consuls who took money for *viséing* the passports of my servants, robbed me, and took it under false pretences?"

"I can say nothing," answered the commissario.

"Is that letter signed by General Singer?"

"I may not say," replied the commissario.

"Let me take a copy of it."

"I may not," said the commissario.

"What is the number of it?"

"I may not tell," replied the poor commissario, hiding it.

"At all events, read it to me once more."

He did so hurriedly; as if he knew he should be dismissed were his courtesy known to General Singer.

"Has General Singer sent any answer to my letter?"

"None."

Polite General Singer!

Without the slightest ill-will towards Austria—no one ever felt any such—without the slightest imputation on the courtesy of her service and the loveableness of her police—to which Italy bore witness—I returned to the Albergo San Michele; paid a bill, the rascality of which was natural in that neighbourhood; and, with my wife and daughters and children, entered upon the alternative left us by the Austrian brute at Como; namely, a return over the Saint Gothard, in order to procure at Berne a valid visé to my passport, in lieu of the imposture affixed to it by the Austrian Legation in London, and most ostentatiously stamped "*gratis.*"

"Thank you for nothing," said I.

We drew nigh once more to Lugano. Pride would not permit us to return to the Donna del Lago; but there was another excellent hotel in the town, and I pulled up at the Grand Hotel Suisse. I had no objection to spend a few more days amid this beautiful scenery, rather than at once resolve to recross the Alps, or even to go by Magadino and the Lago Maggiore. The spirit of opposition was upon me, and I was resolved to brave and conquer General Singer. I enclosed all my passports in a letter to the British Chargé d'Affaires at Berne. For once, I found an English minister abroad who was worth his salt. In a few days, he returned my passports again, with a polite letter, intimating that he had not been aware that English people were exposed to such inconvenience, and would take steps to protect them from such annoyance in future.

I directly sent the passports to the frontier, that they might be forwarded to Como before our arrival; and, on the following morning, rattled triumphantly through the narrow streets of Lugano, and, without stopping at the hateful pothouse of Chiasso, drove straight to the barrier; and, at a sign from the guard, through it, and up to the very gate of the Austrian frontier house.

At the Custom House, I found that somebody had received a reprimand. I was treated with the greatest respect. No baggage whatever was examined. A present of two francs made all right. I directed Paul to drive on with the chariot, and I only waited with the britska until some permit should be made out. An unlucky Custom House guard bethought him to admire the fittings of an English travelling carriage; and, putting his hand on an imperial, asked if it was a cow—a " vache"—a box.

" Yes, it is a cow."

" What is in it ?"

" It contains only my uniform."

" Uniform — uniform! Then there must be arms," he suggested.

" None whatever," I replied, supposing that he referred to fire-arms. " Pistols make no part of the dress."

" But there must be a sword ?" he insisted.

" Only a very small one," I was inclined to say,

as the girl excused herself for having had a bastard child; but I answered, with equal ingenuity, "Yes, an ornamental, gala sword."

"A sword!" he exclaimed with horror. "But no sword whatever can be admitted within the Austrian dominions! I must go and explain this to the chief. Pray excuse. I will be back again in two minutes."

Away he sped.

"Give me that paper," I cried to another guard who came up with the permit for which I had been waiting. Then, while the first guard was inquiring whether the Austrian rule in Italy could withstand the entrance of my sword, I gave a cut to my horses, and trotted bravely forwards without waiting to hear the negative of his chief.

I had done General Singer. He was sold. He was a gone coon, as we used to say on the Wabash.

CHAPTER XXIII.

A MURDER.

San Donnino.—An Italian Inn.—The Waggoner.—A Mysterious Youth.—The Pretore.—The Gensdarmes.—Catholic Deputy-Lieutenants.—How Austria lost Italy.—Mahomet and the Arab.

A FEW days afterwards, I had passed through Milan and Piacenza, and had slept, I know not by what chance, at San Donnino—not a bad baiting-place, but one I would not have selected for the night. I had pulled up at an hotel, where, as usual in these little towns, more accommodation was provided for waggons and their teams than for gentlemen's equipages. In the court-yard, I observed a heavily-loaded waggon, what in England we should call a broad-wheeled waggon, with four wheels, from which had been unharnessed four good horses which the waggoner, a rather elderly and weakly man, attended with much care as he dressed and fed them in the stable adjoining that in which my horses stood.

As I went and came, to see my own horses fed, I chanced to light more than once upon this waggoner as, in some darkened corner, he was in deep converse with a lad, or young man, who looked much startled by my unexpected appearance. The elder of the two, however, seemed to reassure him by saying, that I was a stranger (I heard the word *forestiere*), and should not heed them. He was a fine-looking youth, tall, well-grown, with jet-black hair and eyes, and budding moustaches; and an expression of intelligence and determination. Two gens-d'armes were also lodging in the inn, and these the young man seemed to avoid with peculiar care; and as they kept themselves almost entirely in the tap-room of the house, it was not difficult for him to do so.

I sat up late that night, and having occasion to go into the court-yard before I went to bed, to bathe the shoulder of one of my horses that had been wrung by the collar, I saw, though I scarcely noticed the fact, that the youth I have described, was lying asleep in the swinging hammock or tray which so many waggons and even vetturino-carriages carry slung under the body of the vehicle and just enough raised from the ground to clear large stones or mud. In this swinging tray, were stowed various light articles and the provision of oats and hay intended for the morrow's consumption of the horses. The sleeper was quite covered beneath these; and I should not have seen him, but that a bright ray of the moon happened to glance upon his swarthy face, between two bundles of hay. I thought nothing of the matter, and having dressed my horse went to bed.

We were to start early the next morning, as I wished to make a long bait at Parma, so as to have time to see its interesting cathedral. The bells on the heads of the cart horses showed that the waggoner was leaving two or three hours earlier than our usual time of departure; for we always had breakfast before we left our night's quarters. I looked out of my window as I was dressing myself, and I saw the landlord bring out and consign to the waggoner a canvass-bag containing quite half-a-gallon of something that seemed to be heavy.

"There!" said the landlord laughing; "don't say I have not given it back to you, or I shall call these two signori gens-d'armes as witnesses. Take as good care of it as I have done this last night."

The waggoner thanked him, stowed the bag in a corner amongst the packages behind his own seat, and taking his whip drove out of the yard-door.

My horse's shoulder showed still signs of being wrung, and, resolving that we would give him some hours' more rest and not pass that day beyond Parma, I returned to the inn, and we lingered long over our breakfast. I was standing an hour or two later at the door of the hotel-yard, when I saw the same young man who had secured my attention on the preceding evening, rush wildly up the street towards where I stood with the landlord. His cheeks were as pale as death, and his eyes seemed starting out of his head, as he hurriedly inquired of the host which was the way to the Pretore or chief magistrate of the town.

"Pray, come with me, Signore," he said. "You can speak the truth in this horrible business."

I hastened after, rather than with him, and we soon arrived at the town hall, and made our way to the Pretore.

"Signore Pretore," exclaimed the youth; "I am a deserter from the Austrian conscription. I have been hiding, as this foreign gentleman knows; but it was only to avoid being arrested for the conscription. A most horrible crime has just been committed. You can never learn the truth except from me : the police—the gens-d'armes will never tell you. I will discover it all and will tell who are guilty, if you will give me your word of honour that I shall be freed from the conscription."

"Strange!" said the judge pensively. "Is it really a great crime you can tell?"

"None can be greater. Free me from the conscription and you shall know all."

"I agree to your terms," replied the judge.

"Then let everyone leave the court except this Monsu," said the youth pointing to me.

All retired.

"Your Signoria will see wherefore I have asked him to stay," began the informer. "You saw me more than once Signore, last evening, talking privately to the poor man who drove that waggon and horses?" he asked, turning to me.

"I did."

"You saw me last night lying hid in the tray swung underneath the waggon?" he continued.

"I did; but I thought you were asleep."

"I wished to breathe as long as I could. I covered myself over better with the hay, so soon as you had passed. I was hiding there, Signore Pretore; the waggoner had agreed to let me hide there, and so to try and escape the conscription.

When he drove away his team this morning, I was still lying there; and was carried out of town without having been discovered. The waggon had proceeded about five miles on the road towards Parma, when it was overtaken by two gens-d'armes who had been at the osteria here the night before. Monsu will have seen them."

"I did remark them;" I said, "ill-looking fellows whom I should know again."

"They joined the waggoner, and began talking to him. Suddenly they both seized him and strapped his arms down to his side with one of their own belts. The horses had stopped, and they threw the man on the ground, just before the front-wheel of the waggon; one of the gensdarmes pulled him back by the legs so as to bring his head just before the wheel; the other flogged on the horses and it passed directly over his head. I heard the skull crack and saw the brains squeezed out. The two murderers then unstrapped the belt again, and the one to whom it belonged, replaced it round his own waist. I could do nothing; besides that I was so overcome by terror and sickness at seeing that head crushed so close to where I lay, what could I, unarmed and lying there, have done against two armed soldiers? They would have killed me before I could have freed myself from the hay and the different bundles and sacks that covered me up. So I held my breath and lay without moving—only wondering what could be the object for such a murder.

"It is in that hole, behind where he sat!" said one of them to the other. "Pull it out and let us hasten away."

The one who was spoken to, jumped upon the shafts and pulled out a canvas-bag that seemed to be heavy. They both leaped over the ditch by the side of the road with it; and went into a little copse through which the high road was made. I had held my breath even when the fellow had jumped upon the shaft, for I knew that, if I were seen, they must kill me to prevent me telling; and I now watched them as they withdrew into the copse. As soon as they had gone a few paces and were out of sight, I crept out of my hiding-place on the other side of the waggon; and keeping it between me and the direction in which the murderers had retired, I hastened into the copse that grew on that side of the road, and then took to my heels and came with all the speed I could make, to denounce the crime to your tribunal."

We were horror-stricken, the judge and I; and

neither of us spoke. There was a knock at the door, and an usher entering, announced that two gensdarmes demanded to see the Pretore. He showed the young conscript a door behind his seat, and telling him to wait there, bade the usher introduce the other two. The same two gensdarmes whom I had seen at the hotel entered, with the same look of effrontery and villany.

"Signor Pretore," said one of them, "we have to report a horrible accident by which a poor man has lost his life; but, fortunately, no one appears to be to blame except himself. About five miles from here, on the *stradone* to Parma, we found the body of a poor waggoner lying dead. One of the wheels of his waggon had passed over his head. It was evident that he must have fallen down, perhaps from the shaft on which he was riding; or perhaps he may have been drunk."

The judge made no answer; but writing a few lines, gave the paper to the usher, and ordered him to take it to its address. We all sat or stood in silence for about five minutes. The two murderers once cast a furtive glance at one another; then, as if fearful of being remarked, stood with awkward but motionless consciousness. A corporal, with five or six gensdarmes, entered the court, and advanced towards the judge.

"Arrest those two," he said.

It was done.

"Search them."

They were searched; and in the pockets, in the breasts of the coats, and in the tall jack boots of each of them, five hundred silver crowns were found. They had divided the booty with exact equality.

I have only to add that the magistrate kept his word to the fugitive conscript, and obtained his discharge from the service to which he was liable; and that the Austrians, choosing to impute to the whole Lombard police the treachery of two of their number, decreed that henceforth Lombard policemen should always be accompanied by German soldiers.

In the afternoon, I went on my way; and slept, as I had planned to do, at Parma; and thenceforwards was unmolested by any Custom House official whose suspicions could not be laid by a present of two pauls. With my complete uniform, I arrived at Rome; and at St. Peter's that year, out of nine Catholic deputy-lieutenants who did homage to the Pope, I was the only one who wore his own sword rather than a hired one. All the others had been deprived of theirs at the Austrian frontier, lest they should employ them against that mild, salutary rule in Italy, which they so much admired, and now so deeply regret and deplore. Foolish, suicidal Austrians! Those eight swords, or eight such swords, would have leaped spontaneously from their scabbards to oppose the march of the French and Piedmontese to Solferino and of Garibaldi to Naples! As Gibbon tells us that, at one time, the fate of the world hung on the lance of an Arab, so the fate of Italy hung upon those eight English Catholic swords, by the confiscation of which the Peninsula was lost to Austria!!

CHAPTER XXIV.

SHADOWS OF COMING EVENTS.

Papal Ceremonial.—The Santo Bambino.—New Cardinals.—Pasquinades.—Death of a Roman Prince.—Confirmation.—Head of St. Laurence.—French Army of Occupation, and the Romans.

FAR be it from me to detain the reader from more stirring matter, by descriptions of the religious ceremonies of Christmas or Candlemas, to which I alluded in the last chapter, or of any other of the grand Papal galas at Rome. They have been so often and so fully told, that every one must know all about them:—must know of the scandalous struggles, nay fights between the crowds, who have received ten times the number of admission tickets that the reserved seats will hold, and the Swiss guards, who brutally drive back applicants even before those seats are full; so that every advance is carried by an assault:—must know of the placid, pious, devotional look and manner of good Pius the Ninth himself, and of the far different conduct of many of his assistants—particularly of the *guardia nobile*, who chatter and laugh during the most solemn parts of the service. The political atmosphere was clouding over—or clearing up, as each one may please to consider the impending changes; and I shall prefer to describe the feelings and bearing of the people as these were successively developed.

All have heard of the Santo Bambino—the image of the Infant Saviour, which is kept at the convent of Ara Cœli beside the Capitol, and carried, in a gilt coach, to the bedside of most of the dying Romans who, having faith in its healing presence, often do recover their strength after it has visited them. So great is their veneration for this doll, that, during the short-lived Republic of Rome, Signor Mazzini hoped to conciliate the people by ordering that the state coach, which had belonged to the fugitive Pope, should be dedicated to the service of the Santo Bambino. Knowing all this, my surprise was very great when, on returning one day from the old Forum, I saw large crowds gathered all over the slope that leads up to the Campidoglio, and observed the levity with which they were awaiting, as I was informed, the benediction of the Bambino. The great bell of the capitol—that bell with which so many historic associations are connected—began to toll. It was the festival of the Epiphany, and soon, in commemoration that the Infant Saviour had, on that day, manifested Himself to the Gentiles, the monks of Ara Cœli brought the holy Bambino to the edge of the terrace in front of their church, and, lifting it on high, prayed Him whom it represented to bless the people. The people were almost heedless. Few of them knelt.

"The spirit of irreligion is gaining upon them," I observed to my companion.

But see. The monks have withdrawn with their image. The great bell of the Capitol tolls again, and seems to toll louder than ever. Other priests come out from the convent church; bearing, under a canopy, the consecrated Host. They raise it on high. All fall upon their knees. There is not one of that holiday mob who does not lowly bow his head; and, while the great bell tolls on, and while the priest lifts the Host on high, there is not one of them who does not show reverence and cross himself in pious recollection.

"It is not the spirit of irreligion that is gaining upon them!" I exclaimed to my companion. "They well discriminate; and I rejoice to see it!"

And as these poor people had not necessarily become infidels because they preferred the blessed Host to the figure of the Santo Bambino, so the poor Marchese Gentile of Viterbo might, without abandoning the faith, object to the endless clatter of a convent bell over his house. Poor man! to free himself of a nuisance and by way of frolic, he clomb from the roof of his own house to the steeple of the convent, and quietly detaching the clapper of the bell, hung a Bologna sausage in its place.

> "You had better go about begirt with briars
> Than wear a stitch reflecting on the friars"

says Lord Byron. And so the Marchese found it. He was made to pay a fine of three hundred scudi for his frolic.

Some new cardinals were made about this time, and as the state allows every cardinal a pension of six thousand scudi (about £1000), unless he has private property or church preferment with which to support his rank—the people greeted the nominations with their usual witty malevolence. The spirit of the people was the same that it had been when our own Cardinal Weld, who could not speak Italian, had been created with two others, one of whom had an impediment in his speech, while the other was not considered very wise.

"The Pope has made three new cardinals," they said. "One of them does not know how to speak, the second cannot speak; and the third—had better not speak. Uno non sa parlare: uno non puo parlare; uno—è meglio che non parli."

I do not know whether it was one of these three who was said to have resolved to translate the most popular prayers into Italian; and, beginning with the Litany of Loretto, had sat himself down with a Latin dictionary in hand; but not being able to find anywhere in said Latin dictionary the first prayer *Kyrie Eleison*, had given up the task as a hopeless one, until better Latin dictionaries should be made.

What witty dogs these Romans are! when a certain new-made princely banker married a beautiful girl of the oldest family in Italy, they said that he has put

"Una Colonna vecchia sopra nuovo piedestallo,
Che non ha altro pregio che d'esser di metallo"—
A modern basement for a column old,
Its only value—that it is of gold.

Strange that such sayings should be allowed in a country in which the head of the Congregation of the Index says that "all satire is wicked!"

This, however, is a diversion. Poor old Lord Clifford of Ugbrook died about this time. His coffin was laid on the pavement of the church of S. M. della Minerva, in his quality of a great *noble*. All the minor gentry and others having gratified their feelings by placing their dead relatives during the funeral service on catafalcs, or mortuary scaffoldings, raised in the centre of the church, almost to the ceiling, the real grandees of Rome will not enter into competition with such rivals; and are, therefore, laid on a black velvet pall on the very pavement itself.

Is not this a beautiful aping of humility?

I was told that, when a Roman Prince is thus laid dead on the floor of the church, after the funeral service has been performed, his major domo advances from the body of the household servants who are gathered behind; and, addressing the corpse, says :—

"Your Excellency's valet is here and wishes to know if you have any orders for him ?"

After waiting a few moments and receiving no answer, the major domo turns to the valet and says :—

"His Excellency does not need your services. You may therefore go."

Then, again, he apostrophises the corpse. "Your Excellency's cook is here, and waits to know if you have any orders for him?"

No answer.

"His Excellency has no need of your services; therefore, cook, you may go."

He again advances with solemn reverence :—

"Your Excellency's coachman is here, and wishes to know if you have any orders?"

A pause.

"His Excellency does not answer; therefore, he has no need of your services, and so, coachman, you may go."

My two boys and my wife's lady's maid, a convert, were to receive the sacrament of confirmation; and it was arranged by Monsignor Talbot, that this should be done privately by Monsignor Marinelli, the Pope's sacristan, in his chapel in the Quirinal Palace. All was done most decorously; and I only mention the circumstance because Monsignor Sacristan afterwards showed us a relic, under the altar, in which I was much interested. It purported to be the head of the martyr St. Laurence. All Protestants even know that St. Laurence was roasted on a gridiron, because he would not renounce the faith; and that on this deathbed, he jeered the tyrant judge by exclaiming to him that he was broiled enough on one side, and should be turned on the other. This scull purporting to be his, was most evidently and strangely marked by fire, which had baked and shrivelled the skin to the likeness of parchment scorched by heat. It was very curious. So is the stone or marble slab let into the wall in the great church of St. Laurence; this is pierced with holes and was, evidently, a grating stone through which the water from the street gutter ran into the drain beneath. The legend says that the body of the holy martyr, when taken from the gridiron, was cast on this stone beside which the fire had been lighted; and the stone is most strangely marked or veined with what we are told is grease and blood; not encrusted, but incorporated with the marble. Of course, it may not be so; it is not an article of faith; but I never saw marble veined at all like this slab; and I do not believe any other such exists.

I remonstrated with Monsignor Sacrista that the head of Saint Laurence ought to be in some public church, and not shut up from Christians in a private chapel. He smiled, and answered that many people said the same; but added, "When they ask me to allow it to be removed, I answer that I found it here when I was appointed to my post, and that I cannot allow it to be removed without the Pope's consent. And when they apply to the Pope, his Holiness says, You must ask Monsignor Sacrista. It is in his chapel."

These little incidents, however, were matters of personal feeling or opinion. The general feeling of the Romans appeared to me to be undergoing a change; and this could be best noted in the great religious ceremonies—the only opportunities they have of gathering together and of showing their opinions *en masse*. On the 3rd of June, there was the grand procession of Corpus Domini round the square of S. Peter's; and on this occasion, as on every other of general gathering, rumours of conspiracy, assassination, and tumult were rife in the city. The French Commander-in-Chief, General de Guyon, had four thousand men under arms; and would have placed a battery of cannon before the church, but that the Romans laughed at him, and asked him whether, if his cannoneers fired into the mob, he would guarantee that they should not hit either Pope or Cardinals, who, in case his fears were verified, would be the centre of the tumult raised around them by the revolutionists.

We witnessed the procession from a low window under which it passed; and saw nothing to remark except that the number of strangers collected was infinitely less than usual, and no sign of disturbance save that which was occasioned when Prince de Viano, Colonel of the Guardia Nobile, slid gently from his horse because it caracolled a little, in a manner that would have delighted his wife, who usually rode it. In every other respect, the ceremony went off quietly and decorously.

I had never before been placed so nearly on a level with the Pope as, carried on men's shoulders, he bears the Host aloft in his hands throughout this procession. Of course, he could not really kneel for so long a time on this unsteady platform; and as it would not be decorous that he should be seen to sit, while carrying the Host in adoration, his figure is so made up of pillows and stuffing that, to the crowd below, he seems to kneel, while in reality he sits. This was very evident to us at our window; and, I must say, made of His Holiness a most unnatural and distorted figure.

Better far that he should abandon his Oriental throne above men's shoulders on such an occasion, and do real, rather than sham homage to that which he adores; as he did during a great procession on the octave of Corpus Christi, when he walked behind the blessed Sacrament, in evident accordance with his own devotional feelings.

On this occasion also, the city was threatened with revolutionary tumult; and General de Guyon made awful preparation which nothing occurred to justify.

In fact, he must have found out that the feeling of the Roman people was boiling over against the continued occupation of the city by French soldiery. They thronged everywhere, and the Romans made way for them. On the night of the festival of St. Peter and Paul, (the dome had been illuminated as usual on the preceding evening—I have given a grand description of it in my "Modern Society," and told how, at that very time, the French were taking Rome by assault,) on the evening of this festival, when the famous Girandola was exhibited from the Monte Pincio, instead of from Castle St. Angelo, and when other magnificent fireworks were displayed, the crowd in the Piazza del Popolo, was almost entirely composed of French soldiers. Certainly, two soldiers were there present for one civilian.

This absence of the Romans boded no good to the existing state of things; nor did the indifference, or worse feeling, with which the majority were in the habit of greeting the Sovereign Pontiff, as his carriage passed at other times through the streets. I will not say that hats were not raised; but scarcely a knee was bent to welcome and receive the benedictions he showered around.

They withheld from the temporal sovereign the homage they would have freely granted to the Pope.

CHAPTER XXV.

COUNTS, QUEENS, PRINCES AND CARDINALS

Inventory of my Furniture.—English Toadyism.—The English Lady and the Guardia Nobile.—The Same and the French Prelate.—A Letter and the Censorship.—The English Language.—Judgment by a Roman Tribunal.—Queen Christina of Spain.—My Passport withheld.—Festas and Sundays.

I HAVE said that I had rented the first floor of the Palazzo Albani at the Quattro Fontane until the 30th of June. The palace itself was the property of Prince Chigi, who had let this floor of it to a Signor Zeloni for a term of years. Now this Signor Zeloni was a collector or speculator in old curiosities, "knicknackery," and rococo gilding—a taste I presume he had inherited from his father, who was said to have been a respectable tradesman in that line. But old carved rococo gilded furniture, although most splendid to the eye, is seldom safe for daily use, nor so faultless that it will bear the inspection of one who should verify the inventory at the end of a seven months' lease, and impute to his tenant the breakage of every scroll, leaf, finger or nose that may have been missing for the last two hundred years. I strongly urged, therefore, that the inventory of the furniture should be delivered to me when I took possession of the apartment.

For a long time, I urged this in vain. At length, on one Sunday morning, Signor Zeloni's housekeeper (he lived on the floor above) presented herself with a person bearing a roll of paper, and an inkstand; and informing us that writing was not a servile work, and was not, therefore, forbidden on a Sunday, seated himself at a table; spread out his paper, and opened his inkhorn. The housekeeper walked about the room and dictated.

"Write down," she said, for example, "One large mirror over the stove in a rich rococo gilt frame."

"But the mirror is cracked," I observed.

"Scusare," said the clerk; "I can only write what the signora dictates."

"Write down," she continued, without heeding my remonstrance, "One large pianoforte, *a coda*, the whole case carved and gilded, and resting upon gilt figures of mermaids, tritons and cupids blowing through shells."*

* See note at end of the Chapter.

"But that mermaid nearest the wall has lost her left foot; that cupid has no fingers to his right hand, and that triton is without a nose."

"Scusare," said the clerk; "I can only write down what the signora dictates."

I would not interfere any more.

This Signor Conte Alessandro Zeloni, as he called himself, on his strength of being a count, which was doubtful, and of being a Roman, which was certain, had been received with open arms into the society of many English at Rome, proud of being acquainted with a count, and, still more so, perhaps, with a native of whatsoever class or character. The delight of Tom Moore's "Biddy Fudge" at writing—"only think, a letter from France—with French pens and French ink"—is far from an exaggerated representation of the delight of our country people if they can only entice within their doors a few third or fourth class Italians. That they are Italians, is sufficient recommendation, sufficient introduction. That Italians should condescend to visit English gentlemen and ladies, is an honour on which our dear silly countrywomen pride themselves to one another; and remember, with regret, when they get back to the society of their own equals in England.

Out of many instances of this fatuity which I have witnessed, I will recount one for the amusement and caution of my fair readers.

We visited, at Rome, an English widow with her daughter, who were passing the winter there. They were people whom we had known in England—real English gentry—neither more nor less, and, therefore, the social equals of any foreign gentry, whether with or without titles. I twice met at their house during morning visits, a good-looking young man whom my more accustomed eye discovered to be wanting in the *je ne sais quoi* that marks a foreign gentleman. At length, one morning, my wife brought me a note she had just received.

" Our friend, Mrs. ——," she said, " asks me to permit her to bring to our dance to-morrow Signor ——, whom we have met at her house, and who, she says, is a *guardia nobile* of the Pope. I suppose I had better send him an invitation."

" Not so fast," I replied ; " if he is an Italian, he is not in Italian society, and we never introduce natives of the same town to one another. But the name he gives is not Italian, and I do not see how he can be a *guardia nobile*."

I instituted inquiries ; and my wife was obliged

to write to our friend and decline to receive her favourite, on the ground that he was not a *guardia nobile*, that he was not in Roman society, and that his father or uncle kept a bookseller's shop in Rome.

Our dear English woman thought, of course, that we must be mistaken; that we envied her the acquaintance of foreigners; and she soon sent us a long letter, purporting to be written by a French Prelate, who guaranteed the position of the young man; although he admitted that he had made a mistake in saying that he was a guardia nobile, whereas he had only applied for a commission and had been put off with civil phrases. The Reverend Frenchman then added a page or two of abuse of me, and of laudation of himself. My unfortunate familiarity with continental habits of thought and expression, convinced me that here, also, there was something wrong; and I sent the letter to the authorities at St. Louis des Français, by one who should ascertain who the writer was. I learned from these head-quarters of French Catholicism in Rome, that the writer had never brought any evidence of being a Prelate; that, consequently, the authorities had refused to receive him or to present him to the French Ambassador; that he was thought to be a paid spy of the King of Naples and of others; and, from his habits of intrigue and misrepresentation, was considered a most dangerous man. I was sorry, by sending this information to our dear countrywoman, to deprive her of another foreign hanger-on, and to be obliged to add that, in order to test the real position of the so-called guardia nobile, I had desired a friend to go and buy a book at the shop in which the youth was said to be interested; the which book had, in fact, been sought out and handed to him by that young guardsman himself.

Our fair compatriote never forgave me; and I do not think that she even dropped the acquaintance of either of her two foreign friends.

However, to return to Count Alessandro Zeloni. He had worked his way into several English houses; and was everywhere so misrepresenting my conduct, that I was told I ought to refute his statements. I, therefore, wrote a letter of which I wished to have a few copies lithographed, that I might send them to friends. I now only refer to the letter in order to introduce what the Roman censorship said of it. I wrote as follows:—" To

Signor Count Zeloni. Sir,—You understand English; I write in English, in order that English people, to whom I shall submit this statement, may most clearly understand it. You charge me with refusing to sign your inventory of furniture which you sent to me when I had been three weeks in the house. For my own protection, I gave it to a sworn Roman appraiser to verify, and he finds that it misrepresents almost every article; and that it states the most tattered and worn, and glued and mended rubbish, to be perfect and in a good state.

"You charge me with refusing to pay your rent: according to our contract that rent was to be paid monthly, but not until you had supplied all that you promised. This has not been done; your own lawyer called upon me and admitted that I had done nothing but was most fair and reasonable. The stable in the court-yard, on the faith of having which I took your appartment, as appears by the contract itself, has not yet been given to me.

"Being told that, to all who will listen, you accuse me of refusing to sign your inventory or pay your rent, I write this to show why I have done so. I have documentary evidence to support all I have stated."

I took the original of this letter to a lithographer and desired him to copy it. The poor man was terror-stricken at the idea of printing anything without the permission of the censorship; and so I submitted the MS. to that learned tribunal. It was returned to me in a few days endorsed as follows :—" Senza una genuina e sincera versione nella lingua Italiana, la Censura Eccl'ca non puo ammettere questo scritto.—Without a genuine and sincere version in the Italian language, the Ecclesiastical censorship cannot allow this writing."

And if I send "a genuine and sincere version," you will then require evidence that it is so! A shrug of the shoulders admitted the truth of my supposition.

It seemed to me curious that an ecclesiastical jurisdiction, co-extensive with the habitable and uninhabitable globe, should not be provided with any one who could read a page of manuscript in the language that is more extensively spoken than any other on the face of that same habitable globe. For, let it be remembered that, as England is not only an European but an universal power, so the English language is not only that of a part of this little Europe, but of the inhabitants of the most distant and most widely extended portion of the earth: and these pages will be read by the people of distant lands and communities of whose very existence the Tyberine censors had never heard.

I did not apply again; but took courage and wrote a few copies for friends and left Zeloni to do his worst.

Poor little fellow! It was not much he could do. He went to law; and the following decree was what he got for his pains:—

"Civil Tribunal of Rome.

"On the urgent demand of Count Alessandro Zeloni, that the noble gentleman R. Digby Beste should be compelled to sign an inventory of furniture and objects entrusted to him and which, for four months he has refused to sign, and which Zeloni says he may not deliver up correctly now that he is preparing to leave Rome, unless he be made to sign said inventory, the Tribunal decrees as follows:—

"It absolves and releases the defendant from the improper demand, and condemns the applicant Zeloni to pay all the expenses."

He appealed against this decision and his appeal was again dismissed with costs: every trial being conducted secretly and by written deposition, so that it became proportionally expensive. When my time came for leaving the apartment, he refused to verify the inventory or to receive the keys ; and my lawyer was directed by the court to deliver them to its own offices, who would take charge of them until the troublesome fellow came to his senses. I never heard more of him or his affairs.

For, before my lease was expired, the Dowager Queen Christina of Spain, who had been "spunging" for a long while on the Spanish Legation, in which she had established herself on her first arrival in Rome, purchased the whole Palazzo Albani ; and, one morning, sent me a polite request that I would permit her to call on us and go over our apartment. She came that afternoon— a large, coarse, impudent-looking woman, with a big, handsome, middle-aged man—the Duke of Rianzares, her husband. However, she was very gracious ; walked over the whole suite of rooms, and planned their future destination. I told her that the kitchen was on a floor above, according to the usual Italian system, and she desired her husband to go and look at it. He was recalcitrant ; and her Majesty insisted with a royal and matrimonial frown, till he complied with a bad grace. Meanwhile she seated herself, and drawing my wife and a daughter one on each side of her, urged us to come to her weekly receptions in the Palazzo di Spagna.

While thus engaged, a message came from Zeloni to inform the Queen that his own lease of the apartment had three years more to run; and Her Majesty replied, that he must settle any question about his lease with the owner of the palace.

Some question there was between them, and Zeloni did not leave without a "con-si-de-ra-tion." It was difficult for him to find an apartment large enough to receive all his rococo valuables, or a landlord who would accept him as a tenant. A few months later, I was thinking of taking the first floor of the Palazzo Pamphilj Doria, in the Piazza Navona, belonging to Prince Doria, and when I said to the agent that I would consider of the matter and give an answer on the following day, I was earnestly besought to engage it at once.

"Why so?"

"Because Her Majesty Queen Christina insists upon having Zeloni's apartment in the Palazzo Albani delivered up to her without delay. And Cardinal Antonelli has besought Prince Doria to let Zeloni have this one, so as to set the other free; but the Cardinal will not guarantee the rent, and the Prince does not like to let it without a guarantee, and yet cannot refuse the Cardinal. But if you will engage it at once, we can send to express our regret to his Eminence that it was already disposed of."

Thus do Princes, Queens, and Cardinal Secretaries of State do business at Rome!

In the spring of this year, 1858, I wished to return to England as quickly as possible; but was informed at the police office, that Zeloni had there given notice that my passport should not be delivered to me because I had refused to sign his inventory, and was escaping from the country. The police admitted that it was not very probable that I should be running away to escape my lodging-house debts, while I left behind my five children, horses, carriages, and servants; but, according to the laws of the "Eternal City," no passport could be delivered until twenty-four hours after the reception of such a notice: that time was allowed to the plaintiff to substantiate his statement if he could. Next day, the passport was given; and my wife and I started for Civita Vecchia with post horses.

But, by this delay, we had missed the direct steamer to Marseilles; and, although it was a great pleasure to find our old friends, the Helvétie and Captain Martin, ready to receive us, we knew that we should be delayed three days by having to follow the coast instead of taking the direct line. The 19th March, on which we arrived at Leghorn before sunrise, proved also to be the festival of St. Joseph; and no merchandise could be shipped or unshipped on a holiday. The whole of that day, therefore, the steamer and crew lay idle in port.

In England, the Catholic Church does not require abstinence from work on St. Joseph's day. In Piedmont, as in France, this and all other minor festivals are kept on the Sunday following the day on which they occur. Either political antipathies, unworthy of the church, prevent the same rule being extended to all countries, or else the wish of despotic governments to enervate the people and to check that steady, uninterrupted, and persevering industry, which they know to be fatal to themselves, forbids the change which modern habitudes suggest. The consequence is that, at Naples and elsewhere, I have often heard people, at work on Sundays, excuse themselves by saying that there were one, two, or three festas in the week : and that, as they could not afford to be idle the whole time, they preferred to keep holy the festas rather than the Sunday.

Everybody knows this; and yet the system is unchanged; and churchmen and laymen hypocritically deplore the increasing immorality of the age and its disregard of sacred ordinances.

I know not how much more I should have written in this strain if I had not remembered that, on the Sunday following, I was at Genoa, in Piedmont, and that the vessel was there unloaded and loaded again without any scruple or any observance of the day. Leghorn idleness on the festa, was preferable to this Genoese desecration of the Sunday.

After many delays, we arrived at length in London. I was told that I might sue Zeloni for damages occasioned by the delay that his false charge had created. I quoted the old proverb ——

---

* Note to page 350. I am sorry to be obliged to record the dilapidated state of a pianoforte which the late French ambassador at Rome, M. de Sartiges, has bought for 2,500 francs. It owed its value to the belief that it had belonged to the dissolute Donna Olimpia. Were it possible to produce the instrument of any woman still more infamous, it would, of course, be deemed proportionately more valuable by these modern antiquaries.

CHAPTER XXVI.

CONVENTS AND KIDNAPPERS.

Tableaux Vivants.—Florence Nightingale and the Nuns.—Catherine of the Wabash.—Rev. Mother at Scutari.—Pious Lies.—Cardinal Wiseman and his Attorney.—Ecclesiastical Property.—Pio Nono and the Monks.—A Suggestion.—Division of Property.

I AM perfectly well aware of the deep offence I shall give, of the indignation I shall draw upon myself, by writing the truth, as I purpose doing in this chapter, about certain convents and ecclesiastical dignitaries. I shall be told that I am giving scandal; and that it is my duty to conceal the misconduct of professedly-religious people; and that one ought never to speak against the dead.

I pray good people to be as cautious in condemning me—in attributing bad motives to me, as they would have me to be in reference to those whose misconduct they think I ought to conceal.

Let them ask themselves which is the most likely way to prevent the recurrence of any wrongdoing; whether to conceal the iniquity and permit those who have committed it to shelter themselves under a garb of holiness, or to proclaim the evil that has been committed, and so warn others from doing the like? Is not publicity recognised to be the great preventative of vice in high places? Why should I be called upon to conceal the misconduct of some poor nuns and of Cardinal Wiseman, more than any other writer is expected to deny the pride of Cardinal Wolsey or the infamy of Pope Alexander VII? Religion may deplore the excesses of such personages, but she does not suffer by them. She deplores that, amongst twelve apostles, there should have been one Judas; but she has never thought it necessary to the honour of the eleven to conceal her hatred of the traitor.

In the case which I am about to recite, there is, however, no imputation of Judas-treachery. The good silly nuns thought it their duty to tell lies rather than the truth. Cardinal Wiseman was moved by zeal for religion: he always considered that "*l'état c'est moi*"—that he was the representative, the embodiment of religion; and he always sought to exalt himself in order that he might so exalt that which he represented. If he wished to obtain wealth or power, it was that religion might be more honoured by the wealth, power, and pomp of its representative.

I said in my last chapter that my wife and I had been called suddenly from Rome to England. She had left there an adopted daughter, our Ellen of the Wabash, whom she had educated as her own from its babyhood. On the same day on which my eldest daughter had claimed the fulfilment of a promise that we would no longer oppose her entrance into a convent if she persisted in the wish after she were twenty-one years of age —on the same day on which this Catherine of the Wabash had began her novitiate in the Convent of the Sisters of Charity (or of Mercy, as they are called in England), at Bermondsey, the other had entered a convent of the same order at Blandford Square. The first had been professed, and had gone to the Crimea; the other was still a novice, but in a different house at Chelsea.

I was once at a country house where the young folks got up representations of *tableaux vivants*. In one of these, they showed forth a semblance of good Miss Nightingale, nursing a wounded soldier in the hospital at Balaclava.

"You might improve upon this," I said; "you

might, with equal truth, represent the same Miss Nightingale nursing a Sister of Mercy in her own tent. Hang up the dark dress and the white veil of the nun against the canvas of the tent; and as the Catholic priest goes out after having administered the last Sacraments to the supposed-to-be-dying Sister of Mercy, show Miss Nightingale anxious to discover what it is that disturbs her; and, at last, pull from under her pillow a large rat and kill it with her own hands."

Such a scene had, in truth, occurred between Miss Nightingale and my daughter.

The Right. Rev. Dr. Grant, bishop of Southwark, had been sent for one day by Mr. Fox Maule, Minister of War, as they say abroad. He showed a letter from Miss Nightingale, in the Crimea, which asked for more nurses: " but do not send me Irish nuns," she wrote ; " they quarrel. Do not send me English Protestant lady nurses, they fall in love with the officers, and the officers with them. Try and send me some English Catholic Sisters of Mercy."

Dr. Grant went to the Convent of Mercy at Bermondsey : and, having called the little community together, explained what was wanted; and asked if any of the ladies would volunteer.

The Lady Superior, my daughter, and one other nun offered themselves and went forth with their chaplain on this mission of mercy.

The father of Florence Nightingale was a brother-magistrate of mine in Hampshire. It was curious that he, a protestant, and I, a catholic, should each have a daughter in the same Crimean hospital. He used kindly to send me the letters he received from his daughter as often as they contained anything of personal interest, or relating to my child, whom Florence spoke of lovingly. As both she and Miss Nightingale were sacrificing themselves, if not for the general good of humanity, yet, certainly for that of their own country, English men and English women ought to feel interested in such details as the following, which I copy unaltered, and as they were sent to me by Mr. Nightingale: "General Hospital, Balaclava, June 2nd, 1856. Mrs. Beste, Sister Mary Martha, is now with me here in the Crimea; she has been exceedingly ill with typhus fever.

"I love her the most of all the sisters. She is a gentle, anxious, depressed, single-hearted, single-eyed, conscientious girl—a worker, no talker.

"I am very fond of her. And she is honest and true. She is very interesting; almost too patient and diffident; and she has been recovered from death's door. She is trustworthy and noble."

"In a former letter from Mrs. Shore Smith at Scutari," continued Mr. Nightingale, "she quotes from what she had heard at Balaclava, 'Sister Mary Martha is laid up with feverish cold here— General Hospital, Balaclava. I am glad that her illness should be here rather than at the L. T. Hospital, as we have greater facilities for nursing her.'

"Mrs. Roberts and I, Mrs. Logan and Mrs. Skinner (nurses), sleep in one-half a hut, and the sick Sister in the other half. The three other Sisters in the next hut. We have hardly any time to make any arrangement yet for ourselves."

"Later Mrs. Smith wrote to me how anxious Miss N. had been about Sister M. Martha—that she had been sitting up with her at night and that she hoped she was safely through.

"One night, some one had told her that Miss N. had heard a rat troubling the poor invalid and she had gone and, to her own great surprise, had been able to kill it.

"In one letter Miss N. said, 'the Sisters are well, cheerful, efficient, useful. Our crosses have been many and very sad ones, but God prospers the work. The weather has been tremendous,—snow on the ground, wind and bitter cold; after that, great heat and fear of cholera and fever."

Reader, this was the Catherine of "The Wabash." If you have not read that book, get it; and, as it is out of print, have it reprinted. It can never be out of date, any more than Stern's Sentimental Journey, or Robinson Crusoe.

It is due, also, to the Superior, "the Reverend Mother" of my Catherine's convent, that I should transcribe the following extract which Mr. Nightingale sent me from a letter written to him by his sister, Mrs. Shore Smith, who took Mrs. Bracebridge's place at Scutari:—" Alas! I have just been writing to ask the General for a passage for dearest Rev. Mother, on Monday, by the *Victoria*. I cannot tell you how it upsets one—more than one could have thought, considering that I never spoke a word to her except on business; but it is the love and confidence one feels in pure goodness and much wisdom enshrined in her gentle quiet form, that makes one feel her such a loss. Oh, what a thing it is to love, and trust, and respect! how it supports and makes one better! I have nobody left when she is gone to depend upon as a superior.

"The Bishop writes to her, 'Follow the direction of your medical man.' Dr. Cruikshanks says 'Go as soon as possible.' Rev. Mother, who would step into her grave as willingly as others into their bed, and would not have taken one step to avoid it for her own sake, obeys at once the order of her Bishop. I see Dr. Cruikshanks's is the wise advice. She has now a chronic malady, the disease to which this country is especially prone. If she delays, the vessels will be crowded with returns from hence. If acute fever came on, all would be over.

"How blank, how altered the look of that heavy dark-green curtain behind which was their room! It never looked dull, for one would always find help on the other side of it. It will be a great sorrow to Florence, who, hearing she was better, had been hoping, as she wrote herself, to have the comfort of her presence in the Crimea, where most of the sick are now kept."

This report was signed Mary Shore Smith.

My Catherine had recovered, and had long since returned to her convent in England. We, in Rome, had received a letter informing us that the Community of the Chelsea Convent had decided that our adopted daughter was not really suited to be a Sister of Mercy in their house; and requesting us to say whither she should be removed. My wife immediately sent her own English maid, a steady, confidential person whom she had long known, from Rome to London to fetch her and bring her to us. In due course of steamer and post, a letter arrived informing us that the silly child refused to come to us abroad. I went for my passport, and at last, as mentioned in the former chapter, I and my wife arrived in town.

But, in looking over my notes, I feel so disgusted with the conduct of pious people, that I cannot enter into details. I would not even allude to this subject, but that I had to appeal to the courts and police for protection; and, in this family record, I must not shrink from that which is known to hundreds and which will be misrepresented if I avoid the subject altogether. Suffice it, then, to say, in as few words as possible, that this adopted daughter had entered the convent in Blandford Square, as a novice: that during three years, those ladies had received her pension, and had been unable to decide whether she had a vocation or not; that being pressed to come to a decision, and being assured that she had no property absolutely her own, although we should give the usual handsome dower as to Catherine, they immediately determined that she was not suited to them. She had then insisted upon beginning a new probationary novitiate in the Convent of Mercy at Chelsea, where, also, a community of eight or nine nuns could not judge of her fitness or unfitness until they had drawn her pension for three years—up to the very last day to which her "postulancy" and "novitiate" could be prolonged; having induced us to leave her with them because the Superior had "no doubt of her final profession."

Let me here remind parents and guardians of the danger of allowing young ladies to follow their "vocations"—which, in ninety-nine cases out of a hundred, I believe to be only obstinate resolves to have their own way:—of the great inconvenience, to say no more, of these novitiates. A young girl may be led on for three or even six years—may be forbidden to take any heed of her personal appearance—may be compelled to crop her hair, and to neglect all those accomplishments which had been taught her as proper to her position in life—and may be then sent back to that world for which these conventual habits have quite unsuited her.

When we arrived at the convent at Chelsea, the Superior, showing the whites of her eyes in what was intended to be a most impressive manner, told us that our adopted daughter had left the house three hours and a half before; that, not choosing to let her depart without money, she had given her £10 of the cheque I had sent to pay her journey to Rome with our maid; that, to avoid the scandal that would have ensued if she had gone forth in the community's dress, she had let her have some of the clothes we had sent for her to travel in; that she had not the least idea whither she had gone—that some poor woman had called a cab for her; but she would not say who, or from what stand.

I appealed to the priest of the district, and he compelled this reverend lady to own that the ex-novice had left in a cab which the regular charwoman of the convent had called from the nearest stand. I signed to a policeman, and we soon found the waterman who had heard this charwoman bargain with a cab-driver in the morning to take her and a nun from the convent to Fleet Street, to Lincoln's Inn, and to Hampstead; and who saw them start—not three hours and a half ago—but only a few minutes before I had arrived.

I left directions that, as soon as the cabman appeared, he should harness a fresh horse and come for me at my hotel; and, in the mean time, I went to Cardinal Wiseman, in York Place, and explained to His Eminence how these reverend nuns had cared for a young lady who had been confided to them and had lived under their roof for three years. I knew His Eminence well—had known him for twenty-five years. He expressed the greatest indignation at the conduct of the nuns: ordered his carriage instantly; and requested me to allow my son Kenelm, who was with us and who was then a member of the Brompton Oratory, to go with him and report to us whatever he should learn. In an hour or two, the latter returned, bringing me, in the Cardinal's own handwriting, the address of those to whom the fugitive had gone:

"Messrs. Harting, 24, Lincoln's Inn, and Church Row, Hampstead."

I recognised the names of attorneys who had often appeared for his Eminence in different courts of law. But how could Ellen have got acquainted with any lawyers? And, still more strange—how should she have chanced upon the Cardinal's own lawyers, unless some one had instigated the whole proceeding, and thought thus to secure the connivance of His Eminence?

On our return to our hotel in Albemarle Street, after a useless drive to Hampstead, for the offices in Lincoln's Inn had been long closed—I found the cabman of the convent. He told me that he had taken up two ladies at the convent; that he had driven them to Hoare's bank—whence I found, they had taken not only £10, but the whole amount for which I had drawn the cheque; to 54, Lincoln's Inn; to Spanish Place; back to Lincoln's Inn; back to Spanish Place; to 51, Baker Street, York Place; back to the convent: whence he had dropped one of his fare, and had taken up instead a heavy box, which he had carried with the other lady, and left at 51, Baker Street. This was sufficient. We immediately drove to this last address. The mistress of that house at once owned that the young lady had been recommended to her that morning by the Rev. Mr. Bond, of Spanish Place—let the honour of kidnapping be given where honour is due,—and that she had engaged her apartment by the week.

I interrupted, saying that I was in search of her, assisted by Cardinal Wiseman; and, in proof of my assertion, I showed her Messrs. Harting's address.

"Sure enough that is the Cardinal's handwriting," said the woman. "I know it, because he always sends his niece and other friends to lodge here. But there must be a lie somewhere; because, about an hour and a half ago, while we were at dinner, a woman came in a cab and brought a letter from the Cardinal, which ordered me to deliver up my lodger. The young lady would not even stay to finish her dinner; but went off immediately with that woman and took her box. I must pray you to cross over with me to York Place, that we may inquire the meaning of all this."

We did so. His Eminence was at dinner; but, in answer to an inquiry which I wrote on a slip of paper and sent in to him, he sent me out a note which admitted that he had himself removed her, and that she was in a place of safety.

As she was thus declared to be under the Cardinal's immediate protection, we could have no further present anxiety, and got back to our dinner at nine o'clock.

On the following morning, I saw Mr. Harting, and learned from him that Ellen had been impressed by some one with the idea that she was entitled to a large sum of money and to the accumulated interest of years. Here, then, was the explanation of her flight and of the change of conduct in the Cardinal! *She* had been persuaded that we were over-reaching and robbing her. *He* had declared himself indignant that the nuns should have misled us, until he had referred to the Hartings, and had heard of this money. The very thought of the money had aroused his sympathies, and had urged him to thrust himself into a matter with which he could have no concern; to remove her from a house where he knew that I should easily find her by means of the police and cabman; and to constitute himself her guardian, protector, and kidnapper-in-chief! For Harting, who was soon convinced by our own lawyers, Messrs. Field, of Bedford Row, that they had been engaged for years, at our expense, in an endeavour to recover for the young lady some of the money alluded to, and that there was not the slightest chance that she or anyone else would ever obtain a farthing under the document with which some one had aroused her susceptibilities—Harting declared that he really did not know where she was, and referred us to the Cardinal: and the Cardinal again wrote that he would communicate her address to Harting. The Messrs. Harting, for there were two of them, did no more than their duty to the Cardinal. I believe they really were ignorant of the address, and endeavoured to obtain it, and to get their principal out of a scrape. But he was obstinate, and our researches were foiled for four or five days more, without any certainty that our adopted daughter had been even told that we were in London inquiring for her; although we had the perfect conviction that, even if she did know of our being there and of our willingness to receive her with the affection that had always existed amongst us, her character and natural disposition was such, that she would never forgive herself the injurious imputations which these nuns and priests had instilled against her second mother and only protectors. At length, I went to different police offices and employed detectives; and prepared an affidavit with which we appealed to the Lord Chancellor for a *Habeas Corpus* against the Cardinal. All this was a scandal. These officials delighted to expose what they called "the system:" religion suffered, as usual, from the misdeeds of its ministers. The Lord Chancellor Chelmsford expressed great sympathy for my wife; and declared it to be a most painful case; but he did not think there was evidence that the Cardinal had exercised such physical restraint over her adopted daughter as would enable him to interfere.

And so those pious people triumphed. While under their guardianship, false ideas of independence and unworthy suspicions were first instilled against her only protectors—against those who, under heaven, had made her of the religion those churchmen themselves professed, and had provided for her, as one of their own children, for twenty-four years. Well is the love of money said to be the root of all evil : for no one can suppose these people would have gone out of their own way and mixed themselves up in what, according to their own supposition was a family affair, unless they had expected to go shares in the money to be recovered! Need I add that, when they were convinced that the booty they had hoped to secure was not in existence, these kidnappers no longer cared to exercise their baneful influence? They soon left her whom they had deluded ; and that affectionate connection was restored which they had so scandalously endeavoured to sever.

As I before said, I would not have given this faint outline of the matter had it not been made so public at the time, that unworthy motives would be imputed to me, if I were to shrink from recording it here.

But we, who returned to Rome, knew that monks and nuns had also baffled poor Pio Nono. He had found it as impossible to rule them as to govern the temporal subjects who were casting off his sway. When he had first come to the Pontificate, he had issued many excellent regulations: he had directed, for example, that all members of a religious male community should, in reality, live alike—from a common fund; that no one should be permitted to accumulate a private hoard out of his savings from those unnecessarily-large allowances granted for snuff, for travelling expenses, for preaching and officiating in other churches than their own; that no one should take the final vows without the sanction of the Bishop of the diocese, or before he was twenty-one years old. The poor Pope only raised an outcry against himself; the monks were too strong for him; and his regulations became a dead letter.

I could have suggested a more simple method of diminishing the number of monks, if that were, indeed, as it was supposed to be, the object of his Holiness:—an order directing that the "enclosure" should be enforced in the case of monks as well as of nuns; that no monk should, any more than a nun, pass outside the walls of his convent—such an order would, methinks, have at once lessened the number of postulants.

But how to enforce it?

In the earlier centuries of Christianity, monasteries and convents were most useful retreats from the paganism, the brutality, the wars of the outer world. In the earlier ages of modern Europe, the monasteries alone preserved civilisation, agriculture, literature, from barbarian destruction. In later feudal ages, they were discovered to be useful for a far different purpose: they facilitated the accumulation of wealth and power in families, by drawing off all who might claim a subdivision of either. To insure that none who had thus renounced their rights or natural claims should ever attempt to assert them, the civil law was made to declare that those who had once taken the monastic vows were civilly dead—incapable of inheriting property or titles. The civil power was thus made to recognise the family compact—to force back to their cells all who might attempt to leave them.

When monasteries and convents were turned to such uses, a subdivision and modification of religious establishments totally at variance with the spirit of their founders, became imperatively necessary. The educated members of noble families, who thus withdrew from the world for the aggrandisement of their chieftain, naturally wished to live with people of their own class; and thus houses were established for the exclusive reception of gentlefolks—of monks who had so many quarterings in their coats of arms—who would maintain their superiority by never going forth except in carriages or on horseback—of young ladies who were sufficiently well-born to take a vow of poverty in a rich convent. And thus convents became rich; and the more rich because whatever they accumulated was looked upon as consecrated to holy uses, as church property that could not be sold or taken without sacrilege.

With the progress of centuries, nations agreed to disallow the individuality of man—the right of each one to dispose of his property as he listed. Everybody and everything was declared to belong to the State; it was deemed to be the duty of this latter to regulate everything for the good of all. Almost the whole of Europe agreed to this doctrine. In order to prevent the accumulation of wealth in families and the sacrifice of younger children for the aggrandisement of the elder, it was enacted that parents should be compelled to divide their property more or less equally amongst their offspring. Evidently the accumulation of estates subject to religious corporations and always indivisible and inalienable, was in total contradiction to this new doctrine that had been enforced against secular property. And yet, to compel the subdivision or alienation of monastic property at the death of every abbot or representative of the community, would be equal to giving present occupants the freehold of that in which they had had only a life interest—would be to enforce an application of such property totally at variance with the intentions of original founders or benefactors. . . .

But, without dilating upon any of these problems which must puzzle statesmen and even churchmen, if honest, one fact is patent : the modern Italian legislature has put forth no grand principle, true or false, to justify its war upon religious communities. It has not declared, as did the great French revolutionists, that the idleness and celibacy of monks and nuns were obnoxious to the interests of the state and to the duty of citizens ; it has not forbidden monastic institutions for the future ; it has not even suppressed those now in existence :—it has merely taken their property. It found wealthy communities, existing from time immemorial, and it robbed them. It had need of money; monks, nuns, and churchmen were rich and could not resist; and it committed upon them as barefaced a robbery as was ever perpetrated by Calabrian brigand, by pickpocket or burglar. It promised a small annuity to those whom it dispossessed—an annuity the payment of which is often "deferred," —and it sent them forth, to wear the dress of their several orders if they liked; to live in community elsewhere, if patrons would house them; to found convents again, if they could—and the sooner the better, because they would thus accumulate more wealth for the government again to confiscate. Call you this a revolution on principle?

The mad theories of the old French "Montagne" were more honest.

We had returned to Rome to meet the more stirring events that will be recorded in the next volume.

END OF THE FIRST VOLUME.

www.ingramcontent.com/pod-product-compliance
Lightning Source LLC
Chambersburg PA
CBHW051249300426
CB00011B/948